The Administration and Supervision of Reading Programs

The Administration and Supervision of Reading Programs

Edited by
Shelley B. Wepner
Joan T. Feeley
Dorothy S. Strickland

TEACHERS
COLLEGE
PRESS

Teachers College, Columbia University
New York and London

Published by Teachers College Press, 1234 Amsterdam Avenue,
New York, NY 10027

Quotations (throughout the book) from

Mason, J., and Au, K. *Reading Instruction for Today*. Glenview, IL: Scott Foresman. Copyright © 1986. Reproduced with permission.

Karnowski, L. (1986). "How Young Writers Communicate." *Educational Leadership*, *46*(3), 58–60. Reprinted with permission of the Association for Supervision and Curriculum Development. Copyright © by ASCD. All rights reserved.

McGarry, T. (1986). "Integrating Learning for Young Children." *Educational Leadership*, *46*(3), 64–66. Reprinted with permission of the Association for Supervision and Curriculum Development. Copyright © by ASCD. All rights reserved.

Photo on title page by Cathy A. Labate © 1988.

Library of Congress Cataloging-in-Publication Data

The Administration and supervision of reading programs/edited by
   Shelley B. Wepner, Joan T. Feeley, Dorothy S. Strickland.
     p. cm.
   Bibliography: p.
   Includes index.
   ISBN 0-8077-2929-9.   ISBN 0-8077-2928-0 (pbk.)
   1. Reading.   2. School management and organization.   3. School
supervision.   I. Wepner, Shelley B., 1951–   . II. Feeley, Joan
T., 1932–   . III. Strickland, Dorothy S.
LB1050.2.A36 1989   88-25926
428.4′07′12 – dc19   CIP

ISBN 0-8077-2928-0 (paperback)
ISBN 0-8077-2929-9 (cloth)

Manufactured in the United States of America

93 92 91 90 89   1 2 3 4 5 6

To our parents, our first role models and supervisors:
Carole and Bernard Markovitz
Theresa and Ed Stollmeyer
Evelyn and Leroy Salley

Contents

Foreword

A few years ago, I was an external evaluator for the reading program at a university in New Jersey. In that position, I was invited to observe some of the reading classes being conducted, one of which was on the organization and supervision of a reading program. In the class, the young professor apologized for the photocopies of the text she was using. After class we both bemoaned the fact that there were absolutely no current texts in print that covered the subject matter in the course. I was particularly concerned because a significant portion of my professional life had been spent as a reading supervisor. How awful that there were no good books in print focusing on the preparation of professionals for the administration and supervision of reading programs?

"Why don't you write one?" asked the young professor.

"Why don't you?" I replied.

Well, several years have passed and I'm pleased to see that the young professor, Dr. Shelley B. Wepner, did accept my challenge, and along with her colleagues, Drs. Joan T. Feeley and Dorothy S. Strickland, edited this excellent volume — a work sure to be a classic in the field.

In this book, each of the major parts concerns some of the knowledge areas necessary for administering reading programs. The first part provides a comprehensive overview of the major components of any reading program. This section then serves as an organizer for the rest of the book.

The second part discusses program development and organization from the pre-elementary through the high school level. A particularly unique and relevant aspect of this section is the chapter on pre-elementary programs, a component often overlooked in describing reading programs.

The third part deals with all the activities necessary to implement a successful reading program: program evaluation, staff development, selection and assessment of materials, and community outreach. Certainly, all of these functions are important if a reading program is to be maintained and expanded.

Finally, the last section of this volume focuses on the relationships of reading with other parts of the curriculum and other school personnel. Discussion centers on the interrelationships between reading and writing, and the importance of computers in the language arts program. Some attention is also given to working with special needs students and the special education staff. Lastly, this chapter recognizes that the ultimate goal of any reading program is the cultivation of lifetime readers. Working with library and media personnel helps to insure that this goal will indeed become a reality.

Undoubtedly, with a volume like this, college professors will no longer have to photocopy portions of outdated texts. The material included in this work provides an important sourcebook of recent and relevant research on the organization of a reading program. Furthermore, already practicing supervisors and coordinators will have a handy reference which can provide a bench mark against which they can measure their own programs.

In short, Drs. Wepner, Feeley, and Strickland are to be congratulated for providing the professional educational community with a readable, research-based volume on a heretofore neglected aspect of the field of reading.

Jack Cassidy
Professor of Education
Millersville University
President of I.R.A., 1982–83

Preface

This book is offered as a practical and readable text for those in positions to supervise reading programs. It provides current information about realistic concerns. Although much similar information may be found elsewhere, in a variety of sources, it has yet to be presented in a coherent text addressed specifically to administrators and supervisors.

The Administration and Supervision of Reading Programs aims to help preservice and inservice reading specialists, supervisors, and administrators understand how to organize and supervise reading programs, pre-K through grade twelve. Sound theoretical principles and practices for effective reading supervision in today's schools are offered through examples, observations, and research.

Four parts are written with these goals in mind. Part I provides an overview of reading supervision by describing effective reading program components and the personnel responsible for program implementation. Part II presents guidelines for developing reading programs at the pre-elementary, elementary, middle school and junior high, and high school levels. Part III describes five critical areas for program implementation and evaluation: material selection and use, teacher observations/conferences, staff development, program evaluation, and community outreach. Part IV explores four areas that often are overlooked in reading program development discussions yet are critical for comprehensive program development: reading-writing connections, computers, students with special needs, and the cultivation of lifetime readers. The book closes with a discussion of the connections made throughout the book and a look toward the future in reading supervision.

The strength of this book comes from our authors. By working in the schools in a variety of capacities over the years, our authors have created new visions about delivering reading instruction that they share with us here. We believe that their individual contributions create a unique chorus of harmonized ideas for supervising reading programs. We hope that your sentiments echo ours.

We gratefully acknowledge the following people for enhancing the quality of this book: *administrators and coordinators*, Philip Caccavale, Charmaine Della Neve, Susan Ginsberg, and Hiroko Miyakawa; *photographers*, Arthur Cansor, Sandy Marut, and especially Cathy Labate; *typist*, Helen Wolff.

Part I

OVERVIEW

Part I sets the stage for this book by providing a "structured overview" of guidelines for those responsible for reading program development. In describing the components needed for effective reading program development and the personnel responsible for program implementation, we make basic connections among major concepts addressed in subsequent chapters.

Chapter 1 provides specific guidelines for implementing three essential elements—curriculum, instruction, and assessment—in any effective reading program. Each of these elements then is used as part of a framework for embarking on a systematic process for changing reading programs. Chapter 2 describes the independent and interdependent roles and responsibilities of reading supervisors, reading specialists, principals, and classroom teachers. The technical knowledge and the interpersonal and management skills needed for each role are presented in light of important components for successful reading program development. In combination, these two chapters provide a comprehensive picture of how reading program components are interwoven.

1 Effective Reading Program Development

RITA M. BEAN
University of Pittsburgh

Cathy A. Labate © 1988

Imagine a school superintendent saying this to a teacher: "Our scores on the state reading test are some of the lowest among school districts in this state. This is the time for us to look at our school reading program and to make some decisions as to possible changes. As reading supervisor, we'd like you to chair a study committee, Ms. Reed. You'll report to the School Board at the spring meeting with your recommendations."

Our congratulations to Ms. Reed! The superintendent has just given her an important new responsibility: the task of taking a hard look at the current school reading program (K–12) and making some recommendations about what is effective and what should be changed. Further, she has to decide just how to proceed in making decisions about implementing a

3

change, namely, who should be involved in the change process and with what responsibilities.

Although this task may seem like an overwhelming one, and in many ways it is, there are some principles that can be helpful to individuals responsible for the reading programs in school districts. In this chapter, we describe the essential aspects of a school reading program, discuss a process model that can be used to initiate and implement change, and conclude with suggestions for involving teachers in classroom or action research designed to improve teaching and learning.

ESSENTIAL ELEMENTS OF A SCHOOL READING PROGRAM

Although individual teachers may work effectively in the classroom with students, their individual efforts do not constitute an overall reading program. The effective school reading program necessitates a broad, comprehensive view of reading; it requires a vision of what reading is and demands a concerted effort to help teachers work toward achieving that vision. To achieve an effective school reading program, all individuals involved in helping students become successful readers must be knowledgeable about school goals and directions. These individuals include teachers, parents, administrators, librarians, and resource persons such as reading specialists and counselors. To facilitate the efforts of those involved in developing and implementing an effective school reading program, we identify and describe three essential elements: curriculum, instruction, and assessment. These three elements are portrayed graphically in Figure 1.1.

Curriculum

The reading curriculum is the course of study found in a school; it is the heart and soul of the reading program. The curriculum includes the goals and philosophy of the program and the skills and knowledge identified as important. Materials that facilitate achievement of school goals are also generally included as part of the curriculum. One of Ms. Reed's tasks in studying the school reading program will be to work with others in the school and come to an agreement about the curriculum of reading. We list the following important guidelines related to the development of the reading curriculum.

1. *The school must decide upon goals for reading instruction based upon a sound definition of the reading process.*

Figure 1.1   Essential Elements of an Effective School Reading Program, K–12

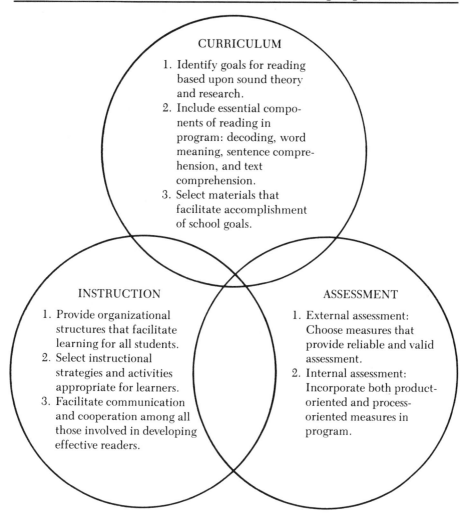

CURRICULUM

1. Identify goals for reading based upon sound theory and research.
2. Include essential components of reading in program: decoding, word meaning, sentence comprehension, and text comprehension.
3. Select materials that facilitate accomplishment of school goals.

INSTRUCTION

1. Provide organizational structures that facilitate learning for all students.
2. Select instructional strategies and activities appropriate for learners.
3. Facilitate communication and cooperation among all those involved in developing effective readers.

ASSESSMENT

1. External assessment: Choose measures that provide reliable and valid assessment.
2. Internal assessment: Incorporate both product-oriented and process-oriented measures in program.

That definition should be based upon knowledge gained from theory and research. The research of the past ten years has led to important understandings about the reading process (*Becoming a Nation of Readers*, 1985; Pearson, 1984). Experts agree that reading is not simply a hierarchically arranged set of subskills easily taught and tested, but that it is a complex skill requiring the coordination of a number of interrelated sources of information. Five generalizations generated from research and discussed in

Becoming a Nation of Readers (1985) provide important considerations for planning a reading program. These are stated as follows: reading is a constructive process, reading must be fluent, reading must be strategic, reading requires motivation, and reading is a continuously developing skill. A curriculum based upon these generalizations limits or discourages what Winograd and Greenlee (1986) call the "reductionist" view of teaching reading, which tends to overemphasize skills and views the teacher as a manager of material. Rather, these generalizations suggest emphasis on providing students with many different purposes for reading and a variety of texts. They stress the importance of self-monitoring and motivation in the reading program. The importance of a K–12 reading program is apparent when one understands that becoming a reader is a lifelong pursuit requiring much practice and refinement, particularly in this technological society with its sophisticated demands of the adult reader.

When working with teachers to define reading, our supervisor, Ms. Reed, also has to raise the issue of reading as one component of communication and must consider how the curriculum will capitalize on the interrelationships among the language arts. Evidence seems to indicate that writing promotes ability in reading and that there is a need for better integration when teaching the formal language skills of reading and writing in the school curriculum (*Becoming a Nation of Readers*, 1985; Stotsky, 1983; Wittrock, 1983). (See chapter 12 for more on this issue.)

2. *The school curriculum should provide the essential components of reading and should identify the foci at various levels and the means for their articulation.*

Although reading is a complex process that requires integrated use of multiple skills, there is a need to separate reading into component parts for the sake of instruction. As stated by Calfee and Drum (1986), the identified components should be simple yet coherent. These authors discuss four components of reading that should be included in all school reading programs: word meaning (vocabulary), word analysis (decoding), sentence comprehension, and text comprehension (narrative and exposition). Within each of these components, it is assumed that teachers will continually focus on developing an interest in and desire to read.

When investigating the various sources (e.g., reading textbooks, state reading guidelines, or basal reader manuals) often used in schools to make decisions about the components of a reading program, one finds somewhat different terminology used for similar components. Thus, for example, *word attack* may be used for *decoding*, or *word meaning* for *vocabulary*. In some cases study skills are treated separately from comprehension. Also, differences in suggestions for sequencing of instruction are found. Where a list is provided, it may be a helpful guide for planning and sequencing instruction. It is not, however, an empirically proven sequence of reading skills and has its limitations, especially if used in a rigid fashion. Careful attention by those working on the reading curriculum to the inclusion of all components and the sequencing of the various skills is essential. Too often the same skills are taught each year (short vowels in first and second grades and, for the poor reader, again in sixth) or there is little or no emphasis on various components of reading (e.g., students may not be introduced to any study strategy or be taught the elements of a story until junior high school English).

Relevant and ongoing issues needing discussion by those concerned include such questions as

- What skills and knowledge are important at the prereading stage?
- When should phonics be introduced? Which phonic elements should be introduced first? How much attention should be devoted to phonics after second grade (especially for those who have not been successful)?
- What should be the focus of the middle school reading program (basal driven, literature based, content based)?
- When and how do students get experience in reading content materials?

Answers to these questions and others specific to one's school district will help curriculum developers identify the foci at various levels of schooling and provide ideas for effective articulation. Chall's (1983) six-stage model of reading acquisition provides an interesting way in which to consider the focus at various levels of schooling. Chall suggests that students progress through each of the following stages of reading: prereading (birth to age six), initial reading or decoding (age six to seven), fluency (age seven to eight), reading to learn (any age), multiple viewpoints (high school), and reconstruction (college and beyond).

It is essential that curriculum developers structure the curriculum so that all components of reading are given appropriate emphasis, and they must consider the focus at each of the levels so that appropriate goals, activities, and materials can be selected.

3. *Materials should help schools achieve their reading goals.*

In an effective school reading program, the materials selected should reflect the curriculum goals and objectives of the school. Too often materials determine and drive the curriculum; they influence both activities and the content that students learn (Duffy, Roehler, & Mason, 1984). At the elementary level, the predominant material and approach to reading is the basal reading program; however, the basal cannot be the total reading program. The selection of trade books for classroom and library is an important dimension of program development. Textbooks used in the various content areas should be assessed to determine how they facilitate literacy instruction. In addition, various supplemental books and nonprint materials such as films, records, maps, and charts add other dimensions to reading and facilitate the view of reading as a communication tool. Moreover, the availability of computer software for classroom reading programs leads to the need for careful scrutiny of these materials.

To help schools select materials appropriate for the curriculum, various guidelines and evaluation suggestions have been developed. The series of guidelines found in the *Guide to Selecting Basal Reading Programs* (1987), developed by the Center for the Study of Reading, is an important aid for evaluating basals (see chapter 7). Kamil (1984) provides an excellent list of criteria for assessing software.

Although published guidelines may provide a basic framework, each school must modify or adapt them so that they complement the school's philosophy and approach to reading.

Instruction

Obviously, the preceding three guidelines are extremely important in the development of the reading curriculum; however, the delivery of the curriculum through instruction is also a critical element in an effective reading program. Ms. Reed knows she must give attention to this area.

When we discuss instruction, we are describing the way in which the curriculum is delivered, for example, the learning activities and strategies and the groupings used to meet the needs of individual learners. Although a teacher working with an individual student must have an excellent understanding of the reading process and reading methodology, this task is "simple" compared to the task of providing instruction for twenty or more students whose range in reading performance may be wide. Generally, a total school reading program will include the following special emphases:

- *Accelerated reading:* The program for students whose progress in reading is greater than expected for a specific grade level (e.g., the child coming to first grade who is already reading; the fifth grader reading at a high school level)
- *Developmental reading:* The overall reading instruction offered for students at normal developmental levels

- *Corrective reading:* The supplemental, selective instruction for students with minor reading difficulties, often taught by the teacher in the regular classroom
- *Remedial reading:* The specialized reading instruction adjusted to the needs of students who do not perform in a satisfactory manner in the regular reading program

One of the important tasks of the individual responsible for a total reading program is to promote communication and congruence between the special programs and the classroom developmental reading program.

There are three major guidelines relating to instruction:

1. *The organizational structure must provide for student differences in background, performance, and ability.*
Currently, the primary means of organizing reading instruction appears to be ability grouping. Although grouping may, in some settings, help teachers adjust the pace and level of instruction to a smaller range, there are concerns about the ability grouping found in most schools, particularly qualitative differences in instruction between the high and low reading groups, which might be detrimental to the students in those groups (Allington, 1983; Gambrell, Wilson, & Gantt, 1981; Hiebert, 1983). Research suggests that, although ability grouping may improve the achievement of the fast child, it may not help the slow child (Kulik & Kulik, 1982). Also, there are more opportunities for learning in high-ability groups (Sorensen & Hallinan, 1986). Finally, there is some concern that ability grouping may have harmful effects on the social and affective development of children, especially for those in the low-ability groups (Esposito, 1973; Rosenbaum, 1980). Therefore, although ability grouping may be one means of providing for student differences, there is a need to think seriously about how to reduce the possible harmful effects of such grouping.

The suggestions listed in *Becoming a Nation of Readers* (1985) encourage variations that may be helpful in reducing the difficulties with ability grouping, such as periodic review and flexible grouping (grouping by interests or topics). The concept of cooperative learning (Slavin, 1984), peer tutoring, and whole-class teaching for some concepts such as vocabulary instruction might also be incorporated into the instructional framework of the reading program.

2. *Select instructional strategies and activities appropriate for learners.*
In this general overview chapter, it is difficult to describe succinctly individual strategies or activities identified by research as helpful in teaching

reading. These will be taken up in detail in the chapters of part II. For the time being, the following critical points regarding instruction might be considered. First, given that reading is an interactive, constructive act, teachers need to consider the text, the learner, and the task in making instructional decisions. Based upon these variables, teachers must decide how much and what kinds of instruction are necessary. Areas of concern are, for example, the amount of prereading preparation, which vocabulary words to teach and how elaborately, the degree of guided reading, and the types of follow-up to text reading. Teachers thus must have an excellent understanding of the reading process and how it affects instruction. They must be able to identify the *what*, *why*, and *how* of reading instruction (Michigan Reading Association, 1984):

- *What* is being read? Is it a poem, a story, a newspaper?
- *Why* are the students reading? Is it for information, for enjoyment?
- *How* should students read? What strategies do students need to use to accomplish the task? Should they study, skim?

Second, classroom time must be provided for reading practice. Research points to the importance of independent reading, both in and out of school, as one of the best ways by which to improve reading performance (Allington, 1984; Leinhardt, Zigmond, & Cooley, 1981; Walburg & Tsai, 1984). Thus, in planning the school reading program, not only must Ms. Reed assist teachers and the librarian in selecting appropriate trade books, but she must facilitate independent reading within the daily structure of the reading program.

Third, writing should be an integral part of the reading program. As mentioned previously, the research evidence supports the relationship of these two formal language skills. The notion of comprehension and composition as "two sides of the same basic process" (Squire, 1983, p. 581) is an important concept for the curriculum developer. Students should participate in experiences that help them see the relationship between the reading and writing process, that is, between being an audience for someone else's writing and writing for an audience (see chapter 12).

Fourth, students should be given opportunities to become independent, to monitor their own reading. From kindergarten on, students need experiences that help them to realize that reading is a task that relies on what readers bring to it, on their purpose for reading, as well as on the type of material or text. All lessons can be planned to help students monitor their reading and to reflect upon what they have learned.

Fifth, a school district should decide how it can incorporate into its instructional programs the results of the research on effective teaching, which has established the value of systematic, step-by-step instruction, particularly in the area of reading at the elementary and junior high school levels. Rosenshine (1986) provides an excellent synthesis of the research on explicit teaching and divides the results into six teaching functions that need to be taken into consideration when presenting new information to students: review, presentation of new material, guided practice, feedback, independent practice, and weekly and monthly reviews.

Finally, the climate in a school must be conducive to the development of students as readers. Not only should the classrooms contain all sorts of reading materials, but there should be an atmosphere in the school that promotes reading as an enjoyable and necessary part of life. There should be opportunities at all grade levels for teachers to read to their students, as well as motivational programs that encourage student reading (see chapter 15).

3. *An effective means of communication and cooperation is essential for those working in an instructional role in reading.*

Although the classroom or reading teacher has a primary role in reading instruction, there are many other individuals who are important in helping students become good readers: parents, the reading specialist, the content teachers (particularly at the middle school and high school levels), the librarian, and the principal, to name a few. In an effective school reading program, there must be a working two-way communication system that facilitates cooperation. Not only can the school share ideas with the parents about what parents can do to help their children become good readers, but the school can obtain important information from the parents regarding student interests and attitudes towards learning.

This notion of communication and cooperation is extremely important when students receive reading instruction from more than one teacher. Often these students are those who are experiencing difficulties in reading, and yet they must handle the demands of two different classroom settings, approaches, and teachers. Johnston, Allington, and Afflerbach (1985) recommend greater congruence between the remedial reading program and the classroom reading program. Leinhardt and Palley (1982) suggest that the setting of instruction is not the primary factor, but rather that the instructional practices are the important ingredients. The key to success appears to be the communication and cooperation that occur between the teachers, which enable the setting of common goals and strategies.

Assessment

Ms. Reed by now is aware that the curriculum and the instructional program are essential elements in the reading program; she also knows the importance of assessment but is not quite certain about how to approach this dimension of the reading program.

The school reading program generally includes two major types of assessment: external (outside the classroom) and internal (in the classroom). The former is generally used to make judgments about the school reading program, such as how well a school is teaching comprehension as compared to others in the nation. Internal assessment is used by the classroom teacher to make decisions that affect daily lessons. Ms. Reed must consider both types of assessment for the school reading program (See chapter 10).

External Assessment.   The standardized measures of student achievement, which generally serve as external measures, do not appear to be very useful to teachers in planning and modifying classroom practice (Salmon-Cox, 1982). However, these test results do provide objective information about school performance to important constituents: parents, board members, and school administrators. Test scores can also be used to "(1) group children on a tentative basis, (2) provide a referral basis for children with reading problems, and (3) provide information about general strength and limitations in the reading program" (Bean, 1976, p. 38). However, anyone selecting a standardized test needs to be concerned about the overlap or match between the reading program and the standardized test (Farr & Carey, 1986). Part of the task in developing an effective reading program, therefore, is that of selecting appropriate assessment measures and determining the grades at which they should be administered as well as the numbers of students who should take the tests so that a reliable sample is obtained.

Using standardized measures as the only criteria for assessing the effectiveness of a school reading program tends to be somewhat limiting and shortsighted, however. These results tend to ignore skills, habits, and attitudes, such as interest in reading and critical reading skills, that should be important aspects of the reading program. As stated by Cuban (1983), "Improved test scores are simply not enough. . . . How can the broader, more complex, and less easily measured goals of schooling be achieved as we improve test results?" (p. 696). Information other than standardized test results can provide important and revealing data. Indicators such as the number of books checked out from the library or the results of reading attitude inventories should be considered by those developing, implementing, and evaluating the reading program.

Internal Assessment.   The internal measures used by the teacher are critical to the success of the reading program. Teachers have a number of informal measures that they can use to assess the progress of individual students in their classroom. Some may be product oriented and assess student outcomes, such as criterion-referenced tests, workbook sheets, and end-of-unit tests in basals. However, internal measures should also include process-oriented measures that focus on assessment of how students relate to or handle a reading task, rather than on how well they have mastered a given task. Observations of how students read orally or handle various reading tasks (e.g., summarizing, categorizing) are examples of process measures. This type of assessment, which is closely related to instruction, can provide an efficient and effective means of helping teachers plan their daily lessons. As teachers observe and interact with their students during a reading lesson, they can assess a student's degree of success in applying various strategies and the amount of teacher guidance needed to assure success. Ms. Reed, in her efforts to develop an effective reading program, may need to work with teachers to help them become more facile with this type of assessment. Johnson (1987) suggests that the expert teacher is also an "evaluation expert" who can describe the extent and quality of a child's literacy development (p. 748).

These three elements—curriculum, instruction, and assessment—comprise the important aspects of a total school reading program and provide the framework for developing, implementing, and evaluating the program. Yet they do not occur instantaneously, nor are they easily achieved. Sizer (1985) states it well: "A good school does not emerge like a prepackaged frozen dinner stuck for 15 seconds in a radar range; it develops from the slow simmering of carefully blended ingredients" (p. 22).

PROCESS FOR CHANGE

The reports from commissions and individuals during the past decade have all described the need for school reform and school improvement efforts, and indeed, many new reform movements and effective school plans have been initiated at district and state levels. Staff development notions such as teacher centers, career ladders, mentoring, and coaching are being "tried and tested," singularly or in combination, in districts across the country. These efforts, which start with much enthusiasm and excitement, too often fall short of reaching their mark. We will describe four principles that are useful in planning school change.

1. *There must be a systematic process for school change.*
Whether one is interested in total school change or in modifications in specific curricular areas or at certain grade levels, there must be a process for change that is ongoing, systematic, and understood by all involved. Bishop (1976) provides a sequential and comprehensive model that has been useful for school change, shown in Figure 1.2. Needs and Diagnosis/ Analysis, the first and second stages in Bishop's model, refer to the importance of identifying goals based upon an understanding of the present situation. One useful activity at this stage is to ask teachers to describe and

Figure 1.2   Bishop's Instructional Change Model

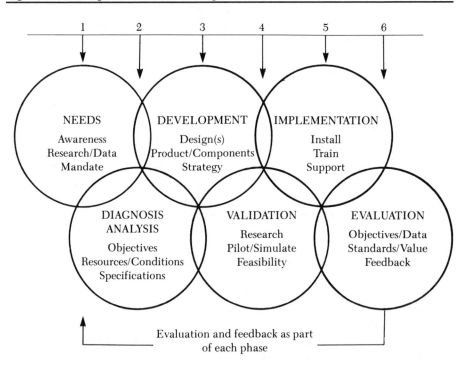

Source: Bishop, L. J. (1976). *Staff Development and Instructional Improvement Plans and Procedures.* Boston: Allyn and Bacon, p. 4. Reprinted with permission.

assess their reading curriculum (the objectives, the content, instructional strategies, and evaluation procedures). Various strengths and weaknesses as well as misunderstandings among teachers become apparent through this type of effort. In the third and fourth stages, Development and Validation, teachers and others (consultants, parents, administrators) investigate various ideas, materials, and so forth that will enable the school to make changes. Also, pilot testing may be necessary to validate the effectiveness of the identified changes. Implementation, the fifth stage, speaks to the importance of helping all teachers understand and implement the specific changes. Too often, good ideas that are placed into curriculum guides or district manuals are not implemented in the daily teaching repertoire of the classroom teachers. Often this is due to inadequate preparation and training for the teachers or other personnel who will actually implement the change. Evaluation, the final stage, refers to the importance of monitoring and assessing the effectiveness of the specific change.

In addition to the need for making changes in a systematic way, the process must also be conducted in a humane and understanding manner. In their concerns-based approach to change, Hall and Hord (1987) discuss the importance of understanding how teachers perceive change and of adjusting the process to teachers' needs and point of view. This aspect of the change initiative is a critical one if Ms. Reed and others involved in change are to be successful in their efforts to implement change in the total school.

2. *The school is the key unit for effective change* (Goodlad, 1984; Lezotte & Bancroft, 1985).
By focusing on the individual school as the unit for change, supervisors or other change agents work with the critical mass necessary to generate ideas and sustain enthusiasm for change. Moreover, the learning that can occur in group activities appears to be important if change is to be initiated and sustained. However, the school does not exist as an island isolated from other schools at the same or different levels in the district. Often at initial phases in a change process, where goals are being determined or questions about the general philosophical basis for the reading program are being discussed, representatives from all schools need to be involved. The key, however, is moving the change process to the school level where as many personnel as possible can be involved.

3. *Collaboration is a key to success in school improvement.*
Collaboration means not only that all constituents must play a part in helping to make decisions about change but also that they must both be responsible and share authority for basic policy decision making (Hoyt,

1978). Most individuals involved in change or reform efforts are aware of the importance of involving all actors in the process: teachers, principals, resource persons (the reading specialist, librarian, and so forth), and community representatives, including students. The role of principal as instructional leader has received enormous support during the past decade. Although the reading supervisor may be given the primary responsibility for initiating change in the reading curriculum, it is paramount that the principal be an integral part of the change process, both in the planning and implementation stages.

Moreover, if one involves parents at early stages of school change, there is greater likelihood of community support and understanding. At the present time, the selection and inclusion of various textbooks has created dissension in some districts across the country. The involvement of community representatives can help a district avoid such controversy and, more importantly, can help those involved in school change select goals and activities that address the values and expectations of the primary stakeholders — the parents and students.

The notion of involving all constituents is commonly accepted; however, the notion of collaborating is somewhat more difficult to achieve. It emphasizes both the central importance of people in an organization and the importance of people working together as equals to solve problems. Collaboration can occur between various combinations of individuals or groups: between university and school, grade-level and content-area teachers, foundations and school districts, and teacher organizations and school districts. Some specific examples are

- Collaboration between university and school to assess the effectiveness of a new approach to teaching middle school reading
- Collaboration between the content-area teachers and reading specialists to develop more congruence between programs
- Collaboration between community library and elementary reading teachers working on a joint program for summer reading

Collaboration appears to hold great promise for creating change. Lieberman (1986) lists guidelines for collaborative work that should be useful. The ten-point definition provided by Hord (1986) provides specific criteria necessary for such an effort.

4. *Staff development efforts must be an integral part of any change process.*
As stated previously, too often good ideas never get integrated into classroom practice. There are many examples of "one-shot" inservice programs

that provided initial enthusiasm but no more. Current efforts at school reform now seem to be focused on helping classroom teachers implement "effective" strategies into their teaching. These efforts are essential if change is to become a reality. Staff development must be ongoing in order to provide continuing support and feedback to teachers. The clinical model of supervision provides one such model for staff development (Acheson & Gall, 1987). Teacher centers, where teachers can leave their classrooms to become involved in professional activities for a period of time, have also proven effective (Bickel et al., 1987). In all cases, ongoing support beyond the staff development period must be provided for participants, to insure continued implementation and usage of the desired behaviors.

The preceding four guidelines point out the need for intimate involvement of the classroom teacher in both generating ideas for change and implementing change in the classroom. They acknowledge the importance of the teacher as a decision maker, a professional interested in creating an excellent learning experience for students. Probably the highest level of involvement for teachers as well as supervisors is to be involved in a deliberate systematic study of what they are doing. Such involvement is known as action or classroom research and probably requires some type of collaboration (between teachers, between teachers and supervisor, or between teachers and university personnel). We now turn to a discussion of this type of research, including ideas for instituting it within the school reading program as a vehicle for creating more effective school reading programs.

ACTION RESEARCH

The notion of action research, sometimes labeled "teacher" or "classroom" research, holds great promise for Ms. Reed and others in similar positions who are interested in improving both their reading programs and the effectiveness of teachers within the system. Action research is the systematic study of educational practice by participants; it requires both active inquiry and reflection upon educational practices (Hopkins, 1985). Action research can range from an informal small study affecting the practices of one teacher to a formal evaluation study that affects education in an entire school or school district. Teachers who become systematic participant-observers of their students can begin to reflect and make judgments about both their teaching processes and student learning. For example, Hess (1986), because of her interest in the writing process and its relationship to reading, incorporated writing into her remedial reading program. Based upon her observations, the writing samples, and responses of students to the process, she was able to make recommendations for further use of the approach in her own teaching and in the school remedial reading program.

Efforts in which teachers serve as members of a research team in order to solve educational problems of a school is also a type of action research. Tikunoff and Mergendoller (1983) describe their "interactive research and development" approach as one that is team-centered, focuses on current concerns of classroom teachers, and is a problem-solving strategy as well as a research process. They describe a large study in an urban school district in which all involved examined the techniques used by classroom teachers to cope with distractions to classroom instruction and to determine the effectiveness of their various techniques. The research goal was established by the school district because of its interest in helping students to engage more often in meaningful learning activities.

Involvement of teachers in evaluation studies of new materials or approaches is another type of action research that can be helpful to those interested in more effective practice. When teachers are involved in conceptualizing, organizing, and implementing the study, they tend to be more willing to participate, less threatened by the notion of evaluation, and more likely to implement the results.

Action research holds great promise for several reasons. First, it may be easier to implement the results of such research. The generalization that results of "traditional" research do not get implemented in the classroom appears to be an accurate one. There are numerous possible reasons for this, but that is not the issue here. Rather, by making teachers partners in the research process, change in classroom practice is more likely to occur. Second, the involvement in the inquiry process necessary for research can be an important tool of staff development. Teachers who become action researchers may assume more control of their professional lives and become more excited and knowledgeable about teaching and learning issues.

How can Ms. Reed involve the reading teachers in her school in action research? First, she and other school district administrators need to provide positive support and reinforcement to individual teachers who express an interest in examining more systematically what they are doing in their classrooms. Not only should she provide the necessary support for these teachers, but she should facilitate the sharing of findings with colleagues and administrators in the district. Second, Ms. Reed and her staff, after identifying some important questions that they believe need to be answered, can reach out to others in the community who might assist in finding answers to those questions. Collaborators may include university educators and individuals from state departments of education or from various educational and business organizations.

With this type of collaboration, the funding that is necessary to support a larger, more systematic study of school practices may be easier to obtain. Moreover, it provides the necessary expertise for investigating an issue and creates an excitement and enthusiasm that helps to sustain the change initiative.

SUMMARY

No one told Ms. Reed that the charge to evaluate and make recommendations about the school reading program would be easy, because it isn't. However, the development, implementation, and evaluation of a well-balanced K–12 reading program is an exciting and challenging task that requires the cooperation, coordination, and involvement of all concerned. In this overview chapter, we have described the three essential elements of an effective reading program — curriculum, instruction, and assessment — which provide a framework by which a program developer can conceptualize the reading program. Specific guidelines have been offered for each of these three elements.

Because a program is useless if it is not implemented, a process for change that is systematic and humane has been described and principles and procedures for implementing such change suggested. Given that teachers provide the key to implementation of any given change, teacher participation and collaboration have been discussed. The notion of action research as a means of staff development, ongoing evaluation, and problem solving has also been described.

REFERENCES

Acheson, K. A., & Gall, M. D. (1987). *Techniques in the clinical supervision of teachers.* New York: Longman.

Allington, R. L. (1983). The reading instruction provided readers of differing ability. *Elementary School Journal, 83,* 548–559.

Allington, R. L. (1984). Oral reading. In P. D. Pearson (Ed.), *Handbook of reading research* (pp. 829–864). New York: Longman.

Bean, R. M. (1976). Guidelines for development and assessment of an effective reading program. In A. Berger & R. Bean (Eds.), *School reading programs: Criteria for excellence* (pp. 34–38). Pittsburgh: University of Pittsburgh.

Becoming a nation of readers: The report of the Commission on Reading. (1985). Washington, DC: National Institute of Education.

Bickel, W., Denton, S., Johnston, J., LeMahieu, P., Soltrick, D., & Young, J. (1987, Spring). Teacher professionalism and educational reform: Clinical teachers at the Schenley Teacher Center. *Journal of Staff Development, 8*(2), 9–14.

Bishop, L. J. (1976). *Staff development and instructional improvement plans and procedures.* Boston: Allyn and Bacon.

Calfee, R., & Drum, P. (1986). Research on teaching reading. In M. Wittrock (Ed.), *Handbook of research on teaching* (pp. 804–849). New York: Macmillan.

Chall, J. (1983). *Stages of reading development.* New York: McGraw-Hill.

Cuban, L. (1983). Effective schools: A friendly but cautionary note. *Phi Delta Kappan, 64,* 695–696.

Duffy, G. G., Roehler, L. R., & Mason, J. (1984). *Comprehensive instruction: Perspectives and suggestions.* New York: Longman.

Esposito, D. (1973). Homogeneous and heterogeneous ability grouping: Principal findings and implementations for evaluating and designing more effective educational environments. *Review of Educational Research, 43,* 163–179.

Farr, R., & Carey, R. F. (1986). *Reading: What can be measured?* (2nd ed.). Newark, DE: International Reading Association.

Gambrell, L., Wilson, R., & Gantt, W. N. (1981). Classroom observations of task-attending behaviors of good and poor readers. *Journal of Educational Research, 74,* 400–404.

Goodlad, J. I. (1984). *A place called school.* New York: McGraw-Hill.

Guide to selecting basal reading programs. (1987). Champaign, IL: Center for the Study of Reading.

Hall, G. E., & Hord, S. M. (1987). *Change in schools: Facilitating the process.* New York: State University of New York Press.

Hess, N. (1986). *Use of the writing process approach for instructing remedial students.* Unpublished master's thesis, University of Pittsburgh.

Hiebert, F. H. (1983). An examination of ability grouping for reading instruction. *Reading Research Quarterly, 18,* 231–255.

Hopkins, D. (1985). *A teacher's guide to classroom research.* Philadelphia: Open University Press.

Hord, S. M. (1986). A synthesis of research on organizational collaboration. *Educational Leadership, 43*(5), 22–26.

Hoyt, K. (1978). *A concept of collaboration in career education.* Washington, DC: U.S. Office of Education.

Johnson, P. (1987). Teachers as evaluation experts. *The Reading Teacher, 40,* 744–748.

Johnston, P., Allington, R., & Afflerbach, P. (1985). The congruence of classroom and remedial reading instruction. *Elementary School Journal, 85,* 465–477.

Kamil, M. L. (1984). Computers, literacy, and teaching reading. In J. F. Baumann, & D. D. Johnson (Eds.), *Reading instruction and the beginning teacher. A practical guide* (pp. 262–272). Edina, MN: Burgess.

Kulik, C. C., & Kulik, J. A. (1982). Effects of ability grouping on secondary school students: A meta-analysis of evaluation findings. *American Educational Research Journal, 29,* 415–428.

Leinhardt, G., & Palley, A. (1982). Restrictive educational settings: Exits or havens? *Review of Educational Research, 52,* 557–578.

Leinhardt, G., Zigmond, N., & Cooley, W. W. (1981). Reading instruction and its effects. *American Educational Research Journal, 18,* 343–361.

Lezotte, L., & Bancroft, B. (1985). Growing use of the effective schools model for school improvement. *Educational Leadership, 42*(6), 23–27.

Lieberman, A. (1986). Collaborative work. *Educational Leadership, 43*(5), 4–8.

Michigan Reading Association. (1984). Reading redefined: A Michigan Reading Association position paper. *The Michigan Reading Journal, 17,* 4–7.

Pearson, D. (Ed.). (1984). *Handbook of reading research.* New York: Longman.

Rosenbaum, J. E. (1980). Social implications of educational grouping. In D. C. Berliner (Ed.), *Review of research in education* (vol. 8) (pp. 361–401). Washington, DC: American Educational Research Association.

Rosenshine, B. V. (1986). Synthesis of research on explicit teaching. *Educational Leadership, 43*(7), 60–69.

Salmon-Cox, L. (1982). Teachers and standardized tests: What's really happening? *Phi Delta Kappan, 63,* 631–634.

Sizer, T. R. (1985). Common sense. *Educational Leadership, 42*(6), 21–22.

Slavin, R. E. (1984). Team assisted individualization: Cooperative learning and individualized instruction in the mainstreamed classroom. *Remedial and Special Education, 5*(6), 33–42.

Sorensen, A., & Hallinan, M. (1986). Effects of ability grouping on growth in academic achievement. *American Educational Research Journal, 23,* 519–542.

Squire, J. (1983). Composing and comprehending: Two sides of the same basic process. *Language Arts, 60,* 581–589.

Stotsky, S. (1983). Research on reading/writing relationships: A synthesis and suggested directions. *Language Arts, 60,* 627–643.

Tikunoff, W. J., & Mergendoller, J. R. (1983). Inquiry as a means to professional growth: The teacher as researcher. In G. Griffin (Ed.), *Staff development: Eighty-second yearbook of the National Society for the Study of Education* (pp. 210–227). Chicago: University of Chicago Press.

Walburg, H. J., & Tsai, S. (1984). Reading achievement and diminishing returns to time. *Journal of Educational Psychology, 76,* 442–451.

Winograd, P., & Greenlee, M. (1986). Students need a balanced reading program. *Educational Leadership, 43*(7), 16–21.

Wittrock, M. C. (1983). Writing and the teaching of reading. *Language Arts, 60,* 600–606.

2 Roles and Responsibilities of Reading Personnel

SHELLEY B. WEPNER
William Paterson College of New Jersey

The role of the reading specialist is often misunderstood and almost always difficult to establish. [Smith, Otto, & Hansen, 1978, p. 233]

The role of the supervisor, having changed frequently in the past, may reasonably be expected to continue to change. [Burg, Kaufman, Korngold, & Kovner, 1978, p. 11]

Today, the principalship is more complex and demanding than at any time in the past. [Barnard & Hetzel, 1986, p. 1]

As our society changes, so do our schools, as microcosms of society. As our schools change, so do the school personnel who run them. Underpinning these changes is a diversity of research to support evolving theoretical principles. We have seen this in the field of reading, particularly in the last two decades. As reading research begins to help us understand the underlying processes in the comprehension of language (Glaser, 1985), we are starting to use this newfound knowledge to help us alter teaching practices, programs, and policies for reading. Accompanying these changes, though, are confusing inconsistencies in reading roles and responsibilities. Who are the people responsible for our schools' reading programs? What are their roles and responsibilities? What are the similarities and differences among the roles of various reading personnel? These are the questions that must be addressed as schools attempt to cultivate an atmosphere that supports reading and reflects the most recent array of reading research. It is these questions that form the basis of this chapter.

OVERVIEW

When we think of an enriched reading program, we think of teachers, administrators, reading specialists, parents, librarians, auxiliary personnel, school board members, community members, and students working closely together. When this happens, a sense of ownership of the reading program is fostered (Cook, 1986). Exactly what they are all working toward is determined, in many respects, by those who are primarily responsible for the reading program; therefore, it is important to understand what characterizes our reading personnel.

Reading personnel have been referred to as an endangered species (Wepner, 1977; Wilson & Becker, 1984) or, at the very least, as unnoticed and ignored (Cohen, Intili, & Robbins, 1978). Some say they are facing an identity crisis in terms of the need and purpose for their jobs. These beliefs are not unfounded. For whatever reasons — the tightening of school budgets, the decrease in federal funding, or the establishment of new priorities (Wilson & Becker, 1984) — reading personnel have been suffering from a great deal of role conflict and role ambiguity in day-to-day interactions and short-term and long-term goals (Pierson-Hubeny & Archambault, 1985). These observations are supported by data from state departments of education. In her survey, Fuccello (1987) found that half of the responding departments reported that there was a decrease in the number of teachers being certified as reading specialists because of differing emphases at the local district levels. Many of the states also reported differing perceptions of the reading specialist's role, supporting Robinson and Pettit's (1978) beliefs that with the reading specialist's multitude of responsibilities come too many role inconsistencies.

Another problem is the varying criteria from state to state and from institution to institution regarding certification of reading specialists. According to a survey conducted by the National Reading Conference (Weisberg, 1986), while all reading specialists need a valid teaching certificate, one to three years teaching experience, and twelve to thirty-four postbaccalaureate credits, their required competencies vary considerably. Only two of the fifteen courses/competencies (Foundations of Reading Instruction or Developmental Reading, and Reading Disabilities) were required by all responding states. Eleven of the fifteen competencies listed were required by 50 percent of the states or fewer, indicating a lack of uniformity among states for reading specialist preparation. One-third of the respondents also indicated statewide exceptions to the reading specialist certification, including differentiated requirements by level — elementary, junior high, and high school; knowledge of the affective basis of reading; knowledge of computer-assisted instruction; and knowledge of supervision.

Even with these variations, reading specialists are needed and used in schools to improve reading programs (Smith, Otto, & Hansen, 1978). For example, according to Wisconsin's legislation in 1977, each district must employ a certified reading specialist to develop and implement a comprehensive K–12 reading program (Vance & Quealy, 1978). Another example is New Hampshire's statute which mandates that when a school has an enrollment of at least 350 children it must provide a full-time certified reading specialist; where there are fewer than 350 children, it must provide the services of a certified reading specialist on a pro-rata basis.

When trained properly, reading specialists have the competencies needed to help students, teachers, administrators, and the community at large to develop appropriately satisfying reading programs. Reading specialists also are an important link between the central office and individual schools in communicating goals and establishing priorities (Wilson & Becker, 1984). To support this notion, Vance and Quealy (1978) reported from a survey that, in most school districts, there is little consistency or coordination except in districts with reading specialists. It is important, though, that the roles of reading specialists be clearly delineated to promote effective reading program development and foster positive staff relationships. While local needs usually dictate the specific job descriptions, it is critical that the roles of reading personnel be explicit in order to help them understand the parameters of their own positions as well as those of other staff members (Rice, 1987).

READING SPECIALIST'S ROLES AND RESPONSIBILITIES

Some believe that the designation *reading specialist* is so broad that the meaning given in any particular situation should be determined by what the specialist does and what training he or she has or needs (International Reading Association, 1986; Smith et al., 1978). For example, reading specialists in one district have released time to confer with other classroom teachers, order material, and perform inservice sessions. In another district, reading specialists are totally responsible for helping content teachers incorporate reading into teaching. Obviously, both would require different training for adequate job performance (Smith et al., 1978). In my own varied experience as a reading specialist, I have been a glorified remedial language arts teacher at a middle school; a K–6 resource teacher; a Chapter 1 reading teacher (then Title I); and a reading lab housekeeper of yesteryear's exotic reading machines. While my title always was or resembled "reading specialist," I have performed the different duties desired by each district.

Obviously, the role of the reading specialist is affected by many factors: the size and type of school, institutional policy and practice, the personality of the individual specialist, financial exigencies (Bean & Eichelberger, 1985), and statewide proclivities. For instance, Fuccello (1987) found that, while most states had reading specialists spending most of their time teaching (often in Chapter 1 programs), many states were beginning to require specialists to devote 50 percent of their time to the resource role, with one state (Wisconsin) firmly establishing the resource role as the main one.

The International Reading Association's (IRA) *Guidelines for the Specialized Preparation of Reading Professionals* (1986) include five distinct roles under the rubric of reading specialist: diagnostic-remedial specialist, developmental reading-study skills specialist, reading consultant/reading resource teacher, reading coordinator/supervisor, and reading professor. For purposes of this chapter, the first three are considered appropriate to the job of reading specialist. The designated role responsibilities, as defined by the IRA, are as follows:

• *Diagnostic-remedial specialist:* Assesses, remediates, and plans instructional intervention at the elementary or secondary level, or in a laboratory or clinic (public, private, or commercial), or a resource center at all levels. Provides service to students designated as having reading disabilities, reading difficulties, or environmental/educational deprivation (for example, Chapter 1 students). Coordinates reading services provided to each disabled learner in conjunction with the classroom teacher and those in allied professions.

• *Developmental reading-study skills specialist:* Teaches developmental and/or corrective reading, writing, and thinking skills at the secondary school, community college, college, or university/professional school levels. May be responsible for teaching developmental reading in corporate educational, vocational, penal, or social agencies. Responsible for teaching higher-order developmental and study skills as well as for providing diagnostic corrective and/or remedial services.

• *Reading consultant/reading resource teacher:* Organizes and administers a school site reading program. Responsible for providing leadership to classroom teachers, diagnostic-remedial specialists, and/or developmental reading study skills specialists in planning, organizing, managing, and evaluating the schoolwide reading program. Tasks may include (1) applying current research/theory to practice in all programs, (2) articulating a balanced reading-language-thinking program through the grades, (3) providing staff development consistent with assessed needs of program and staff, (4) coordinating the work of reading specialists and special services personnel, and (5) advising administration and community about the school reading/language arts program.

In addition to knowing how the IRA defines role responsibilities, it is important to be aware of three areas of concern regarding reading specialists' roles. The first area that needs to be resolved is the debate over balancing student instruction with resource responsibilities. An IRA survey (1979) found that reading specialists' four most frequent functions were remedial reading, diagnostic work, developing instructional materials, and teaching developmental reading. Even with the current thrust to establish more of a resource role, most survey reports seemed to indicate that classroom teachers and administrators valued the reading specialist's role as an instructional position in which the focus was on working with students with reading problems (Bean & Eichelberger, 1985; Cohen et al., 1978; Hesse, Smith, & Nettleton, 1973; Mangieri & Heimberger, 1980; Pikulski & Ross, 1979). Bean and Eichelberger (1985) referred to these responsibilities as student-centered; in contrast, reading specialists saw themselves more as resource teachers, for example, assisting classroom teachers to plan instruction, offering inservice training, and developing materials. Some of these same studies indicated, though, that teachers or administrators became very interested in the resource role when they had experienced some of the benefits. Bean (1979) found that three of the most highly valued roles of the specialist (inservice training, development of materials, and conferencing) were resource oriented. This was despite the fact that the fourteen teachers surveyed had spent a year working with these reading specialists, who acted more as instructors than as resource teachers. Wilson and Becker (1984) found that principals rated the resource role services of reading specialists very highly. In one particular district, the reading specialists were more like resource teachers, working closely with teachers and parents. In addition, teachers' instructional strategies improved when reading specialists had the opportunity to give suggestions, provide diagnostic feedback, or share materials (Cohen et al., 1978).

While some recommend that the specialist work with both students and teachers (Bean, 1979; Garry, 1974), we believe that serving in a resource role enables the specialist to help teachers become better instructors of reading. Nichols (1979) recognized how the role was changing, primarily from that of dealing with reading problems in a clinical environment to that of training teachers. Obviously, closer cooperation between reading specialists and teachers needs to be cultivated so that the resource role is regarded as a viable responsibility.

This leads to the second area of concern, regarding misconceptions of the various roles. It is imperative that reading specialists, principals, classroom teachers, and reading professors share information about the role of the reading specialist, so that their perceptions are more closely aligned to what reading specialists actually do. Rupley, Mason, and Logan (1985) found that, while reading professors' perceptions closely matched the overall impressions of reading specialists and administrators, reading professors nonetheless retained some anachronistic notions, for example, that reading specialists still were giving vision and hearing tests. Similarly, administrators believed that reading specialists seldom taught a regularly scheduled remedial reading class and seldom taught in more than one school. There needs to be more communication at all levels to reduce the amount of role conflict mentioned earlier. State departments of education must include reading professionals at all levels, as new legislation is enacted and implemented. Reading professors must work in the field or, at the very least, communicate with people in the field, to keep abreast of changing role responsibilities. Administrators must confer with reading personnel at the building, district, college, and state level to insure optimal program development. Together, these communicative inroads will help to clarify any existing misconceptions.

A third area of concern is the need to study reading specialists within the context of various educational systems. In addition to seeking a definition of their roles, reading specialists should work to implement these activities within the limitations of local situations. Robinson and Pettit (1978) suggest ways in which to give meaningful assistance to the classroom teacher. They identify three time frames established in schools — no resource time, minimal resource time, and optimal resource time — and provide creative strategies for expanding the role in each situation.

READING SUPERVISOR'S ROLES AND RESPONSIBILITIES

In contrast to reading specialists, reading supervisors have supervisory and administrative responsibilities. Reading supervisors are responsible for designing, implementing, and evaluating all of the reading programs offered by the school or school system. Usually assuming a leadership position, reading supervisors coordinate and appraise all facets of the reading program, including teacher observation and evaluation.

The following scenario may help to visualize role differences between reading specialists and reading supervisors. These descriptions represent a combination of personal experiences and observations.

Mrs. L. is the reading supervisor in a medium-sized school district in central New Jersey which has five elementary schools, two middle schools, and one high school. Having had experience as a remedial reading teacher at the elementary level and as a reading resource teacher at both the elementary and secondary levels, she feels very comfortable in her role as a supervisor. To improve her ability to observe and evaluate teachers in an official capacity, she went to a number of supervision training sessions at a regional educational office run by the State Department of Education.

Her days are busy. As the person responsible for the district's entire reading program, she knows that she must be constantly on her toes in terms of teacher performance, materials, inservice, and text scores. She feels lucky because her reading specialists are excellent: knowledgeable, motivated, and organized. She can concentrate on the bigger picture while they focus on their individual schools. While her office is located at the district's central office, she is available and visible to the district's teachers and administrators. She constantly visits the schools and does so with a purpose, whether it be to observe teachers, work with the principal and/or reading specialist, help to implement a new program, or plan staff development. Recently, she, along with a committee of reading specialists and elementary and secondary teachers, was able to convince the other administrators to try sustained silent reading (SSR) on a regular basis. (See chapter 15 for a description.) As a result, she has been working diligently with the principals and reading specialists to develop a plan. Another recent concern of hers has been the purchase of new reading basals, since each of the five elementary schools had been using different basals. She has been meeting weekly with a committee of K–8 classroom teachers, working to resolve some of the disparities in teaching philosophies and attempting to establish an appropriate set of criteria for textbook selection. She also is ready to unveil the new reading curriculum, a modified version of the curriculum developed seven years ago.

Of course, she has many concerns: Will the students perform adequately on the statewide reading achievement test? Will the local school board accept her committee's recommendations for a new basal system plus collections of tradebooks? (See chapter 7 for more on implementation.) Will the superintendent accept her budget for the forthcoming year, especially since she wants to begin to order computers for her reading specialists? Will the teachers stage a revolution against the new assessment tests for the modified reading curriculum?

Accompanying her position of power is her constant struggle to prove herself. Unaccustomed to having to master the art of polemics, she has had to depend on her tireless ability to work at her job to convince others of her competence as a supervisor.

Mr. M. is one of the elementary reading specialists in Mrs. L.'s district. His biggest concern has been the development of the resource role. Having worked closely and successfully with Mrs. L. and his principal, Mr. P., on the development of his remedial reading program, he is ready to begin to work with his teachers. He knows he has credibility because he has worked hard at being reliable and helpful. Whenever the teachers have wanted materials or ideas for some of the students, he has been there to help. Whenever the teachers have needed advice on how to deal with some of the parents regarding students' reading progress, he has been there. Teachers know they can come to him for materials and that their students are in good hands.

Mr. M. has wanted more. He is tired of just working with his group of three to five students every period, day in and day out. He wants time to work with teachers. He wants to share what he has learned from his own reading and conference participation. He is excited about the sustained silent reading plan he has worked out with Mrs. L. and Mr. P. He actually will provide inservice training for the staff and be the resource person responsible for its implementation. He will need to make sure that everyone in the school has books and understands SSR's purpose. He also wants to use journals as a vehicle for recording everyone's thoughts about SSR. He told Mrs. L. that he will work on that so that it's ready for their first staff development day. At least it's a start in terms of resourcing. His next goal is demonstration lessons.

As with reading resource teachers, reading supervisors provide specialized help and service to teachers, both individually and in groups. However, because it is impossible to devote adequate time to all teachers, other reading personnel are needed for more direct and extended teacher contact. That is where Mr. M. comes in; he is helping to execute Mrs. L.'s administrative visions. Simply stated, Mr. M. works directly with the students and teachers in one school so that the district's reading program is implemented and maintained. Mrs. L., on the other hand, is responsible for the operation of the entire reading program in all the schools, so her involvement with teachers and students is less frequent.

Even with the IRA's (1986) definition of a reading coordinator/supervisor, statewide and districtwide policies differ for reading personnel positions so that widespread variations in responsibilities exist. Nevertheless, it is important to know the IRA's delineation of role responsibilities for a supervisor:

> [A person who] supervises a district-wide reading and language arts program as central office staff person, or directs public, private, or corporate educational, vocational, penal, or social agency serving learners at any level. Responsible for student progress toward reading maturity through: (a) improvement of curriculum, methodology, and management of district-wide reading/ language arts programs and policies; (b) application of current research/theory in the refinement of reading and language arts instruction; (c) coordination and implementation of collaborative reading research; (d) attainment of resources through budget processes and grant applications; (e) development of community support for the reading/language arts program; (f) supervision and evaluation of classroom teachers, diagnostic-remedial specialists, and reading consultants; and (g) support of professional development through provision for attendance at workshops, conferences, and conventions. [p. 3]

In developing a reading curriculum, reading supervisors need to determine what is to be taught, by whom, when, where, and in what pattern. They need to build into their plan a cyclical procedure for assessing the district's program needs, revising or reconfirming goals, developing a coherent plan, and implementing and evaluating this plan. Reading supervisors also need to organize instruction, both developmental and remedial, at the elementary and secondary levels. With developmental programs, this entails dealing with conflicts between the self-contained mentality and the departmentalized mentality, a major concern in itself in terms of teacher commitment and involvement. It also involves an understanding and appreciation of different grouping patterns within and between classes. With remedial reading programs, it means being able to establish credible entrance and exit criteria after devising a suitable adapted program. Furthermore, reading supervisors must make sure that pupils, staff, space, and materials are coordinated (Harris, 1975). In addition to designing, organizing, and evaluating the reading curriculum, reading supervisors are responsible to and for the teachers. With both elementary and secondary teachers, reading supervisors must disseminate information and materials, usually through inservice and teacher observations. This means that supervisors must know what teachers need before planning to assist. Reading supervisors should have enough reading expertise to know how to diagnose teachers' instructional strengths and weaknesses and enough supervisory expertise to predict what conferencing and inservice strategies will work with the teachers.

Two other responsibilities are inherent in the supervisory role: budgeting and community outreach. Supervisors who are indeed immersed in their districts' programs will show a level of commitment to the district's overall welfare that will help in getting budgets approved, especially if appropriate requests are made. With community outreach, there should be a continuous, free flow of information, whether through face-to-face communication, news media, or specialized school publications (Burg et al., 1978), so that the community is aware of the reading program and the parents appreciate what goes into developing diversified reading experiences for students.

Effective reading supervision is nothing more than an amalgam of different experiences that reflects the ideals and initiatives of those involved in reading instruction.

OTHER SCHOOL PERSONNEL

The Principal's Role

In effective schools, principals have five broad instructional and leadership areas: working with teachers, working with students, creating a school atmosphere, providing policy leadership, and building community support. All levels of the reading program need attention in these five areas (Mottley & McNinch, 1984), to develop an effective reading program. Barnard and Hetzel's (1976, 1986) belief that principals are the key to good reading programs has been strongly supported by other principals, who advocate strong involvement with the administrative, pupil, and policy facets of reading programs, through, for example, inservice presentations in reading, instructional support to teachers, and acquisition of new information that bears on reading programs (Manning & Manning, 1981; Rice, 1987).

In one study of two schools with high achievement scores in reading, the principals played very different roles; however, the teachers from both schools followed similar schoolwide policies and practices to promote reading. While both principals were extremely supportive and knowledgeable about the reading program, one chose to be involved with every facet of the program while the other managed from a distance, using other faculty leaders as program coordinators. However, because there were no real differences in interest or awareness, students from both schools performed similarly on the reading achievement tests and teachers from both schools were equally satisfied with the program's progress (Hallinger & Murphy, 1987).

Unfortunately, most principals have received insufficient training for teaching reading or developing reading programs (Smith et al., 1978).

Because of their lack of reading program expertise, many principals default on their responsibility in this area and rely upon classroom teachers, reading specialists, and/or central office staff to provide the major ideas for decision making. While it is important to value staff participation and decision making, it also is important for principals to know enough about reading to evaluate the effectiveness of reading instruction and to supervise their staff in reading. Even if they are not experts, they must acquire enough knowledge of the reading process and of methodology for teaching reading to communicate intelligently with their staff.

Some of the best schoolwide recreational reading programs observed emanated from principals. For example, one principal, well versed in reading, started up a "Mickey Mouse Club." Each week she had a different group of students meet with her and Mickey Mouse (a huge stuffed version of the Disney character) in her conference room, to discuss a student-selected novel. Since she would randomly pick a group (usually students from the same grade level) the preceding week to prepare for the following week, the students were very excited about whom she would pick. The students were constantly buzzing about different books to suggest (multiple copies of books were ordered by the librarian) and the principal, of course, had the opportunity to work with her students and put herself on a weekly regimen of reading books.

Another principal created all types of buttons related to reading. When members of the school (students, teachers, secretaries, custodial staff, paraprofessionals, and the principal) completed a book, they would receive a button. Everyone walked around decorated in colorful buttons that proclaimed the virtues of reading. Principals, as the educational leaders of schools, make the difference in whether children learn (Barnard & Hetzel, 1986).

The Teacher's Role

All classroom, subject, and special needs teachers are key contributors to a sound reading program. They need to provide appropriately planned instruction by stimulating, extending, and reinforcing learning. They should create effective reading environments and model appropriate reading behavior. They need to demonstrate reading strategies by reading aloud, encouraging silent reading time, encouraging student interaction, and communicating realistic student expectations. Teachers also should participate in inservice programs for professional growth and effective instruction. Classroom teachers provide the developmental reading program, which is reading instruction paced to the needs of children who can be expected to learn to read as part of their normal maturation (see chapter

1). They also provide corrective instruction, which is mainly a review of skills and concepts, with one or more children who have gaps in knowledge and for whom instruction has already begun (Burg et al., 1978; Thompson & Allen, 1984). Smith et al. (1978) have bemoaned the insufficient attention given to the training of teachers in teaching reading. The IRA (1986), in its guidelines for reading professionals, has identified each of the necessary reading competencies for both early childhood and/or elementary teachers (K–8) and secondary teachers (7–12). These competencies, in varied degrees, need to be acquired by those responsible for reading instruction.

The Local School Board's Role

School boards should be informed continuously by superintendents or their designees so that the members of the board are able to make knowledgeable decisions concerning curriculum, staffing, and budget (Cook, 1986). Wisconsin law requires that the school board be legally responsible for developing a program of reading goals for the district for grades K–12, making an assessment of existing reading needs based on the reading goals established, and making an annual evaluation of the reading curriculum of the school district (Vance & Quealy, 1978). While most states do not have such stringent policies for reading, it is important to appreciate the value of the school board for endorsing, both privately and publicly, the strides made in the district's reading program. The more apprised they are of what is going on, the more likely they will be to support your endeavors.

The State Department of Education's Role

State department of education personnel oversee the statewide operation of curriculum and instruction. If a department is well developed, it will provide specialists in such areas as science, social studies, and reading (Oliva, 1984). Otherwise generalists (those with responsibilities across curricular areas) assume reading/language arts tasks among other content-area instruction. As with reading supervisors at the local level, these supervisors assist teachers by disseminating information, providing inservice programs, demonstrating effective teaching methods, and suggesting materials. Some spearhead statewide textbook selection committees. Others direct statewide publications. For instance, Doris Cook, Supervisor of Reading Education at the Wisconsin Department of Public Instruction, developed *A Guide to Curriculum Planning in Reading* (Cook, 1986). Although one step removed from the local district level, state supervisors are in key positions to move local districts forward with reading/language arts instruction.

SIMILARITIES AND DIFFERENCES AMONG THE VARIOUS ROLES

Having examined each role separately, it is important to understand the interrelationships among the roles of reading specialist, reading supervisor, principal, and classroom teacher. Examining their similarities and differences will help us to understand how to design effective reading programs.

Essentially, three basic categories of skills are required for leadership performance in the schools: technical knowledge, interpersonal skills, and management skills. Technical knowledge refers to an understanding of facts and principles and a proficiency with methods and processes related to the field of reading/language arts, which are available to dispense or apply as needed. Interpersonal skills refer to the personal-social qualities and attitudes that enable the professional to work effectively and efficiently with students, teachers, administrators, and people in general, on a one-to-one basis and in group settings. Six essential interpersonal characteristics enable successful functioning in this skill area: acceptance, genuineness, sensitivity, empathy, assertion, and initiative (Bean & Wilson, 1981). Management skills refer to the ability to contribute actively to the organization, guidance, and direction of the reading program by being able to see the class, the school, the district, and the total education program as a whole (Burg et al., 1978; Pikulski & Ross, 1979; Sergiovanni & Carver, 1973).

While persons in each of the four roles discussed in this chapter need to possess skills in all three of these areas, they do so in varying degrees, due to the nature of their positions. First, it is important to distinguish their roles in two other dimensions: administrative versus instructional and generalist versus specialist. Administrative personnel (in this case, the reading supervisor and the principal) have the responsibility of overseeing the work of others and evaluating their performance in each of the three skill areas. Instructional personnel (in this case, the classroom teacher and the reading specialist) are primarily responsible for teaching and assisting students and other teachers. Generalists are those whose duties cut across subject-matter lines and grade levels, whereas specialists are those whose tasks fall within a subject area or grade level, in this case, reading/language arts (Oliva, 1984). Figure 2.1 shows how the various roles, leadership areas, and dimensions are interrelated.

Within each of the three basic skill areas (technical knowledge, interpersonal skills, and management skills), there are a few subcategories. For example, with technical knowledge, four subcategories exist: evaluator, instructor/trainer, diagnostician, and consultant. (The evaluative duties of the reading supervisor include evaluating classroom teachers, diagnostic-

Figure 2.1   Personnel Interrelationships

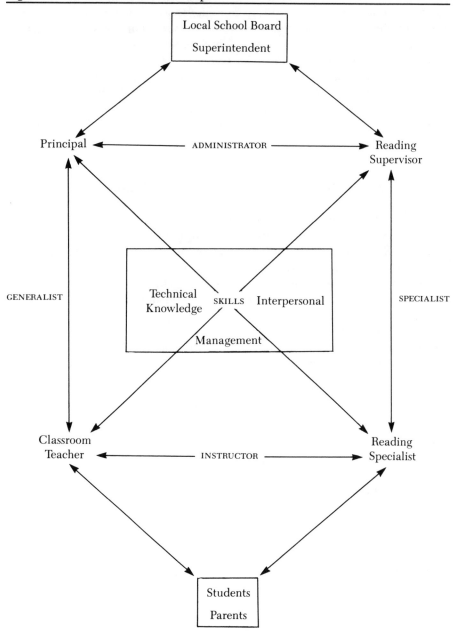

remedial specialists, and reading consultants.) The inclusion of these sub-categories should help to facilitate an understanding of some of the major responsibilities subsumed under each of the three skill areas. Tables 2.1, 2.2, and 2.3 show how each of the four roles (reading supervisor, reading specialist, principal, and classroom teacher) are interrelated in terms of role responsibilities in each of the three basic skill areas.

It is important to note that, while the categories and subcategories are included to highlight similarities and differences in roles, they are not ironclad divisions. Any of the responsibilities could easily flow into another subcategory or category.

GUIDELINES FOR READING PERSONNEL

According to *Becoming a Nation of Readers* (1985), there now exists enough knowledge to make worthwhile improvements in reading through-out the United States. As reading personnel, we are charged with seeking ways in which to help teachers and administrators understand and repli-cate some of the better reading practices. It is up to us to prove our value. A few simple guidelines are offered to help promote our role.

1. *Assess your skills.*
Periodically assess your technical/knowledge skills, interpersonal skills, and management skills in relation to other reading personnel, teachers, and administrators.

2. *Market yourself.*
Use school and district newsletters and bulletins, local newspapers, local television stations, local school board meetings, inservice programs, and professional organizations to share your reading ideas and initiatives (Gaus, 1983).

3. *Be available.*
Meet formally and informally with teachers, administrators, parents, and students to find out about satisfactions and dissatisfactions with the read-ing program (Smith et al., 1978).

4. *Start small.*
Get involved with a modest reading project or begin to work with a few interested classroom teachers to initiate an idea. Once successful, use those involved to help promote it.

5. *Be aware.*
Know the complexion of your school community in terms of group dynam-ics for schoolwide and districtwide initiatives.

Continued on page 43

Table 2.1 Technical Knowledge Skills of Reading Specialist, Reading Supervisor, Principal, and Classroom Teacher

	READING SPECIALIST	READING SUPERVISOR	PRINCIPAL	CLASSROOM TEACHER
EVALUATOR	Evaluates reading curriculum in relation to schoolwide needs	Evaluates classroom teachers, reading specialists, and consultants	Monitors reading program through formal and informal data	Evaluates how reading programs work in class
	Evaluates new instructional materials	Evaluates districtwide reading program	Observes classroom reading and evaluates teachers' performance	Evaluates students' reading progress
	Analyzes and interprets reading test data			
INSTRUCTOR/ TRAINER	Demonstrates reading lessons in classroom	Provides inservice sessions	Works with students	Stimulates, extends, and reinforces learning
	Provides remediation with individuals and groups	Works with specialists and students	Provides inservice presentations	Demonstrates appropriate reading strategies
	Demonstrates new materials and techniques	Works with classroom teachers		Provides developmental and corrective reading program
	Trains new teachers in school reading program			

(continued)

Table 2.1 (*continued*)

	READING SPECIALIST	READING SUPERVISOR	PRINCIPAL	CLASSROOM TEACHER
DIAGNOSTICIAN	Diagnoses students' reading strengths and weaknesses and prescribes appropriate instruction	Diagnoses teachers' instructional strengths and weaknesses	Diagnoses teachers' instructional strengths and weaknesses	Uses informal and formal data to assess students' strengths and weaknesses
CONSULTANT	Assists teachers with student diagnosis	Assists classroom teachers, reading specialists, and consultants with reading program	Assists teachers in effective classroom instruction	Works with parents to improve reading performance
	Suggests changes for classroom reading program			Works with paraprofessionals
	Develops reading materials			
	Assists content-area teachers to incorporate reading instruction into content areas			
	Consults with parents on individual cases			

Table 2.2 Interpersonal Skills of Reading Specialist, Reading Supervisor, Principal, and Classroom Teacher

	READING SPECIALIST	READING SUPERVISOR	PRINCIPAL	CLASSROOM TEACHER
ADVISOR	Informs administrators of services provided for school Helps parents and community promote reading at home	Confers with teachers to help with instructional strengths and weaknesses	Provides supervisory feedback	Assists students, parents, and administrators with effective reading practices
COLLABORATOR	Works with administrators to support and implement reading curriculum Works with principals and teachers regarding social, emotional, and instructional needs of pupils Works with teachers and administrators to develop programs for students with special needs	Works with teachers to do collaborative research Works with administrators and reading specialists to develop reading program	Works with teachers, reading specialists, and reading supervisors on schoolwide reading practices Helps staff to identify classroom management expectations (for example, instructional time schedule)	Works with other teachers and principals to establish roles, expectations, and rewards for student control

(continued)

Table 2.2 (*continued*)

	READING SPECIALIST	READING SUPERVISOR	PRINCIPAL	CLASSROOM TEACHER
COMMUNICATOR	Provides frequent feedback to classroom teachers about students and instructional methods used	Cultivates community support for reading/language arts program	Uses newsletters, bulletins, etc. to communicate schoolwide reading initiatives	Models appropriate reading behavior
	Conducts workshops for parents to build community support	Supports teachers attending workshops, conferences, and conventions	Builds community support	Encourages student interaction
	Uses newsletters and bulletins to report to parents on purpose and progress of reading program	Provides presentations to school board regarding reading program	Communicates value of staff participation and decision making	Communicates realistic student expectations
	Articulates balanced reading program through grades	Engages in discussions with superintendent	Interacts with staff frequently to communicate reading program goals	Communicates enthusiasm, warmth, and expectations and provides good classroom climate
		Disseminates information and materials	Reinforces desired teaching behaviors while making classroom visitations	
		Provides feedback to teachers in terms of quality of work	Becomes involved with classroom teacher initiatives	

Table 2.3 Management Skills of Reading Specialist, Reading Supervisor, Principal, and Classroom Teacher

	READING SPECIALIST	READING SUPERVISOR	PRINCIPAL	CLASSROOM TEACHER
COORDINATOR	Coordinates reading program with classroom teachers Coordinates reading curriculum with other reading programs Coordinates work of reading specialist and special services personnel	Coordinates all facets of districtwide reading/language arts program, including pupils, staff, and materials	Coordinates reading program in school Works closely with reading personnel in school and district	Coordinates all facets of the reading program in the classroom Works with other teachers for grouping and teaching
LEADER	Creates change for students' program Provides innovative staff development, consistent with assessed needs of program and staff	Conducts staff meetings in central office Writes grant proposals to obtain resources Initiates new programs for students and staff	Initiates and institutes policy changes Creates positive school atmosphere Acquires new information that bears on reading Moves teachers toward goal of improved reading instruction Initiates recreational schoolwide program	Creates effective reading environments Leads inservice sessions

(continued)

Table 2.3 (continued)

	READING SPECIALIST	READING SUPERVISOR	PRINCIPAL	CLASSROOM TEACHER
ORGANIZER	Assigns pupils to specific classes for reading	Develops districtwide reading budget to reflect requests from all schools	Develops schoolwide reading budget to reflect classroom teachers' and reading specialists' requests	Develops list of budgetary items for reading
	Maintains pupils' records containing test data and conference records	Designs and implements districtwide reading program	Commits resources to help with reading program	Provides appropriately planned instruction
	Develops, organizes, and maintains reading program	Provides districtwide inservice program	Monitors instructional practices	Organizes classroom for recreational reading
	Maintains resource room of current reading materials			
	Develops schoolwide reading budget and helps order materials			

6. *Establish your credibility.*

Be reliable, efficient, and effective in assisting with any facet of the reading program. When you have credibility, you have the allegiance needed to effect change.

CONCLUSION

In defining reading personnel role responsibilities, ideals need to be tempered with the realities of individual situations. Well-defined, functional roles need to be created from an amorphous set of characteristics. Clear-cut directions for assuming instructional or supervisory positions in reading cannot be offered. What can be offered, though, is the challenge of knowing that your responsibilities not only will continue to change to reflect societal changes but also will continue to develop to reflect your professional/personal growth. In trying to cast one small vote in the race to develop national literacy, you are offered the opportunity to create your own community of readers.

REFERENCES

Barnard, D., & Hetzel, R. (1976). The principal's role in reading instruction. *The Reading Teacher, 29,* 386–388.

Barnard, D. P., & Hetzel, R. W. (1986). *Principal's handbook to improve reading instruction* (2nd ed.). Lexington, MA: Ginn.

Bean, R. (1979). Role of the reading specialist: A multifaceted dilemma. *The Reading Teacher, 32,* 409–413.

Bean, R. M., & Eichelberger, R. T. (1985). Changing the role of reading specialist: From pull-out to in-class programs. *The Reading Teacher, 38,* 648–653.

Bean, R. M., & Wilson, R. M. (1981). *Effecting change in school reading programs: The resource role.* Newark, DE: International Reading Association.

Becoming a Nation of Readers: The report of the Commission on Reading. (1985). Washington, DC: National Institute of Education.

Burg, L. A., Kaufman, M., Korngold, B., & Kovner, A. (1978). *The complete reading supervisor: Tasks and roles.* Columbus, OH: Charles E. Merrill.

Cohen, E. G., Intili, J. K., & Robbins, S. H. (1978). Teachers and reading specialists: Cooperation or isolation? *The Reading Teacher, 32,* 281–287.

Cook, D. M. (1986). *A guide to curriculum planning in reading.* Madison: Wisconsin Department of Public Instruction.

Fuccello, J. (1987). [National survey of reading supervisor/reading specialist roles in the schools.] Unpublished raw data.

Garry, V. V. (1974). Competencies that count among reading specialists. *Journal of Reading, 17,* 608–613.

Gaus, P. J. (1983). The indispensable reading teacher. *The Reading Teacher, 37,* 269–272.

Glaser, R. (1985). Foreword. In *Becoming a nation of readers: The report of the Commission on Reading.* Washington, DC: National Institute of Education.

Hallinger, P., & Murphy, J. (1987). Schools show improvement in reading skills. *AARSIC Abstracts, 2*(4), 2–4.

Harris, B. M. (1975). *Supervisory behavior in education* (2nd ed.). Englewood Cliffs, NJ: Prentice-Hall.

Hesse, K., Smith, R., & Nettleton, A. (1973). Content teachers consider the role of the reading consultant. *Journal of Reading, 17,* 210–215.

International Reading Association. (1979). What's in a name: Reading specialist? *Journal of Reading, 20,* 623–628.

International Reading Association. (1986). *Guidelines for the specialized preparation of reading professionals.* Newark, DE: Author.

Mangieri, J. N., & Heimberger, M. J. (1980). Perceptions of the reading consultant's role. *Journal of Reading, 23,* 527–530.

Manning, G. L., & Manning, J. (1981). What is the role of the principal in the excellent reading program? Principals give their views. *Reading World, 21,* 130–133.

Mottley, R. R., & McNinch, G. H. (1984). The principal and the reading program. *Reading World, 24,* 81–86.

Nichols, J. N. (1979). Providing reading inservice on a shoestring budget. *Journal of Reading, 23,* 233–235.

Oliva, P. F. (1984). *Supervision for today's schools* (2nd ed.). New York: Longman.

Pierson-Hubeny, D., & Archambault, F. X. (1985). Role stress and perceived intensity of burnout among reading specialists. *Reading World, 24,* 41–52.

Pikulski, J. J., & Ross, E. (1979). Classroom teachers' perceptions of the role of the reading specialist. *Journal of Reading, 23,* 126–135.

Rice, R. (1987). Clearly defined staff roles: A key to effective programs. *AARSIC Abstracts, 11*(3), 4.

Robinson, R. D., & Pettit, N. T. (1978). The role of the reading teacher: Where do you fit in? *The Reading Teacher, 31,* 923–927.

Rupley, W. H., Mason, G., & Logan, J. W. (1985). Past, present and future job responsibilities of public school reading specialists. *Reading World, 24,* 48–60.

Sergiovanni, T. J., & Carver, F. D. (1973). *The new school executive: A theory of administration.* New York: Dodd, Mead.

Smith, R. J., Otto, W., & Hansen, L. (1978). *The school reading program: A handbook for teachers, supervisors and specialists.* Boston: Houghton Mifflin.

Thompson, R. A., & Allen, I. A. (1984). *Effective reading instruction.* Springfield, IL: Charles C. Thomas.

Vance, D., & Quealy, R. (1978). Reading program legislation in Wisconsin. *Journal of Reading, 22,* 28–32.

Weisberg, R. (1986). [Survey of state policies in reading specialist training and reading instructional practices.] Unpublished raw data.

Wepner, S. B. (1977). Are reading teachers becoming obsolete? *The Reading Teacher, 30,* 402–404.

Wilson, R. M., & Becker, H. L. (1984). An educational audit of a district's reading personnel. *Reading World, 24,* 69–72.

Part II

PROGRAM DEVELOPMENT

Part II focuses on the various settings for which administrators and supervisors must plan and carry out reading programs. The variance in age and development of the students and the differences in the curricular goals emphasized at each level demand different responses to the issues administrators and supervisors confront.

The expansion of pre-elementary programs, particularly in the public schools, has presented a variety of challenges relevant to teaching reading to very young children. Issues related to screening, testing, and the nature and content of reading instruction at this level often provoke heated debates. Chapter 3 describes these issues and provides the background knowledge to help administrators and supervisors set policy, plan programs, and ask good questions of those teachers responsible for helping the very youngest children attain a good start.

Chapter 4 sets forth goals for the elementary program in broad, comprehensive terms. Stress is placed on offering students variety in materials and methods, with many opportunities to explore reading from a personal perspective. Guidelines, accompanied by many concrete examples, are given for implementing a sound, diversified elementary school reading program.

Middle and junior high schools tend to vary greatly from district to district. Confusion about the nature of these programs is frequently manifested in uncertainty about what is appropriate reading instruction at this level. Chapter 5 helps to clarify the goals of middle school and junior high programs. It describes the reading development of preadolescent and adolescent students and offers guidelines for developing reading programs for children of this age. Numerous programs commonly found at this level are examined.

"The best high school reading programs are often the most invisible." This statement from chapter 6 reveals a view of reading instruction that is integral to every aspect of the curriculum. Attention to reading is so pervasive that it becomes a natural part of every discipline and every lesson where print materials are used. When reading is viewed in this way, it no longer stands separate and apart from the remaining curriculum as the business of a particular teacher or a particular period in the day.

Broadly interpreted, the principles and guidelines presented in each chapter may be applied to all the others. This is reassuring for administrators, supervisors, and teachers, since it means that the essence of sound, effective reading instruction remains the same for children at any level.

3 Pre-elementary Reading Programs

DOROTHY S. STRICKLAND
Teachers College, Columbia University

Imagine a kindergarten classroom. The bulletin board is covered with brightly colored pictures, the windowsill lined with beautiful plants. There is a block-building center, a homemaking area, and a place for books and games. The children sit at tables arranged in the center of the room, their cherubic faces turned to the teacher as they await instructions for the next activity.

A typical developmental kindergarten, you say? Perhaps, but let's take a closer look. As we move toward the block-building center we notice that the blocks have accumulated a considerable amount of dust. We wonder if their neat appearance might indicate a lack of use. A closer inspection of the homemaking area reveals an absence of the many little items that we normally associate with housekeeping. We look for a dishcloth folded on the stove, some utensils on the table, and some cereal boxes stored in the cupboard. The area looks rather barren. In fact, the furniture appears to be lined against the wall rather than arranged in a manner that would indicate its use.

We move toward the book area. We are pleased to see that some of the books look worn from use, yet there are no pillows or carpeting to make the area inviting. We wonder if this corner functions more as a place to store books rather than as a comfortable place to browse and enjoy them.

We glance at our watches and note that it is already 9:30 A.M. The children have been sitting at the table since their arrival at 8:30. Their day began with the usual opening activities: attendance, the calendar, and the weather. This was followed by a lesson on the letter *B*, accompanied by a phonics workbook page. Now the teacher is announcing a brief break for outdoor play before they return to their seats for math. The children are told that they will work on the number *4* in their number workbooks. They are praised for their good work on the letter *B*. Only two people will need to stay indoors to redo their workbook pages. Everyone else will be allowed to go outdoors to play. The children clap. Most look happy and proud of what they are accomplishing.

Later, we talk with the teacher. She is concerned about the time the children spend doing what she calls academic work. This is an experienced teacher with a child development background, yet she says she feels compelled to do things she considers developmentally inappropriate because, as she puts it, "This is what the parents and the administration want." She is pleased that the kindergarten program is being extended to a full day but worries that the newly proposed prekindergarten will mean a further downward shift of formal academics.

A brief talk with the school principal reveals that he, too, is concerned about providing a sound program for these children. This community is deeply committed to its very young. They know the importance of a good educational start. Neither he nor the reading resource teacher, from whom he often seeks advice on curriculum, is very familiar with early childhood education. They want to do what is right, yet they are not at all sure of what "right" is.

TRENDS AND ISSUES IN READING AT THE PRE-ELEMENTARY LEVEL

In recent years, an ever-increasing amount of attention has been given to strengthening and expanding public school education at the earliest levels. Several factors have contributed to this trend:

1. Increasingly, children of working parents are enrolled in child care centers where they receive day care services from as early as infancy. It is felt that these children are more socialized to the school experience and better prepared for formal school activities.
2. Added to the increased socialization due to prekindergarten educational programs are the apparent intellectual effects of educational television, which have caused many to feel that most children are ready for more rigorous instruction at an earlier age.
3. Research indicating a positive relationship between academic learning time and pupil achievement (*Beginning Teacher Evaluation Study*, 1980) has caused some to recommend a longer school day as a means of promoting excellence through increased time on task. Many school districts construe the expansion of early childhood programs to mean more time on task, particularly for those children who are deemed "at risk."
4. Research in the language and literacy development of young children (Hiebert, 1978; Goodman, 1980; Taylor, 1983; Harste, Woodward, & Burke, 1984) indicates that, given a supportive, print-rich environment, young children are capable of understanding far more about reading and writing than was previously realized.
5. Longitudinal studies have shown that effective early childhood education has long-term effects on the academic, social, and economic well-being of children (Schweinhart & Weikart, 1980).

The trend toward greater emphasis on early childhood education in the public schools has served to raise a number of issues for parents, teachers, and administrators. Several of these issues have direct implications for teaching reading.

Tests for Screening and Achievement

In recent years, excellence has become the watchword of educational reform. Unfortunately, public pressure for educational excellence is often translated into demands for increased pupil performance on measures of evaluation. In many school districts, evidence of excellence is equated with improved test scores. The quality of a program and even the effectiveness of teachers may be judged largely on the basis of pupil test performance.

The practice of screening children for learning problems or delayed development is a growing trend, which many believe threatens the nature of pre-elementary programs. The concern rests with the use that is made of the results of screening. Rather than use the information to adjust the program to the child, screening is frequently used to deny children entry into kindergarten or first grade. An editorial in *Young Children* ("Two Viewpoints," 1986) states the concern well:

Since so many children experience kindergarten failure, the problem lies in the programs, not the children! Why do so many educators expect children to conform to the schools? As early childhood educators, we share a professional commitment to plan programs that are appropriate for young children. [p. 9]

Although most of the emphasis on achievement tests begins at the mid-elementary levels, any attempt to increase test scores at one level affects the curriculum at each preceding level. Test stress at third grade is felt at the first- and second-grade levels. Changes in the first-grade program affect the kindergarten program, and what happens in kindergarten ultimately changes the way prekindergarten is perceived.

Increased Focus on Reading

Because reading is viewed as the foundation of learning and the key to success in school, it has been a particular source of controversy in the early childhood curriculum. Schools that engage in entry-level screening often focus on what they consider to be the precursors for reading instruction — a set of discrete skills and knowledge that indicate a child's readiness for kindergarten or first grade. Because what is tested usually includes knowledge of letter names and the sounds letters represent, these often become central to the curriculum. Many educators are concerned that the early stress on literacy leaves little time to promote the traditional goals related to children's social, emotional, and physical growth. They say that kindergarten programs are beginning to look more and more like those of first grade. Others express even more fundamental concerns, going beyond the issue of imbalance to question the philosophical underpinnings of most literacy programs at this level. They suggest that the content and methods are frequently far removed from the research base on literacy and the young child.

Disagreement over Content and Methods

Even when schools agree that reading has a legitimate place in kindergarten, there is controversy over what forms the instruction should take. Should the stress be on direct instruction of a prescribed set of skills and knowledge, in preparation for formal reading instruction? Or should instruction be more process oriented, capitalizing on children's natural curiosity and desire to learn about print and books? Those who believe in the latter approach would respect and build on whatever language competence children bring to school and attempt to stretch children as far as their interests and abilities allow. Writing as process (see chapter 12) would receive a prominent role in an integrated approach to literacy. Fostering children's emerging abilities to read and write would not be done in preparation for some future task, but for children's immediate use and enjoyment.

Administrators and supervisors who are seeking to initiate, expand, or improve pre-elementary education in a school or district are likely to struggle with the issues just raised. Fortunately, child language research has expanded rapidly in recent years. We know a great deal about how children learn and the kind of curriculum that fosters language development. This knowledge, which will be summarized next, can be used by administrators to inform their decision making.

THE CONDITIONS OF FIRST LANGUAGE LEARNING

Learning language is perhaps the most marvelous of all human accomplishments. In a very short period of time, very young children acquire extremely complex systems of knowledge and rules. Indeed, the rules of their language are internalized with such a high degree of proficiency that prekindergartners are able to use them to generate utterances they have never heard before. This feat alone is marvelous enough. But, perhaps for educators, the most amazing aspect of first language learning is that children accomplish it without the benefit of lesson plans, skills checklists, or competency tests (Strickland, 1987).

Because language development is such a marvelous human accomplishment and because it is fundamental to every aspect of an individual's social and cognitive development, it has received considerable attention from educational researchers. By examining the conditions under which very young children undergo the remarkable acquisition of spoken language, we can deepen our insight into how we might shape the language curriculum of the school. The following key factors seem to be universally present when first language learning occurs:

1. *An atmosphere of success.* Children acquire spoken language in a warm, rewarding atmosphere. The nature of the learning environment is positive. Parents are delighted with whatever the child accomplishes; moreover, they show it. Anxiety about first language learning is rare. Not only are the child's miscues or mistakes accepted, they become the content of family stories right through adulthood.
2. *Respect for individuality.* Children acquire spoken language in an atmosphere that conveys respect for the uniqueness of each individual. There is little temptation to mold the child to fit a group standard or method. Individual styles and approaches are generally respected. Par-

ents are most apt to judge achievement in terms of what a child can do today that he or she could not do yesterday.

3. *Child-centered atmosphere.* During first language learning, adults and children frequently interact on an individual basis. The child is an active participant — curious about the environment, asking endless questions and demanding to know the answers.

4. *Meaningful, functional context.* First language learning is always related to meaningful activities, objects, and situations. If there is no meaning for the child, an idea or element of language is quickly discarded. Each new word or concept must find its place in the child's existing schemata or frameworks of knowledge. Adults act to help bridge the known and the unknown. Throughout, the adult uses language with the child to do something besides teach language.

5. *Holistic learning.* In first language learning, children are presented with the whole system of what is to be learned. Language is neither sequenced nor segmented into skills. All of the components of language are presented as they exist — as an interrelated, integrated whole. Yet children learn the rules of their language and apply them with ever-increasing facility, in order to form new utterances they have never heard before.

The conditions of first language learning cannot and need not be prescriptively duplicated at school. Awareness of these conditions, however, has direct implications for pre-elementary curricula. A sound pre-elementary curriculum will be characterized by an atmosphere of success; by respect for individuality; by child-centeredness; by a meaningful, functional context; and by holistic learning. It will be important to keep these factors in mind as we consider the kind of curriculum that fosters language and literacy.

CURRICULA FOR FOSTERING READING IN YOUNG CHILDREN

The reading program at the pre-elementary level should be embedded within the framework of a developmentally appropriate curriculum. According to the National Association for the Education of Young Children (Bredekamp, 1987), a developmentally appropriate curriculum:

1. Takes into account all areas of a child's development, including physical, emotional, social, and cognitive factors
2. Integrates all aspects of the curriculum so that children's learning does not occur in narrowly defined subject areas
3. Includes curriculum planning based on teachers' observations and

recordings of each child's special interests and developmental progress

4. Emphasizes learning as an interactive process in an environment where children are encouraged to learn through active exploration and interaction with adults, other children, and materials
5. Stresses learning activities and materials involving concrete, real experiences relevant to the lives of the children
6. Accounts for a wide range of interests and abilities
7. Provides a variety of activities of increasing difficulty and materials of increasing complexity

An example of a sound strategy for teaching reading at the pre-elementary level is the use of "big books." These enlarged texts are perfect for use in shared reading activities with young children. Big books often contain humorous stories with predictable and repetitive language, causing even the most restless youngsters to become quickly engrossed. Largely inspired by the work of Don Holdaway (1979), big books offer teachers opportunities to help children develop concepts about print and an understanding of the reading process. They offer teachers an opportunity to develop the objectives of a reading program for young children in a whole-language context. Table 3.1 provides some examples of big-book activities suggested for use before, during, and after the reading. Each is organized according to what a teacher might be doing, what the children would be doing, and the curricular objectives that would be being met (Strickland, 1988).

Early in this chapter we discussed the issue related to the content and methods of the reading program at the pre-elementary level. The importance of treating writing as an integral part of a literacy program that links reading, writing, and literature was made. Listening, speaking, and thinking are also active ingredients in the literacy program. Harste et al. (1984) suggest that children create a "linguistic data pool" into which they feed what they learn from each language encounter, to be drawn upon in a subsequent language encounter. Oral language encounters provide data for written language encounters, and vice versa. Growth in a given expression of language must be seen as a multilingual event. Whether the child is listening to a big book, sharing in the reading or retelling of one, or attempting to write a story independently, literacy is supported. This new way of viewing early literacy has stimulated numerous books and articles about introducing writing into the curriculum at the pre-elementary level.

Karnowski (1986) offers guidelines for early childhood writing programs. She suggests that teachers determine what children understand

Table 3.1 Some Tips for Shared Book and Chart Experiences

TEACHER	CHILD	OBJECTIVES
Before the Reading:		
• Asks children what they think story might be about, based on title and cover. Or, thinks aloud about what he/she thinks this story might be about.	• Uses clues from title and cover, together with background knowledge, to formulate predictions about the story. Or, observes teacher model the same.	• Using clues from text and background knowledge to make inferences and formulate predictions.
• Shows pleasure and interest in anticipation of the reading.	• Observes as teacher models personal interest and eagerness toward the reading.	• Building positive attitudes toward books and reading.
During the Reading (teacher reads aloud):		
• Gives lively reading. Displays interest and delight in language and story line.	• Observes teacher evoke meaningful language from print.	• Understanding that print carries meaning.
• Hesitates at predictable parts in the text. Allows children to fill in possible words or phrases.	• Fills in likely words for a given slot.	• Using semantic and syntactic clues to determine what makes sense.
• At appropriate parts in a story, queries children about what might happen next.	• Makes predictions about what might happen next in the story.	• Using story line to predict possible events and outcomes.
After the Reading:		
• Guides discussion about key ideas in the text. Helps children relate key concepts.	• Participates in discussion of important ideas in the text.	• Reflecting on the reading; applying and personalizing key ideas in a text.
• Asks children to recall important or favorite parts. Finds corresponding part of the text (perhaps with help of children) and rereads.	• Recalls and describes specific events or parts of text.	• Using print to support and confirm discussion.

Source: Strickland, D. (1988). *The Reading Teacher.* Newark, DE: International Reading Association.

about communication in general and writing in particular. In order for this to happen, children must be in an environment that will allow them to experiment with writing and to share with others their growing communication awareness. This also requires a teacher-observer who is informed by the growing body of information on communication and early writing. Such teachers will operate under a definition of writing that values scribble writing and invented spelling, recognizing that convention should never come before language expression. Karnowski describes concrete ways that teachers can offer invitations to write throughout the day:

> Because young children often combine writing with other alternative communication systems, teachers should include tools in other areas of the classroom, as well as in the writing center. Writing tools in the music area encourage the writing of musical notes or words to go with a rhythm. Writing tools in the home-making area encourage the writing of shopping lists, phone messages, notes, and reminders. Writing tools in the art center encourage children to write about their pictures, and writing tools in the block area encourage the labeling of structures and buildings. Writing flourishes in a social environment where young children are free to use oral language, art, music, and drama to explore and enhance their writing. [p. 60]

ELEMENTS OF A GOOD PRE-ELEMENTARY READING PROGRAM

One of the great dilemmas of school administrators and, to a lesser degree, supervisors, whether they be assigned to the district level or be school based, is that they can never hope to be experts in all the disciplines, developmental levels, and areas of concern for which they are responsible. Everyone concedes that this is true. It is possible, however, for administrators and supervisors to become well enough acquainted with each area under their supervision to become effective observers and questioners of those who are expected to have the expertise. The material offered so far in this chapter is intended to help them acquire general background knowledge about pre-elementary reading. Further assistance is provided by the following list of descriptions of recommended elements of such programs. This list is based on *Literacy Development and Pre-First Grade* (IRA, 1985), a joint statement of concerns about present practices in pre-first-grade reading instruction. The original document was endorsed by the Association for Childhood Education International, the Association for Supervision and Curriculum Development, the International Reading Association, the National Association for the Education of Young Children, the National Association of Elementary School Principals, and the National Council of Teachers of English. For our purposes, the recommendations have been reformulated as characteristics of what an administrator or supervisor will observe in good pre-elementary reading programs.

1. Instruction is built on what the children already know about oral language, reading, and writing. It will focus on meaningful experiences and meaningful language rather than merely on isolated skill development.
2. The language the child brings to school is respected and used as a base for language and literacy activities.
3. Success is insured for all children. They are helped to see themselves as people who can enjoy exploring oral and written language.
4. Reading experiences are provided as an integrated part of the broader communication process, which includes speaking, listening, and writing, as well as other communication systems such as art, math, and music.
5. Children's first attempts at writing are encouraged without concern for the proper formation of letters or correct conventional spelling.
6. Risk taking in first attempts at reading and writing are encouraged and what appear to be errors are accepted as part of children's natural patterns of growth and development.
7. Familiar materials, such as well-known stories, are used for instruction because they provide children with a sense of control and confidence.
8. Children are presented with models to emulate. In the classroom, teachers use language appropriately, listening and responding to children's talk and engaging in their own reading and writing.
9. Children are read to regularly from a wide variety of poetry, fiction, and nonfiction.
10. Time is provided for children's independent reading and writing.
11. Children's affective and cognitive development are fostered through opportunities to communicate what they know, think, and feel.
12. Evaluative procedures are developmentally and culturally appropriate for the children being assessed. The selection of evaluative materials is based on the objectives of the instructional program, with consideration for each child's total development and its effect on reading performance.
13. Parents are made aware of the reasons for a total language program at school and provided with ideas for activities to carry out at home.
14. Parents are alerted to the limitations of formal assessments and standardized tests of pre-first graders' reading and writing skills.
15. Children are encouraged to be active participants in the learning process, rather than passive recipients of knowledge. This is accomplished

through activities that allow for experimentation with talking, listening, writing, and reading.

ADMINISTRATIVE AND SUPERVISORY SUPPORT

It is extremely important for administrators and supervisors to become involved in the decisions made on behalf of pre-elementary children. Awareness of the language and reading development of young children and the increasing public demands for academic programs at this level are only first steps. Administrators need to let teachers at this level know that their work and the children they serve are every bit as important as the many other programs within a district. They must be sure to assign teachers to this level who have the training and experiential background needed to work with very young children. In addition, it is the administrative and supervisory staff who are in the best position to promote professional cooperation among kindergarten teachers and teachers in the primary grades — an extremely important aspect of program continuity.

Allocation of resources is a critical administrative consideration at this level. The initial outlay of monies for pre-elementary programs is typically much greater than that for other grade levels. Administrators who are planning new pre-elementary programs need to be aware of these costs and plan accordingly. Establishing programs that maintain close relationships with parents is another area in which administrators play a key role. It should be kept in mind that, for many parents and children, the pre-elementary program represents an introduction to a school or district. In districts in which new programs are being implemented or old programs are undergoing major revision, administrators have an excellent opportunity to share in making an important statement to the entire community of children, teachers, and parents. Thomas McGarry (1986), then an administrator in the Fairfax County (Virginia) Public Schools, describes several important measures that were taken in his district to insure the successful implementation of an integrated kindergarten curriculum:

> The school district organized a day-long "Great Beginnings" convention for kindergarten, first- and second-grade teachers and for special education teachers of young children, to reinforce project themes and purposes and to encourage teachers to share successful ideas and practices in workshop sessions.
>
> All required print and nonprint lesson materials were assembled and provided to teachers. Furniture, equipment, and techniques for managing instructional materials were also supplied. Simple as it sounds, this action received almost embarrassing praise.

Each teacher attended four full-day inservice training sessions over the year. These relatively small-group meetings were conducted close to teachers' schools — an important consideration in a large district.

Training sessions used teacher-presenters extensively.

Teacher feedback was encouraged on all aspects of the program. Staff both preached and practiced that this project was a partnership.

Ample time was allowed for teachers to interact informally at inservice training sessions.

Developers visited classrooms regularly to solve problems, provide materials, answer questions, and stay in touch. [p. 66]

CONCLUSION

Throughout this book, we have reminded administrators and supervisors of the key role they play in every aspect of the reading program. As the educational leaders within a district, they help to determine policy. Once policy is established, it is their leadership that helps to initiate, implement, and maintain the programmatic decisions that support it. Finally, the articulation of both policy and program to the public is largely an administrative responsibility. Reading at the pre-elementary level is a highly important, issue-laden topic, one in which the public is increasingly interested and about which they are likely to have questions and opinions. For these reasons, it is essential that administrators and supervisors have sufficient background to serve as active, informed participants in its discussion. It is our hope that this chapter will provide the foundation needed to help those in administrative and supervisory positions to take a true leadership role in an area in which change and controversy are likely to remain for some years to come.

REFERENCES

Beginning teacher evaluation study: The final report. (1980). Sacramento, CA: California State Commission for Teacher Preparation and Licensing.

Bredekamp, S. (Ed.). (1987). *Developmentally appropriate practice in early childhood program serving children from birth to age 8* (exp. ed.). Washington, DC: National Association for the Education of Young Children.

Goodman, Y. (1980). The roots of literacy. In M. P. Douglass (Ed.), *Claremont Reading Conference forty-fourth yearbook* (pp. 1–32). Claremont, CA: Claremont Reading Conference.

Harste, J., Woodward, V., & Burke, C. (1984). *Language stories and literacy lessons.* Portsmouth, NH: Heinemann.

Hiebert, E. H. (1978). Preschool children's understandings of written language. *Child Development, 49*, 1231–1234.

Holdaway, D. (1979). *The foundations of literacy*. Sydney, Australia: Ashton Scholastic (distributed in the United States by Heinemann).

International Reading Association. (1985). *Literacy development and pre-first grade: A joint statement of concerns about present practices in pre-first grade reading instruction and recommendations for improvement*. Newark, DE: Author.

Karnowski, L. (1986). How young writers communicate. *Educational Leadership, 46*(3), 58–60.

McGarry, T. (1986). Integrating learning for young children. *Educational Leadership, 46*(3), 64–66.

Schweinhart, L. J., & Weikart, D. P. (1980, November). Young children grow up: The effects of the Perry Preschool Program on youths through age 15. *Monographs of the High Scope Educational Research Foundation, 7*. Ypsilanti, MI: High/Scope Press.

Strickland, D. (1987). Whole language: What does it mean? How does it work? *Scholastic Teacher, 44*, 4.

Strickland, D. (1988). Some tips for using big books. *The Reading Teacher, 41*, 966–967.

Taylor, D. (1983). *Family literacy: Young children learning to read and write*. Portsmouth, NH: Heinemann.

Two viewpoints: A challenge to early childhood educators. (1986). *Young Children, 41*(2), 9.

4 Elementary Reading Programs

KATHRYN H. AU
Kamehameha Schools, Honolulu

JANA M. MASON
University of Illinois

Cathy A. Labate © 1988

When it comes to elementary school reading programs, parents and others often want to know, "What is the best way to teach reading?" Phrasing the question this way assumes that there is one reading method that will give the best results for all students in all schools. After more than two decades spent in attempts to answer this question, we find that no one reading program or method has been proven best for all students. According to Barr (1984), reasons for this lack of conclusiveness include the following:

- Schools and classrooms are complex settings, so there are many different factors that can affect how well a particular program works.

- Teachers in the same program may carry it out in quite different ways.
- Students are different from one another, so what works well with some will not necessarily be best for others.

What this means is that developing an effective elementary reading program is a matter of making a series of good decisions, not a matter of choosing the right program or applying a simple formula. Decisions should be informed by knowledge of the research on effective reading instruction and of the features associated with success in different settings. Fortunately, this base of knowledge is extensive. Of course, decisions should also be informed by knowledge of the students and community being served, and of the school and its staff.

In this chapter we offer ten guidelines for shaping a successful elementary school reading program. Supporting research is discussed, and practical examples are included from two exemplary reading programs: the Kamehameha Elementary Education Program (KEEP) in Hawaii and Structured Teaching in the Areas of Reading and Writing (STAR) in New York City. Both programs are long-term efforts to improve reading instruction in elementary classrooms with large numbers of educationally at-risk students. Both offer instruction based on the findings of current research in reading and the language arts and have been shown to be effective. (For further information on KEEP, refer to Au et al., 1986; for further information on STAR, see Smith-Burke & Ringler, 1986.)

The initial goal of the KEEP program was to enable young, disadvantaged Hawaiian students to achieve at average levels in reading. KEEP began as a program for the primary grades and gradually expanded into the upper elementary grades. The hallmark of KEEP is its emphasis on small-group reading comprehension lessons. It emphasizes the delivery of instruction in a style compatible with the children's own culture, which places a high value on group cooperation rather than individual achievement. KEEP reading consultants help teachers master new teaching strategies, become familiar with a range of instructional materials, and organize appropriate activities for independent practice and recreational reading.

The STAR program targets students in grades three through nine. It was originally developed in East Harlem, a low-income area with a large percentage of Hispanic and black families. STAR emphasizes activities integrating the use of reading, writing, speaking, and listening, with real-life materials such as tradebooks, magazines, and newspapers. Teachers in the program learn to ask higher-level questions, elicit responses from students, and facilitate discussions.

Ongoing research and development are characteristic of both KEEP and STAR, and program improvement is seen as a continual process. Both programs are complex and do not present teachers with simple solutions.

Sound judgments, informed decisions, and principled problem solving are concepts that should capture the spirit of reading program development, as we see it. Close collaboration with all stakeholders — students, teachers, other school staff, and parents — leads to a strengthening of the process of creating a successful program. Guiding these program development efforts, like teaching itself, is a matter of both art and science and requires a feeling for the human dynamics of the situation, as well as an understanding of reading instruction.

Let us turn now to our ten guidelines for achieving these ends.

1. *Take a broad view of reading, as part of literacy, and set broad goals for the reading program.*
The overall goal of the elementary school reading program is to give students a foundation for lifelong literacy. That is, we want to prepare students to use literacy for a variety of purposes throughout their lives. We can think of these purposes as falling into two general categories:

- Recreational and aesthetic, involving reading for pleasure
- Functional, involving reading as a tool for obtaining information in the context of the family or community, at work, and in school

These categories encompass both reading for enjoyment and insight into human nature, and reading to get a job done or to extract specific information.

Reading is a social process, one of the ways people communicate with one another and make sense of their world. Mature readers are capable of using reading for a wide variety of purposes, according to many different patterns. For this reason, teachers want to give students the opportunity to develop fully as readers, while being sensitive to their individual tastes and preferences. Thus, the elementary school reading program should be broad in scope, exposing students to many of the ways reading can be useful and enjoyable. The idea is eventually to give students the ability to use literacy for the purposes they choose.

Of course, students' achievement of recreational and functional reading goals is not the sole responsibility of the elementary school. For one thing, many children receive a good start toward achieving these goals in the home, before they ever come to school (Taylor, 1983). For another, their reading ability will continue to develop for a long period of time, through their secondary school and perhaps college careers, and into their adult lives. The aim of the elementary school reading program is to lay a solid foundation for future growth in literacy through these phases of life.

In short, the goals of the elementary school reading program are best thought of in very broad terms. Even from the very beginning, in kindergarten and first grade, the reading program should reflect a vision of children as literate citizens of the future. Such a vision will encourage us to present students with a wide variety of text materials, lessons, and opportunities to explore reading from a personal perspective.

2. *Develop a reading program that incorporates a broad range of literacy events and activities.*

When we think of reading in a broad, multipurpose way, we see that we need to call children's attention to the many, many uses of reading in the school and community, to everything from print on cereal boxes to street signs, from newspapers to storybooks, from directions in a cookbook to notes sent home to parents. During their elementary years, we want to impart to students a view of reading as an integral part of life in a literate society.

From this point of view, a key school literacy event is guided discussion of different kinds of text. Guided discussions provide teachers with opportunities to teach students to comprehend and critically evaluate text. Conducting a guided discussion in a responsive manner is a complex and challenging task. Often staff members benefit from the opportunity to learn about strategies for teaching comprehension through guided discussion.

At KEEP, teachers learn to conduct guided discussion lessons following the experience-text-relationship (ETR) approach for narratives (Au, 1979). Teachers begin by having students talk about background experiences (E) related to the theme of the story. Next, sections of the story are read silently and discussed (T). Finally, teachers help students draw relationships (R) between story ideas and their own background experiences. Teachers also learn to use the concept-text-application (CTA) approach for developing students' ability to comprehend informational text (Wong & Au, 1985). CTA lessons are similar to ETR lessons, except that greater emphasis is placed on helping students learn the concepts and vocabulary needed to understand the text. This building up of background knowledge is necessary because the comprehension of informational text often requires a grasp of concepts and vocabulary unfamiliar to many students.

In the STAR program teachers learn to ask higher-level questions about stories and literature and to use techniques such as the PreReading Plan (Langer, 1981). Like the ETR and CTA approaches, the PreReading Plan calls for teachers to draw upon students' background knowledge relevant to the topic of the text. Teachers ask students to give initial associations to key words in the text, then to reflect upon their association, and finally to reformulate their ideas.

All students, but especially poor readers, can be helped through specific instruction in strategies for thinking about text. For example, students can be given instruction in making inferences (Hansen & Pearson, 1983) and in generating questions, summarizing, predicting, and clarifying (Palincsar & Brown, 1986). They also benefit from explicit explanations and responsive elaborations, which focus their attention on the mental processes required to comprehend text (Duffy & Roehler, 1987a, 1987b).

In many elementary schools in the United States, the reading program is operationally defined as involving the use of a particular basal reading program. Research suggests that teachers tend to center lessons with basal materials on round-robin oral reading and do not discuss the meaning of texts or provide instruction on comprehension (Durkin, 1978–1979). When this pattern is present, little sound instruction occurs and students' school literacy experiences are severely restricted. Basal activities and materials can be the basis for a good developmental reading program, but they should be seen only as a starting point and should be heavily supplemented with other activities and materials.

To supplement basal instruction, some literacy activities favored by experienced teachers at KEEP are

- Reading aloud to students from novels (many teachers read their students a chapter a day)
- Sustained silent reading (the students and teacher read silently from books of their choice, perhaps for ten to twenty minutes a day; see Levine, 1984)
- Dialogue journals (students keep journals and the teacher writes responses to students' entries; see Staton, 1980)
- Voluntary sharing among students of books read for recreation
- Cross-grade sharing (older students read aloud to younger ones, or listen to younger ones read)

Both KEEP and STAR incorporate a wide variety of reading materials. These include

- Picture books, novels, and other fiction
- Articles from magazines and newspapers, especially those written for younger readers
- Informational books, such as those about science and social studies topics
- Pieces written by the students themselves, including stories based on personal experiences, poems, and research reports

All of these materials may be the subject of guided discussions intended to sharpen students' reading comprehension.

3. *Schedule ample time for reading instruction, but also encourage the application of reading strategies throughout the school day.*
According to Goodlad (1983), the average amount of time set aside for reading/language arts instruction in the early grades is about one hour and forty-five minutes. In the primary grades, this is probably the minimum amount of time that should be allocated. In primary grade classrooms in the KEEP program, approximately two hours are scheduled for the teaching of reading and writing. In the upper grades less time may be scheduled for reading instruction per se, because students are doing more reading in science, social studies, and other subject areas.

Of course, the scheduling or allocation of adequate time for reading instruction is only a first step. Close attention must also be paid to what actually happens in classrooms during this time. Thus, this guideline about *quantity* of time should be considered along with guideline 2, which speaks to the *quality* of instruction.

Teachers should be encouraged to look for natural opportunities throughout the school day when students can apply reading and writing skills. Especially in the upper elementary grades, teachers should emphasize reading for meaning and the learning of new vocabulary during content-area lessons. Good models for content-area reading instruction are described by Herber (1978), Moore and Readence (1983), and Roth, Smith, and Anderson (1984). Examples of reading in the content areas include

- In math class children learn how to interpret word problems in terms of mathematical operations.
- In science class children learn to follow step-by-step directions in setting up experiments.
- In a social studies class children learn to follow the logic of a written argument.

Besides content-area lessons, other times when reading and writing can be highlighted for children are

- During the planning of classroom projects, such as performing a play (students can write down materials needed for sets and costumes, mark their parts in the script, and so forth)
- During classroom routines, such as taking attendance (a student needs to be able to read classmates' names and to mark those who are absent)
- During excursions, when notes can be taken and signs read

By highlighting reading throughout the day, teachers show students the situations in which they should be applying reading skills.

Teachers who are not accustomed to thinking of reading as spanning the entire curriculum may profit from a group brainstorming activity, in which teachers think of all the occasions (outside of the scheduled time for reading) when the value of reading and writing can be reinforced for students.

4. *Provide children with a wide range of experiences for learning about the purposes served by reading and writing, as well as for learning how to read. Favor balanced instruction, including word identification and phonics, but not to the exclusion of all else.*

Recent research in the area of emergent literacy, which focuses on the beginnings of young children's development as readers and writers, is changing our views about the shape of the elementary school reading program in kindergarten and first grade (Mason & Allen, 1986). We are moving away from the concept of "readiness," which assumes that children need a general mental maturity or that they must know the alphabet and letter sounds, before beginning to read easy stories. Studies of emergent literacy reveal that young children begin learning about reading and writing long before they enter school, by handling books, hearing stories, drawing, and attempting to write. The result is that they are actually learning about reading and writing at the same time that they are learning to listen and speak (Teale & Sulzby, 1986). The research shows that behaviors such as young children's retellings of a favorite storybook, or their scribblings, are signs of their knowledge of literacy.

The implication for the primary school reading program is that formal, teacher-directed lessons are not sufficient. We need to include open-ended reading and writing activities in kindergarten and first-grade classrooms, to allow children to experiment with print and show us what they already know. Children should have opportunities to read books and to write on topics of their own choosing. By becoming familiar with the forms of early reading and writing behavior shown by young children, teachers can recognize and celebrate these steps toward becoming literate in more conventional ways (see chapter 3).

A sound beginning reading program is balanced, giving students the opportunity to develop knowledge of strategies both for identifying words and for comprehending text. Kindergarten and first-grade reading instruction should *not* consist almost entirely of lessons on word identification, especially phonics and sight words. Quite clearly, children need to have memorized common English words such as *the*, *was*, and *of*, so these words can be recognized automatically. They also need to learn about sound-symbol relationships in English (phonics) and how these can be applied to reveal the probable pronunciation of an unknown word. But an overemphasis on phonics can be detrimental to reading achievement, particularly for educationally at-risk, cultural minority students. At KEEP, for example, the students' achievement increased only when instruction shifted to an emphasis on comprehension (Tharp, 1982). In KEEP classrooms, comprehension instruction occupies roughly two-thirds of the time in teacher-led lessons, with instruction in word identification taking roughly one-third of the time.

When comprehension is given a good share of instructional time, it becomes possible to familiarize students with the wide range of functions served by literacy. All children who grow up in a literate society like that of the United States have knowledge of some functions of literacy. However, the functions of literacy children experience or witness will differ from community to community (Heath, 1983). For example, not all children have stories read to them at bedtime (Heath, 1982). Thus, teachers need to be sure that children understand the functions literacy serves in typical classroom activities, and to give them time to become comfortable with such classroom routines as large-group storyreading.

Here are examples of reading/literacy activities used by kindergarten and first-grade teachers at KEEP:

- Reading and rereading big books (Holdaway, 1979)
- Sharing of children's writing through the Author's Chair (Graves & Hansen, 1983)
- Morning message (the teacher writes a message about the day's events and helps the children to decode and interpret the message (Crowell, Kawakami, & Wong, 1986)
- Expression of story events through painting, drawing, and writing

5. *Make sure that systematic instruction continues through all grades, so that students are moved gradually toward independence.*
Students need to be able to comprehend literature as well as narratives, content-area as well as expository text. The best way of helping students develop the ability to comprehend both types of text is to provide them with comprehension instruction beginning at the primary level and continuing on through the grades.

In KEEP classrooms, lessons in the strategies needed to comprehend both narrative and expository texts start in the first grade, with ETR and CTA lessons, as mentioned earlier. These lessons may be founded on basal reader selections, tradebooks, or articles in periodicals such as *Ranger Rick*. By the third or fourth grade, at least some reading lessons center on novels. In these lessons, teachers guide students in thinking about the central theme, cause-effect relationships, characterization, new vocabulary, and other aspects of literary understanding and appreciation. Among the novels students and teachers enjoy reading and discussing together are *A Wrinkle in Time* by Madeleine L'Engle, *The Big Wave* by Pearl Buck, and *Mrs. Frisby and the Rats of NIMH* by Robert O'Brien. Sometimes teachers read and discuss a novel with the whole class. More often, different novels are read by different reading groups. Work with a particular novel often extends over three or more weeks. Teachers feel this is time well spent, because of the deeper learning and interest in reading that develop when students deal with good literature.

In most settings, the key issue in the upper elementary grades is to insure that students receive systematic instruction in study skills and in comprehending expository text, such as that found in science and social studies articles. In the STAR program, teachers help students develop study techniques such as note taking and summarizing (Anderson, 1980; Brown, Campione, & Day, 1981). Students may also benefit from instruction in identifying the main idea (Baumann, 1984) and outlining (Taylor, 1982).

Both STAR and KEEP make extensive efforts to turn reading instruction in the upper elementary grades into a worthwhile learning experience for students, by involving them in teacher-led lessons to promote comprehension ability. Research on elementary education in general suggests that, even in the third and fourth grades, instructional events often center on skill-based assignments and students receive little uninterrupted time in guided discussion lessons following the ETR or a similar instructional framework (Mason, 1983). In many schools, then, teachers may benefit from learning about strategies for teaching comprehension and study skills. Because many of these teaching techniques are quite complex, it may be helpful for teachers to see classroom demonstrations and participate in discussion groups.

6. *Provide for continuity of instruction across the grades.*
Successful elementary school reading programs are whole-school efforts that provide for continuity in the development of students' reading ability as they progress through the grades (Hallinger & Murphy, 1985). Agreement about the overall nature of the program and what it should accomplish is probably the key to insuring continuity across the grades. In both KEEP and STAR, extensive staff discussion about the program and numerous workshops and small projects contribute to a shared understanding among program participants, including classroom teachers.

Arranging for cross-grade discussions and observations is a specific step that can be taken to build continuity of instruction across grade levels. In many schools teachers do not have many opportunities to learn about the concerns in reading instruction of teachers at other grades. Even more rare are opportunities for teachers to observe in classrooms at other grade levels. When teachers have these opportunities, they are able to take a broader view of the reading program, beyond the bounds of their own classroom and students. They can appreciate the progress students have made in earlier grades, as well as see the goals students will need to reach later on. An approach based on cross-grade discussions and observations is essentially a staff development approach to building reading program continuity.

The main approach in many schools and districts relies on the use of a single basal reading program, rather than on a staff development process, although the two approaches can be compatible. Having schools select and then adhere to the use of their chosen basal program was the first step taken by the school district that later developed the STAR program. Using a particular basal program across all grades is a reasonable step, especially when the process of developing a shared understanding about the goals and emphases of the school's reading program has already begun.

A different approach to maintaining continuity across the grades is taken at KEEP. Here a scope-and-sequence chart of goals for student reading is used. Like most such charts, it provides goals by reading level rather than grade level. Comprehension objectives are prominently displayed at the top of the chart, so that the comprehension emphasis of the program is readily apparent. There are criterion-referenced tests for all objectives, so that assessment directly supports program emphases. A profile sheet is maintained for each student, and, in the fall, the information on this record is passed on to the student's new teacher. Because continuity is maintained through the KEEP testing and record-keeping system, most teachers do not limit themselves to use of a single basal reading program. Instead, they teach lessons designed around high-quality selections from different sources, including tradebooks and several basal reading programs.

A basal program or scope-and-sequence chart should be seen as only one part of the school's total reading program. Following a staff development approach in working out a total reading program will allow individual teachers to integrate their own ideas, understand the goals of others, and work cooperatively. The selection of a basal program and the development of a set of goals for student learning can be taken on as schoolwide projects. Later, when the program or set of goals is put into place, staff members will understand the reasons behind it.

7. *Be aware of pros and cons of different patterns of grouping students for instruction, and consider social and emotional as well as academic outcomes.*

Children in most elementary school classrooms in the United States are placed in ability groups for reading instruction. The use of three groups appears to be the norm. Grouping decisions are usually permanent arrangements, as few children are moved from one instructional group to another over the course of the school year. We are now discovering that these practices, while long-standing and in many ways sensible, can be detrimental to some students. Grouping sometimes has the effect of limiting opportunities for learning. Being placed in the bottom group often means that students receive low-quality instruction. As a result, they progress poorly in learning to read and gradually lose motivation and confidence.

Recent research suggests that teachers teach different kinds of lessons to good and poor readers. In a study of high- and low-ability groups in grades one, three, and five, Allington (1984) found that low-ability groups had much less opportunity to read silently, in some cases only 5 percent as much as high-ability groups. Poor readers read fewer stories and were given more skill drills and worksheets. On the basis of these findings, we can reach two conclusions. First, isolated skills instruction, the commonest approach for poor readers, probably does them more harm than good. When students focus so completely on separate skills, they are likely to miss the broad view of literacy that should be the foundation of the elementary school reading program. The very students who need to understand the larger picture of reading, especially its functions, are those for whom reading instruction tends to be the most fragmented. Second, while high-ability learners can move at a faster pace, the differences in instruction are often greater than necessary and tend to hold low-ability children back.

In KEEP classrooms, possible detrimental effects of grouping are avoided in four ways. First, groups are not static. Most classrooms have four or five reading groups (enrollment in most classes is from 25 to 30 students). Students are assigned to groups on the basis of criterion-referenced test results. Regrouping takes place every quarter, and in a typical classroom three or four children usually move from one group to another. Second, each group meets with the classroom teacher for the same length of time each day, usually twenty to twenty-five minutes. Additional instruction of poor readers supplements but does not replace classroom instruction. Third, while lessons vary with the children's level of reading development, all receive an emphasis on comprehension, silent rather than oral reading, and work with a variety of texts. All children are encouraged to develop the habit of reading for enjoyment, although extra assistance with book selection is provided to lower-ability children. Fourth, an effort is made to break away from homogeneous grouping when the children are working independently. During this time children are seated with those from other reading groups. Thus, students experience work in both homogeneous and heterogeneous groups during the reading/language arts period.

Possible alternative approaches to typical homogeneous grouping for reading instruction include the following:

1. Keep an ability grouping arrangement but foster a multidimensional concept of ability for your students, the view that children have different special abilities and that no one is best in every way.
2. Take special steps to give low ability students the chance to achieve higher status.
3. Encourage cooperative learning by using different kinds of peer work groups.
4. Use various types of heterogeneous (mixed ability) grouping. [Mason & Au, 1986, p. 412]

8. *Make provisions for continuous communication about students with special needs, so extra instruction helps (not hinders) progress.*
In many schools students with special needs are taken from the regular classroom and given reading or language instruction by a resource teacher. This type of pull-out procedure is often used in programs for poor readers. The danger in many of these situations is that the classroom teacher loses touch with the children's needs in learning to read and fails to provide continued classroom support in reading. Then, neither the classroom nor the research teacher assumes responsibility for the students' overall development as readers.

For children who are experiencing difficulty with learning to read, the absence of classroom support may be quite damaging. Allington's (1983) findings point to the importance of setting aside adequate time to teach special students to read. For many children with reading difficulties, the time provided in resource room instruction is inadequate in and of itself. Further classroom instruction is also needed. Thus, pull-out instruction should be viewed as *supporting* or *supplementing* classroom reading instruction, rather than replacing it entirely. Also, pull-out instruction seems to be more effective if it is coordinated with classroom reading activities rather than being completely separate or different (Carter, 1984).

Part of creating a successful reading program is establishing the means for insuring ongoing communication between classroom and resource room teachers. The instruction provided by resource teachers should dovetail with classroom instruction, as well as fit in with the overall school philosophy for the reading program. Classroom and resource teachers need to meet regularly to determine how supplemental instruction can best reinforce the students' learning to read. Meetings should occur weekly but do not have to be lengthy. Longer meetings can be scheduled quarterly, or whenever significant changes in instruction are being contemplated.

Our view, supported by the experience of the KEEP staff, is that responsibility for the students' overall progress in reading should rest with one person — the classroom teacher. An important reason classroom teachers should communicate frequently with resource teachers is to insure that supplemental activities lead to success in the regular classroom. Too often, students experience successes in the resource room that do not carry over to the regular classroom. Continued failure of students outside of the resource room is an outcome counter to the major purpose of supplementary instruction, which is for students to become independent learners, able to function well in the regular classroom. On the one hand, resource room teachers may be able to suggest ways of altering classroom activities so that poor readers can participate more successfully. On the other hand, classroom teachers may be able to suggest ways that resource room activities can be used to bolster students' success in the classroom. For example, at KEEP, classroom teachers inform resource teachers of the units of study the class will be covering. Resource teachers can then equip poor readers with relevant background knowledge by having them read and write about the topic, such as insects or plants, before the whole class begins the unit. Poor readers then are well prepared to participate in content-area whole-class discussions and reading and writing activities.

9. Involve parents in their children's learning to read.

If they understand the school's philosophy, parents can often do much to support the overall goals of the elementary school reading program. To insure that interested parents have the opportunity to become involved in their children's learning to read, multiple ways of communicating with parents need to be worked out. Beginning in kindergarten, books can be sent home for parents to read to children. One book a week sets a good pattern. Communication can be started with a school newsletter, including information about the reading program and suggestions for ways that parents can help. Many parents are willing to support their children's recreational reading and may also be interested in suggestions for fostering writing. Parents of younger children may read aloud to them. Schools following a process approach to writing may give parents information about the importance of drawing and letting children try out their own invented spellings. Parents of older students may give their children some quiet time to read on their own and encourage the keeping of a diary, note taking, or story writing. Parents may arrange regular visits to the library so their children always have access to interesting books.

Parents, and other family members such as grandparents, can be invited to serve as volunteers in the classroom. For example, parents can read to children or listen to individual children read aloud. Or parents can accompany students to the library to look up information needed for research projects. Parents can help with school reading activities, such as setting up a book fair where children can purchase or trade books.

At open houses and parent conferences, teachers can be encouraged to provide parents with complete explanations about their children's progress in learning to read and write. Parents may be interested in seeing samples of their children's writing and the kinds of materials they currently are reading. Some schools even hold "back-to-school" sessions, where parents come to school and participate with their children in typical school activities.

10. *View people, not commercial programs or curriculum guides, as the key to a successful reading program. Treat the reading program as a whole-school effort, allowing for staff discussions and the building of an attitude of continuous innovation.*

The key to a successful elementary school reading program is a shared vision of what the program should accomplish for the students, along with a sense of its important elements. This shared vision can rarely be transmitted in a top-down way but generally develops as all involved with the program meet to air their views.

Time for staff to meet for discussions is essential. No program, however wonderful in design, can be successful if staff members have not contributed to shaping it and do not feel ownership over it. A possible way of stimulating discussion would be to share an article or a chapter such as this one with other staff members, and then to meet for a discussion. Questions for discussion should be open ended; for example,

Was there an idea you found especially interesting?
Did you come across an idea you might like to try?
Which idea do you think might be most important for our school?

The idea would be for staff at the school level to become involved in thinking the issues through for themselves. As we said in the beginning, there is no simple formula for success, and abstract ideas need to be made concrete through an infusion of knowledge about the students to be served, the community, the school setting, and the staff members themselves.

Finally, once an effective program is in place, there must be room for improvement and individual initiative. The process of discussion should continue so that the program can be updated constantly on the basis of new experiences at the school and in the classroom, of new research knowledge, and of new insights.

REFERENCES

Allington, R. L. (1983). The reading instruction provided readers of differing abilities. *Elementary School Journal, 83,* 548–559.

Allington, R. L. (1984). Content coverage and contextual reading in reading groups. *Journal of Reading Behavior, 16,* 85–96.

Anderson, T. H. (1980). Study strategies and adjunct aids. In R. J. Spiro, B. C. Bruce, & W. F. Brewer (Eds.), *Theoretical issues in reading comprehension* (pp. 483–502). Hillsdale, NJ: Lawrence Erlbaum Associates.

Au, K. H. (1979). Using the experience-text-relationship method with minority children. *The Reading Teacher, 32,* 677–679.

Au, K. H., Crowell, D. C., Jordan, C., Sloat, K. C. M., Speidel, G. E., Klein, T. W., & Tharp, R. G. (1986). Development and implementation of the KEEP reading program. In J. Orasanu (Ed.), *Reading comprehension: From research to practice* (pp. 235–252). Hillsdale, NJ: Lawrence Erlbaum Associates.

Barr, R. (1984). Beginning reading instruction: From debate to reformation. In P. D. Pearson (Ed.), *Handbook of reading research* (pp. 545–581). New York: Longman.

Baumann, J. F. (1984). The effectiveness of a direct instruction paradigm for teaching main idea comprehension. *Reading Research Quarterly, 20,* 93–115.

Brown, A. L., Campione, J. C., & Day, J. D. (1981). Learning to learn: On training students to learn from texts. *Educational Researcher, 10*(2), 14–21.

Carter, L. F. (1984). The sustaining effects study of compensatory and elementary education. *Educational Researcher, 13*(7), 4–13.

Crowell, D. C., Kawakami, A. J., & Wong, J. L. (1986). Emerging literacy: Reading-writing experiences in a kindergarten classroom. *The Reading Teacher, 40,* 144–149.

Duffy, G. G., & Roehler, L. R. (1987a). Teaching reading skills as strategies. *The Reading Teacher, 40,* 414–418.

Duffy, G. G., & Roehler, L. R. (1987b). Improving reading instruction through responsive elaboration. *The Reading Teacher, 40,* 514–520.

Durkin, D. (1978–1979). What classroom observations reveal about reading comprehension. *Reading Research Quarterly, 14,* 481–533.

Goodlad, J. (1983). *A place called school.* New York: Harper & Row.

Graves, D., & Hansen, J. (1983). The author's chair. *Language Arts, 60*(2), 176–183.

Hallinger, P., & Murphy, J. (1985). Characteristics of highly effective elementary school reading programs. *Educational Leadership, 42*(5), 39–42.

Hansen, J., & Pearson, P. D. (1983). An instructional study: Improving the inferential comprehension of fourth-grade good and poor readers. *Journal of Educational Psychology, 75,* 821–829.

Heath, S. B. (1982). What no bedtime story means: Narrative skills at home and school. *Language in Society, 11*(2), 49–76.

Heath, S. B. (1983). *Ways with words: Language, life, and work in communities and classrooms.* Cambridge, England: Cambridge University Press.

Herber, H. L. (1978). *Teaching reading in content areas* (2nd ed.). Englewood Cliffs, NJ: Prentice-Hall.

Holdaway, D. (1979). *The foundations of literacy.* Sydney, Australia: Ashton Scholastic (distributed in the United States by Heinemann).

Langer, J. A. (1981). From theory to practice: A prereading plan. *Journal of Reading, 25,* 152–156.

Levine, S. G. (1984). USSR – A necessary component in teaching reading. *Journal of Reading, 27,* 394–400.

Mason, J. (1983). An examination of reading in third and fourth grades. *The Reading Teacher, 36,* 906–913.

Mason, J., & Allen, J. (1986). A review of emergent literacy with implications for research and practice in reading. In E. Rothkopf (Ed.), *Review of Research in Education* (Vol. 13) (pp. 3–48). Washington, DC: American Educational Research Association.

Mason, J. M., & Au, K. H. (1986). *Reading instruction for today.* Glenview, IL: Scott, Foresman.

Moore, D. W., & Readence, J. E. (1983). Approaches to content area reading instruction. *Journal of Reading, 26,* 397–402.

Palincsar, A. S., & Brown, A. L. (1986). Interactive teaching to promote independent learning from text. *The Reading Teacher, 39,* 771–777.

Roth, K. J., Smith, E. L., & Anderson, C. W. (1984). Verbal patterns of teachers: Comprehension instruction in content areas. In G. G. Duffy, L. Roehler, & J. Mason (Eds.), *Comprehension instruction: Perspectives and suggestions* (pp. 281–293). New York: Longman.

Smith-Burke, M. T., & Ringler, L. H. (1986). STAR: Teaching reading and writing. In J. Orasanu (Ed.), *Reading comprehension: From research to practice* (pp. 215–234). Hillsdale, NJ: Lawrence Erlbaum Associates.

Staton, J. (1980). Writing and counseling: Using a dialogue journal. *Language Arts, 57,* 514–518.

Taylor, B. (1982). A summarizing strategy to improve middle grade students' reading and writing skills. *The Reading Teacher, 36,* 202–205.

Taylor, D. (1983). *Family literacy: Young children learning to read and write.* Portsmouth, NH: Heinemann.

Teale, W. H., & Sulzby, E. (Eds.). (1986). *Emergent literacy: Writing and reading.* Norwood, NJ: Ablex.

Tharp, R. G. (1982). The effective instruction of comprehension: Results and description of the Kamehameha Early Education Program. *Reading Research Quarterly, 17,* 503–527.

Wong, J. W., & Au, K. H. (1985). The concept-text-application approach: Helping elementary students comprehend expository text. *The Reading Teacher, 38,* 612–618.

5 Middle School and Junior High Reading Programs

MARK W. CONLEY
Michigan State University

In theory, middle schools differ from junior high schools in fundamental ways. Middle schools are supposed to be more like elementary schools. In many middle schools, teachers work in teams, with a focus on the individual and on personal development. Junior high schools, on the other hand, are supposed to look more like secondary schools. They are often departmentalized, with a focus on academics and college preparation (Lipsitz, 1984).

In practice, confusion persists about the nature of middle and junior high schools. Few schools entirely adopt a middle school or junior high emphasis. Criticized for a lack of academic rigor, middle schools are pressured to become junior high schools. Criticized for not attending to the needs of the adolescent as an individual, junior high schools are pushed to become middle schools. Though current trends favor the movement toward middle schools, junior high schools are still much in evidence.

The confusion about middle schools and junior highs is also evident in the reading curriculum. Like the schools themselves, approaches to middle and junior high reading have been drawn from both the elementary and secondary levels. Little is known about reading programs in the context of the goals of middle and junior high schools. Like the schools, middle and junior high reading programs struggle to establish and maintain an identity and meet the various needs of early adolescent learners.

The purposes of this chapter are to

1. Distinguish between the goals of middle and junior high schools
2. Describe the reading needs of the early adolescent
3. Examine various programs that are commonly found in middle schools and junior highs
4. Provide guidelines for developing middle and junior high school reading programs

THE GOALS OF MIDDLE AND JUNIOR HIGH SCHOOLS

Before middle schools, there were junior high schools. Junior high schools were first organized at the turn of the century (Peeler, 1974). First thought of as "little high schools," junior highs were supposed to prepare students for the vocational and academic subjects they would experience at the secondary level.

Then and now, junior highs typically cover grades seven, eight, and nine, with a curriculum that parallels the high school. Emphasis is usually on mastery of subject matter, though attempts have been made to extend the curriculum to encourage exploration and personal development. Peeler's (1974) goals for the junior high are a good example of a broader perspective on what junior highs should do. According to Peeler, junior highs should stress the needs of the early adolescent, especially the need for a smooth transition from the elementary to the secondary school. In addition, junior highs should offer opportunities for students to discover their interests and capabilities, providing vocational education and programs that will reduce the number of dropouts. Ultimately, suggests Peeler, junior highs should assist students in realizing their fullest potential to offer service to the society in which they live.

Unfortunately, though Peeler's goals promise to broaden the focus of the junior high to students' personal and social adjustment, most reform efforts lead back to an exclusive focus on academics. Personal exploration in the junior high usually involves entertaining different vocational and academic choices. Personal development often means making decisions about educational opportunities but not about extracurricular activities (Wiles & Biondi, 1981).

Middle schools, typically covering grades five through eight, emerged in the late 1950s and early 1960s, in part as a reaction against junior highs. Critics argued for a reorganization of schools in the middle levels, based on the junior high's neglect of the physical, intellectual, and emotional needs of the early adolescent (Peeler, 1974).

Several other factors contributed to the development of middle schools (Wiles & Biondi, 1981). Concerns over the quality of schooling in the United States created an obsession for academic achievement in the middle and upper grades. Calls came for a four-year high school (grades nine through twelve), viewed as a college preparatory school. Grades five and six were combined with grades seven and eight so that teachers could introduce more specialized content and instruction at earlier levels.

Racial desegregation and increased enrollments also contributed to middle school development by creating incentives for reorganization. Segregation and overcrowding at the elementary level were often relieved by moving grades five and six to the middle school. The factor that continues to influence middle school development is the "bandwagon effect." Favorable reports on middle schools convince many administrators that middle schools are "the thing to do."

A recurring problem of middle schools is that reorganization often occurs without a clear conception of what middle schools should accomplish. The National Association of Secondary School Principals (NASSP, 1985) recently described the goals of the effective middle school. Rather than rigidly emphasizing academics, these goals focus on teaching students to become lifelong learners, with attention to developing students' knowledge, skills, and motivation. Specifically, the NASSP recommends that middle schools should

1. Articulate and disseminate core values that address personal responsibility, the importance of learning, and respect for diversity in the school and community
2. Develop a climate in the school that supports excellence and achievement
3. Support students' personal development, offering frequent opportunities for responsible social behavior as well as promoting a positive self-concept

4. Implement a curriculum that effectively balances skill development with content coverage, offering lifelong skills for the future along with an understanding of different content areas
5. Challenge each student at his or her ability level
6. Use a variety of instructional approaches (e.g., lectures, simulations, discussion, demonstrations, and labs), combined with high expectations and guidance

These goals illustrate how middle schools try to deal with many different aspects of a student's life, from personal and academic development to helping students understand their place in the community. Note how many of these goals resemble those meant to reform the junior high. Effective middle schools take these goals seriously. In a recent survey of exemplary middle schools, a large percentage stated a commitment to students' personal development and development of skills for continued learning and exploration. These goals are often addressed through use of interdisciplinary teams, a home-base period, and a teacher advisor for each student, as well as flexible scheduling (George & Oldaker, 1986).

In contrast to these promising signs, several problems persist with the middle school curriculum. The middle school's commitment to student development sometimes translates into an overemphasis on facts at the expense of abstract thought. This stems from the belief that middle school students are not ready for more sophisticated types of thinking. In addition, while there is a concern for reading instruction in some form, there is uncertainty about what kind, how it should occur, and who should be served (Lipsitz, 1984).

The goals of the middle school and junior high have become more clearly differentiated over the years: Junior highs stress academics and preparation for secondary school, while middle schools emphasize the development of the student as an individual. Despite this clarity in goals, middle schools and junior highs continually strive to translate them into actual practice, striking a balance between academics and meeting students' needs. An important part of this balancing act is a concern for identifying and addressing the reading needs of the early adolescent.

THE NEEDS OF THE EARLY ADOLESCENT READER

Despite differences in emphasis, middle schools and junior highs set high goals for the early adolescent reader. These goals, in turn, create specific requirements for students, or expectations for what students need to do in order to succeed. Duffy and Roehler (1986) describe students' needs in terms of three areas of the curriculum: content, process, and attitudes. At the middle school and junior high level, the content that students are expected to read can be very complex. The simple stories students are exposed to in the early grades are replaced by more sophisticated stories, poetry, and folklore. Simple expository texts are exchanged for specialized texts in science, mathematics, and social studies. Students at this level need to be able to deal successfully with more complicated types of content.

The shift to more complicated content also creates a need for students to know more about the process of comprehension. Simply stated, comprehension is the ability of the reader to use prior knowledge to gain meaning from text. Prior knowledge that facilitates comprehension can either be topical knowledge (knowledge that relates to the topic of a particular lesson) or knowledge of a particular reading skill (e.g., forming interpretations). Students need both the appropriate prior knowledge to complete the tasks required at this level and the ability to apply their knowledge at the right place and at the right time. The same knowledge, particularly knowledge about reading, needs to be applied differently as students deal with various types of text across the curriculum.

At the elementary level, instruction on attitudes about reading centers on helping students build positive feelings about reading and themselves. For the early adolescent, the emphasis on attitudes becomes more functional in nature: getting students to see themselves as readers who can use reading as a tool for understanding. Students at this level need to perceive themselves as enthusiastic, successful readers who can use reading to understand better not only their school subjects but also the world around them.

The goals created by the curriculum — what students are expected to accomplish — must be considered alongside the needs of the students themselves — what they are actually capable of doing. Early and Sawyer (1984) have described the features of three different types of early adolescent readers: problem, average, and superior readers. All vary in the extent to which they are capable of meeting the challenges posed by the curriculum at this level.

Problem readers experience difficulty in virtually every curriculum area. These students are still struggling to master basic learning-to-read skills. They tend to use phonics as their only approach to reading. Because they have not learned to make sense of what they read, their attitudes about print are generally poor. In addition, because of their inability to process information and their poor attitudes, they view the content of what they read as inaccessible and uninteresting.

As a group, average readers have mastered phonics and are often accurate and fluent in their oral reading. Mistakes they do make orally generally do not interfere with their understanding. Average readers have also, for the most part, acquired basic comprehension skills, yet they have not necessarily integrated skills adequately to be flexible and strategic in their comprehension. Some of these students can be slow in their reading, that is, they need more time than others to comprehend. Others may read too fast, only to sacrifice their comprehension (Singer & Donlan, 1980).

The main characteristic of this group is that they don't read much. Many in this group can read proficiently but won't read. Like problem readers, they need good reasons for reading. They especially need to see connections between themselves and the content they are learning.

Superior readers have a great deal of background from experience with reading, yet they still need to refine their approach. They may be especially proficient at factual learning and even be capable of forming sophisticated interpretations. These students need to enhance their ability to apply what they know. This includes using their imagination for self-motivation and creative thinking and developing both speed and flexibility while reading.

The challenges posed by the middle school and junior high curriculum and the strengths and weaknesses of the early adolescent have created a diversity of needs in the early adolescent reader. The response in schools has been a diverse range of reading programs. While these programs can be tailored to the needs of the early adolescent, they are also subject to middle school and junior high constraints.

READING PROGRAMS FOR THE MIDDLE SCHOOL AND JUNIOR HIGH

Many different types of programs are available to help the early adolescent reader (Early & Sawyer, 1984). Beyond the elementary level, reading is most often taught as a separate course. As of 1982, remedial courses were the most prevalent, followed by corrective and developmental courses and courses with labels like "Recreational Reading," "Everyday Reading Skills," and "Independent Reading" (Greenlaw & Moore, 1982).

Remedial programs are intended for problem readers, the students who have acquired few if any basic skills. These programs are characterized by intensive, one-on-one or small-group instruction outside the regular classroom. The emphasis is almost always on learning-to-read skills, such as phonics and basic comprehension, that these students have yet to master. Teachers in these programs are specialists who have been clinically trained (Early & Sawyer, 1984).

Corrective programs are for students who have mastered most basic skills but need selective instruction in areas they have not mastered. Corrective programs are usually administered in a reading or English class by a reading or English teacher. Students work on specific skill weaknesses in corrective programs.

In general, reading instruction in remedial and corrective classes focuses on the identical basic reading skills taught at the elementary level. All too often, this instruction consists of workbooks, skill-builders and boxes or machines that offer a carefully controlled environment for learning about reading. Not only do students become cynical about this type of instruction, these experiences fail to prepare students for the variety of content and sophisticated concepts they will encounter in their content-area classes (Nelson & Herber, 1982).

Developmental programs help average students refine and extend their existing skills. For the average reader, this means learning how to apply the comprehension and study skills they already know. Developmental programs are also used for superior readers. For them, the emphasis is on creating interest and challenge through reading. Elective courses, such as courses in personal reading and studying, are frequently reserved for better readers as part of a developmental program (Early & Sawyer, 1984).

In contrast to the learning-to-read skills characteristic of remedial programs, developmental programs emphasize "reading-to-learn" skills, or the use of reading for functional or personal reasons (Singer & Donlan, 1980). Developmental programs take place in many types of settings, from specialized classes outside the regular classroom to instruction in all content areas. Teachers in the developmental program may be reading or English teachers, or teachers from any curricular area.

Content reading is a term applied to some developmental programs. This involves helping all students comprehend and apply the materials they are required to read in their school subjects. Reading skills in content-reading programs are taught functionally; that is, skills are taught as they are needed, particularly when students need assistance in comprehending materials they are required to read. Content-reading programs are typically administered in the regular classroom by the content-area teacher, sometimes with the support of a reading teacher or specialist (Herber, 1978).

A feature of many content-reading programs is the use of guided reading. Figure 5.1 illustrates a comprehension guide used to help students understand the relationship between fractions and decimals. Notice how the guide focuses on helping students understand the content of the lesson (part I) while emphasizing the function of the information students are learning (part II). This can be especially important in mathematics.

Figure 5.1   Comprehension Guide: Fractions and Decimals

Content Objective: To understand that fractions can be written as decimals and decimals can be written as fractions.

Part I: Below are pairs of fractions and decimals. Check the pairs that are equal. Be ready to tell why they are equal.

		FRACTION	DECIMAL
_____	1.	$\dfrac{3}{10}$	.30
_____	2.	$\dfrac{27}{100}$	.27
_____	3.	$\dfrac{3}{4}$	.75
_____	4.	$2\dfrac{4}{5}$	2.80
_____	5.	$\dfrac{3}{8}$	.375
_____	6.	$\dfrac{3}{500}$	.006

Part II: Check the statements below that can be used to support the ideas presented in part I. Think about what we have learned in this and other lessons so far.

_____ 1. Some fractions are easier to rewrite as decimals than others.

_____ 2. Knowing about fractions and decimals could save you money.

Another type of guided reading strategy heightens students' awareness of question-and-answer relationships (QARs) (Raphael, 1984). During QAR instruction, students are taught three different ways that questions and answers may be related when they read a text: (1) "right there" — words used to create the question and words used for the answer are in the same sentence, (2) "think and search" — the answer is in the text, but words used to create the question and those used for the answer are not in the same sentence, and (3) "on my own" — the answer lies outside the text. Teachers can introduce students to these concepts and create specific activities for students to complete. (For example, they can generate and then label different types of questions and related answers.) This training offers students opportunities to practice and then independently apply their understanding of QARs.

Reasoning can be stressed with a guide like the one in Figure 5.2, a prediction guide used in social studies. Notice how the guide gets students to think about their own perspectives first, before they consider the U.S. Constitution. This builds background and motivation for what could otherwise be a very difficult and abstract topic. Once students have completed the first part and read about the Constitution, they should be well prepared to think about how constitutional issues continue to affect their own lives.

A structured overview, a guided reading strategy used to teach vocabulary, appears in Figure 5.3. This type of strategy goes by many names, including "semantic map" and "graphic organizer" (Conley, in press). Its main purpose is to organize discussion and provide students with a familiar framework within which to understand the meaning of new words and concepts. This overview has been successfully used to teach words that offer insight into different worlds represented in "The Secret Life of Walter Mitty" (Thurber, 1965). Words and concepts taught within this overview become the key to appreciating characters and themes in this story and in other types of literature read throughout the year.

Figure 5.2   Prediction Guide: The U.S. Constitution

Content Objective: To know that the U.S. Constitution balances the rights of the many with the rights of the few.

Part I: Place a check in the blank if you think the statement is true. Be ready with one example from your own experience to support each decision.

_____ 1. Without freedom, you have nothing.

_____ 2. The majority should *always* rule.

_____ 3. The individual is the most important part of any society.

_____ 4. It is important to compromise whenever possible.

_____ 5. Though all people are created equal, not everyone has the same opportunities.

Part II: Now that you have studied the U.S. Constitution, circle the number of the statements you can support, based on what you have learned about the U.S. Constitution. Be ready with evidence from what you have read to support your decisions.

Figure 5.3   Vocabulary Development: "Walter Mitty"

Content Objective: To understand how some people use fantasies to escape their troubles in the real world.

WALTER MITTY

REAL WORLD ◄─────────────────────────────────────► FANTASY WORLD

henpecked husband	famous anesthesiologist
drives his wife to town	flies hydroplane
washed-up old man	famous defendant
mocked by people with "insolent skill" and "derisive whistling"	"intimate airways" of Mitty's mind

An unresolved question in content reading concerns whether or not students gain a greater understanding of the reading process through use of these and other types of approaches. Guided reading typically occurs in the context of whole-class and small-group discussions. If teachers use guided reading to encourage memorization rather than reasoning, then students will leave with little if any knowledge about content or process. In addition, students' attitudes about what they are reading will not be particularly affected. If, on the other hand, teachers use guided reading to show students how to integrate new information with what they already know, students' knowledge of content and process can be enhanced, along with their perception of the usefulness of what they are learning (Conley, 1986; Roehler & Duffy, in press).

Developmental programs typically face at least two problems: a lack of clearly defined purposes and a tendency to reserve more worthwhile (and motivating) reading experiences for better readers. In some schools, electives in developmental reading programs may be plentiful yet lack a coherent focus, either in relation to one another or in terms of how the courses will eventually benefit students. Speed reading is an example of a frequently offered course that can give students the wrong impression about proficient reading, namely, that reading faster means reading better. Instead, students should become aware of the need to be flexible in light of different materials and purposes while reading.

Reserving some of the better offerings in developmental programs (such as courses in study skills) for superior readers ignores the needs of problem and average readers. While problem and average readers need some type of instruction in basic skills, they also need to learn how to deal with the increasing demands of the curriculum at the middle school and junior high levels. Offering developmental reading to better readers over-looks the benefits that problem and average readers might receive from enrichment in reading.

A major issue for remedial, corrective, and developmental programs for early adolescents concerns how to involve students and teachers. It has been popular to recommend that every early adolescent be provided with specialized reading instruction (Cooper & Petrosky, 1976). It has also been suggested that every teacher should be a teacher of reading (Karlin, 1984). Many middle schools and junior highs recognize the need to offer services in reading to their students, but the cost of extra reading classes for every student can be prohibitive (Early & Sawyer, 1984). Because of limitations in resources, many schools are faced with the unfortunate choice between hiring a reading teacher to meet reading needs or hiring a content-area teacher to keep class sizes at reasonable levels.

Middle schools, with their tendency to emphasize teachers working in interdisciplinary teams, are often in the best position to deal with these issues. Shared responsibilities at the middle school should help teachers focus on reading as a way to integrate learning experiences (Aulls, 1978). Content reading is a natural choice for middle schools to use in helping students learn from text as well as develop and refine the processes and attitudes they need for success at this level. A problem with this approach, however, is that content-area teachers don't have the time or the expertise necessary to meet all of the reading needs of students in their classrooms. It is not always clear how remedial issues are addressed in middle schools or how a remedial specialist can contribute to middle school teams. Some teachers resist becoming involved in reading at the middle school level because they are uncertain about the relationship between reading and their content area (Ratekin, Simpson, Alvermann, & Dishner, 1985).

The response of the junior high to reading needs and limited resources has been either to set up separate reading classes or to incorporate reading into English departments (Early & Sawyer, 1984). This is consistent with the tendency of the junior high to departmentalize subjects (Lipsitz, 1984). These solutions contribute to at least two other problems in meeting the needs of the early adolescent reader. First, reading or English teachers can become overly burdened, while other teachers get the impression that reading is not their responsibility. Second, the reading skills taught in separate classes have not been shown to transfer to the successful reading of content-area textbooks (Nelson & Herber, 1982). By setting up separate classes or making reading the responsibility of the English department, junior highs run the risk of isolating reading and failing to help students with the increasing demands of the curriculum. Given the organization and the constraints of many middle and junior high schools, the challenge remains of how to build an effective reading program for the early adolescent.

BUILDING EFFECTIVE MIDDLE SCHOOL AND JUNIOR HIGH READING PROGRAMS

This section provides five guidelines for developing successful reading programs for students in the middle school and junior high.

1. *Involve reading specialists, reading coordinators, content-area teachers, building principals, and district-level administrators in the planning.*
Planning and involvement by these key participants are crucial to building an effective middle school or junior high reading program (Nelson, 1981). Some schools and districts opt for using reading committees with representatives from each of these areas. Their job is to initiate, improve, extend, or evaluate reading programs (Early & Sawyer, 1984).

Each participant in the planning process serves an important function. Reading specialists gather information about the needs unique to students and staff in their own building. Reading coordinators provide consistent support for those in different buildings, and they facilitate communication among administrators and other planning staff. It is especially desirable to involve content-area teachers representing all subjects, in order to avoid the misconception that reading is isolated from the rest of the curriculum. Pay special attention to ways of developing interdisciplinary teams responsible for decisions about remedial and content-area reading. Though it is unreasonable to expect the content-area teacher to conduct remediation, she or he needs to participate in developing a relationship between the remedial and content-area curriculum.

Without administrative support, chances for building a reading program can be severely limited. In one school district, a content-reading program developed outside the regular framework for staff development. This effort began with content-area teachers and reading coordinators who participated in the program based on the strength of their own commitment. Building-level administrators, believing in the objectives of the program, began to reward the participants with release time. As the program became popular, more and more teachers volunteered to participate. District-level administrators eventually killed the program, however, when they learned that an unofficial staff development program was using up district resources. Planning that took into account the need for administrative awareness as well as ownership over the program could have avoided this problem (Whitford, 1987).

2. *Base your program on clear goals for the role reading should play in what and how students learn in your building.*
Arriving at these goals requires both a research and a classroom perspective. For middle schools, developing a research base may involve gathering information about how reading contributes to the personal development of the early adolescent. Junior high programs might focus on how reading is used to help students become independent learners, especially in their academic subjects.

Any examination of research on middle school and junior high reading programs should be balanced by a study of the unique needs and constraints of classrooms in your school or district. Doing this requires a needs assessment and then a careful consideration of existing needs in relation to types of programs and available resources. This examination should help middle schools and junior highs alike, not only to design and clarify program goals but also to avoid the pitfalls of overly stressing academics or students' personal and social development.

3. *Use reading materials and instruction, even for remedial and corrective programs, that emphasize success and independence with students' own content-area textbooks.*
Reading kits and workbooks divorced from the rest of the curriculum do not encourage this kind of success. Instead, students need to learn specific reading strategies *while* they are learning content in their other classes. These strategies should help students unlock meaning not only for the immediate lesson but also in other situations that require independent reading. Vacca (1977) offers several recommendations for helping students to master content while they simultaneously learn to use reading as a functional, thinking process in the content-area classroom. Vacca (1977) states that reading instruction should

- Encourage students to relate their experiences to their reading
- Help students consider what they already know about what they are going to learn
- Set clear purposes for reading
- Offer students opportunities to discuss their reading
- Pose problems and encourage different interpretations
- Involve questions that require thinking rather than recall

Techniques that are consistent with these recommendations focus on comprehension, reasoning, and vocabulary development and emphasize independence. Study guides, like the one in Figure 5.1, can be used to facilitate independent comprehension on a personal level. For example, knowing how fractions and decimals are sometimes used interchangeably to mislead can help students become wary consumers.

4. *Integrate guided reading strategies with whole-class and small-group discussions.*

In classroom discussions, teachers and students share ideas that help them construct meaning and think about the content. Teachers, however, need to know how to conduct discussions that are responsive to students' needs during instruction (Conley, 1987). Otherwise, study guides or other approaches to guided reading become no better than a teacher's manual that replaces rather than supports effective classroom decisions.

To avoid this problem, teachers must be sensitive to the need to phase in greater sophistication and student responsibility during discussions (Pearson & Gallagher, 1983). Early in a lesson, teachers must be able to recognize when students have misconceptions that could interfere with the concepts they are required to learn. Teachers must be capable of providing alternative explanations and model processes necessary for students to grasp the content. In addition, they must be able to verify that students are understanding the content and processes important in the lesson. Finally, students need opportunities to practice and apply new concepts. Using whole-class and small-group discussions as part of this phasing-in of student responsibility is one way for teachers to guide students toward greater independence.

5. *Plan reading programs so that they are implemented over long periods of time.*

This approach is essential, first because of the organization of the junior high and second because of the natural reluctance of content-area teachers to participate in reading programs. Junior high faculties that thrive on departmentalization are naturally resistant if content reading is presented without a concern for the uniqueness of each subject area. Planning should focus on eventually breaking down the departmentalization and isolation of reading, gradually implementing programs intended to assist readers throughout the school. Teachers who participate in any program should be volunteers. Many middle school and junior high reading programs that fail do so because programs have been thrust on content-area teachers who are not ready for them. When this occurs, remedial and corrective programs can become dumping grounds for problem students or students who experience difficulty interacting with others in the regular classroom.

The complexity involved in implementing content-reading strategies in the classroom is yet another argument for taking a long-term approach to developing reading programs in the middle school or junior high. In one school district, a content-reading program was built over a three-year period. In the first year, content-area teachers learned how to implement content-reading approaches like those described in this chapter. In the second year, teachers refined their understanding by reviewing concepts, focusing on classroom implementation, and designing curriculum units. In the third year, teachers were given the opportunity to help other teachers learn about content reading. At the end of the third year, content-area teachers had acquired considerable expertise in adapting content reading to the specific needs of their students (Conley, 1986).

Approaches to reading program development should be both long-term and continuous. Middle schools and junior highs are faced with changing expectations about the best ways to meet the needs of students at that level (Hargreaves, 1986). An ongoing analysis of the reading needs of the early adolescent reader in relation to the organization and the resources of the middle school and junior high can contribute substantially toward meeting those expectations.

CONCLUSION

While the current structure of middle schools and junior highs is due mostly to changes in population or just the desire for change, goals have emerged that make middle schools and junior highs truly distinct. In particular, the middle school emphasizes the whole student while the junior high focuses on preparation for success in later academic subjects. Within each view, reading holds a special place. Designed appropriately, remedial and corrective programs offer students a chance both to build and to refine skills in ways that directly influence their success in the content-area classroom. Content-area teachers can apply strategies that simultaneously teach students content and the attitudes and processes necessary for lifelong learning. Reading programs that are both sensitive to the needs of the early adolescent and responsive to the changing organization of middle schools and junior highs stand the best chance of fostering achievement.

REFERENCES

Aulls, M. (1978). *Developmental and remedial reading in the middle grades.* Boston: Allyn and Bacon.

Conley, M. (1986). The influence of training in three teachers' comprehension questions during content area lessons. *Elementary School Journal, 87*(1), 17–28.

Conley, M. (1987). Teacher decisionmaking. In D. Alvermann, D. Moore, & M.

Conley (Eds.), *Research within reach: Secondary school reading* (pp. 142–152). Newark, DE: International Reading Association.

Conley, M. (in press). *Content reading instruction: A communication approach.* New York: Random House.

Cooper, C., & Petrosky, A. (1976). A psycholinguistic view of the fluent reading process. *Journal of Reading, 20,* 184–207.

Duffy, G., & Roehler, L. (1986). *Improving classroom reading instruction: A decision-making approach.* New York: Random House.

Early, M., & Sawyer, D. (1984). *Reading to learn in grades 5 to 12.* New York: Harcourt Brace Jovanovich.

George, P., & Oldaker, L. (1986). A national survey of middle school effectiveness. *Educational Leadership, 43*(4), 79–85.

Greenlaw, M., & Moore, D. (1982). What kinds of reading courses are taught in junior and senior high school? *Journal of Reading, 25,* 534–536.

Hargreaves, A. (1986). *Two cultures of schooling: The case of the middle schools.* New York: Falmer Press.

Herber, H. (1978). *Teaching reading in content areas.* Englewood Cliffs, NJ: Prentice-Hall.

Karlin, R. (1984). *Teaching reading in the high school.* Philadelphia: Harper & Row.

Lipsitz, J. (1984). *Successful schools for young adolescents.* New Brunswick, NJ: Transaction Books.

National Association of Secondary School Principals. (1985). *An agenda for excellence at the middle level.* Reston, VA: National Association of Secondary School Principals.

Nelson, J. (1981). *A staff development program for teaching reading in content areas.* Binghamton, NY: A Network of Secondary School Demonstration Centers for Teaching Reading in Content Areas.

Nelson, J., & Herber, H. (1982). Organization and management of programs. In A. Berger & H. A. Robinson (Eds.), *Secondary school reading: What research reveals for classroom practice* (pp. 143–158). Urbana, IL: ERIC Clearinghouse on Reading and Communication Skills and the National Conference on Research in English.

Pearson, P., & Gallagher, M. (1983). The instruction of reading comprehension. *Contemporary Educational Psychology, 8,* 317–344.

Peeler, T. (1974). The middle school: A historical frame of reference. In G. Duffy (Ed.), *Reading in the middle school* (pp. 7–15). Newark, DE: International Reading Association.

Raphael, T. (1984). Teaching learners about sources of information for answering comprehension questions. *Journal of Reading, 27,* 303–311.

Ratekin, N., Simpson, M., Alvermann, D., & Dishner, E. (1985). Why teachers resist content reading instruction. *Journal of Reading, 28,* 432–437.

Roehler, L., & Duffy, G. (in press). The content area teacher's instructional role: A cognitive mediational view. In J. Flood & D. Lapp (Eds.), *Instructional theory and practice for content area reading and learning.* Newark, DE: International Reading Association.

Singer, H., & Donlan, D. (1980). *Reading and learning from text*. Boston: Little, Brown.

Thurber, J. (1965). The secret life of Walter Mitty. In R. Pooley, A. Grommon, V. Lowers, & O. Niles (Eds.), *Accent: USA* (pp. 242–247). Glenview, IL: Scott, Foresman.

Vacca, R. (1977). Reading comprehension in the middle school. *Middle School Journal, 8*(3), 12–13.

Whitford, B. (1987). Effects of organizational context on program implementation. In W. T. Pink & G. W. Noblit (Eds.), *Schooling in social context: Qualitative studies* (pp. 83–104). Norwood, NJ: Ablex.

Wiles, J., & Biondi, J. (1981). *The essential middle school*. Columbus, OH: Charles E. Merrill.

6   High School Reading Programs: Out of the Past and Into the Future

RICHARD T. VACCA
Kent State University

Cathy A. Labate © 1988

Imagine stepping into a DeLorean-styled time capsule and taking a trip "back to the future." The DeLorean transports you back in time and space to 1962 in Hometown, the place where you grew up. Hometown's high school is typical of most secondary schools in the 1960s, and this suits you fine. The trip back is intentional. As someone interested in the supervision and organization of reading programs, you want to develop — firsthand — an understanding of secondary school reading as it was then. What did it mean to teach reading at Hometown High School in 1962? How will your exploration of the meaning of secondary school reading then better inform you about the *what, why,* and *how* of high school reading programs today? As you compare and contrast the past with the present, what will you need to take into consideration as you plan and organize high school reading programs for the twenty-first century?

So, reacquaint yourself with the corridors of Hometown High. Introduce yourself to Mr. Crippen, the principal, as the new reporter in town who's been assigned to cover the local school scene. You want to do a feature story on the high school's reading program. With pad and pencil in hand, you're ready to listen and observe. Take good notes!

HIGH SCHOOL READING: THE WAY WE WERE

As you stroll the halls of Hometown High, you soon recollect the "feel" of being in high school again. Class periods are fifty minutes long. When the bell rings, ending a class, a mass of humanity spills into the halls for three minutes or so, amid the din of slamming locker doors, hoots and hollers, and "true love" tête-à-têtes, only to be followed by a remarkable calm and silence at the ringing of the late bell. Throughout the school day, students trek from their homerooms to content-area classrooms to study halls, with occasional forays to the library or the restroom, and to the gym and cafeteria.

So where's the reading program at Hometown High? When you were a student at Hometown, you were totally unaware that something called a "high school reading program" existed. Mr. Crippen gladly informs you that high school reading programs are still a novel concept, educationally speaking, but at Hometown High, his hope is that the reading program will become an integral part of the total school curriculum. He hands you the work of the reading curriculum committee—a course of study—to investigate for yourself. The course of study reflects the latest thinking in the field of reading and provides Hometown High with a blueprint for curriculum planning and instruction.

The Curriculum Course of Study

As you read the opening philosophical statement of the course of study, you are encouraged by these strong words: "The teaching of reading cannot be approached in isolation from the content material of high school subjects." The statement goes on to say that "reading is best viewed as an integral part of all content-area courses taught at the secondary level." Thus, awareness on the part of the teacher about such instructional matters as "vocabulary development, comprehension, and study skills is imperative." Pretty impressive, you think to yourself.

The committee that prepared the course of study followed the philosophy section with an overview and description of the three broad components of the high school reading curriculum, the gist of which is characterized below:

- *Developmental:* For students near, at, or above grade level in reading, where reading instruction takes place in regular classroom settings
- *Corrective:* For students below grade level who are capable of reading effectively if provided with instructional assistance from the classroom teacher within the regular classroom setting, or from the reading teacher in a special classroom setting
- *Remedial:* For students who need concentrated assistance from a reading specialist in a laboratory setting

As you continue to study the curriculum document, you peruse lists of course objectives and materials to be taught at various grade levels for each of the major skill areas associated with reading instruction. The program components identified by the reading curriculum committee are fairly conventional by today's standards. You wonder how the content-area teachers at Hometown High respond to the heavy emphasis placed on their role in the school's reading program. "Every teacher, a teacher of reading" isn't the most endearing slogan ever devised. Nonetheless, the committee's members certainly had their heads and hearts in the right place.

The Reading Program in Action

Because you recognize that a curriculum guide reflects what "ought" to be and does not necessarily depict what actually happens in a schoolwide setting, you ask Mr. Crippen if you might freely visit classrooms to observe how teachers put the "developmental" and "corrective" components of the reading program into action.

In most of the content-area classrooms that you visit, teachers are either lecturing or talking to students in a language that can best be described as "questionese." While the teachers are talking in questions, students, in turn, are either listening, taking notes, daydreaming, or talking to teachers in one or two-word answers. After a week's worth of observation, you begin to liken the search for reading instruction in content classrooms to a game of hide-and-seek. Nevertheless, you persevere.

The more you observe classrooms, the harder it is to find reading instruction taking place. You note that textbooks are part of the physical environment of Hometown High. You find them stacked on window ledges, tables, desktops, and in bookcases. You also find that some teachers are using textbooks during class lessons. But are they teaching reading? It appears from your observations that the lower the ability of the class, the more students are asked to read aloud from textbooks, in round-robin fashion. In some classes, textbooks are being used to verify answers to questions that teachers ask during recitation. In higher-ability classes, especially in the social studies and science areas, some of the teachers require students to take in-class notes from their textbooks or to outline chapters. In practically all of the classrooms you visit, whether of low, average, high, or mixed ability, students are assigned homework from textbooks; that is, they are given material to read and end-of-chapter questions to prepare for the next day's class sessions.

Interviews with teachers are revealing. Most say they're not trained to be teachers of reading. If elementary teachers did a better job of teaching reading, then the secondary teacher wouldn't need to be burdened with an additional instructional responsibility. After all, content-area teachers are prepared to teach the subject matter of their disciplines, not reading skills. Reading is something that students do in their classrooms; it is one of many activities that the teacher must juggle in the course of a school day.

Déjà vu? What you see and hear at Hometown High is no illusion. Throughout the 1980s you have observed one instructional situation after another quite similar to those you have recorded at Hometown High. High school teachers today generally share similar perceptions with their 1960 counterparts about the role of reading in their classrooms.

Discouraged, you ask Mr. Crippen to show you the way to the reading specialist's room. "The remedial reading lab," he notes, "is housed in the basement, next to the boilers, in a recently renovated room . . . " Enough. You're ready to return to the 1980s.

Your trip back to the future may have proved somewhat frustrating, but it was not without its rewards. You learned that the promise of the past is still the promise of the present. With the concerted efforts of today's teacher education and staff development programs, that promise may become a reality in the near future. More is known today about the nature of the reading process, how children and youth learn, and what it takes to make secondary reading programs workable for and sensible to classroom teachers.

INSTRUCTIONAL ROLES: MAKING DISTINCTIONS

High school reading programs hinge upon the distinction teachers make between *direct* and *functional* instruction. Direct reading instruction centers around the development of skills and strategies. Direct instruction in reading often takes place in a specialized situation, such as a reading class. In some high school programs, however, content-area teachers may be responsible for direct instruction in reading and studying. Skills and strategies are taught with the expectation that they will be used by students when a reading situation demands their use. Acquisition and use of these skills and strategies are the objectives.

There are inherent risks involved when the burden for direct, explicit reading instruction is placed on the shoulders of content-area teachers. They are likely to misconstrue their instructional role. Often the very idea of teaching reading is viewed by classroom teachers as an imposition, an additional instructional responsibility, rather than as a vehicle for textbook learning. If content-area teachers believe they are deviating from the development of concepts integral to their discipline, they are quick to question the wisdom of such a move, and rightfully so. They are, by training, subject-matter specialists. Recognizing the utility of explicit instruction in reading and study strategies comes only when content-area teachers have experienced directly the value of such functional instruction.

When textbooks are used as tools for learning, classroom teachers have a significant role to play. That role involves functional reading instruction. A functional approach to teaching reading suggests that the classroom teacher is in a position to influence how students effectively learn from text reading. Rather than teach skills and strategies apart from content learning, with the expectation that, once acquired, they will be used by students, the content-area teacher helps students to apply the skills and strategies required to meet the demands inherent in actual text assignments. Thus, functional instruction means that skills and strategies are taught as they are needed and required by the material. Herber (1978) put it this way:

> Reading is taught functionally (1) when the skills being taught are those which must be used by readers in order to understand the content of an information source . . . , (2) when those skills are taught *as* the students read the information source, [and] (3) when that information source is assigned in order to teach the content it contains rather than to teach the reading skills it requires. [p. 26]

Margaret Early (1964) maintained that, once the difference between direct and functional instruction was clarified in the minds of content teachers, confusion over their instructional role would fade. She suggested that a spiral concept of learning can be adapted to provide insights into the meaning of secondary reading programs. In Figure 6.1, two cone-shaped spirals are superimposed upon one another to signify direct and functional instruction throughout the grades. The widest part of the direct instruc-

Figure 6.1 The Spiral Reading Curriculum: Direct and Functional Instruction

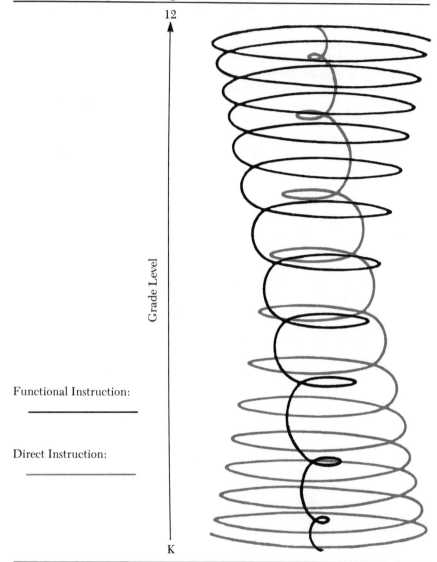

Source: Vacca, R. T., & Vacca, J. L. (1986). *Content Area Reading* (2nd ed.). Boston: Little, Brown, p. 13. Reprinted with permission.

tional cone lies in the elementary grades, representing the heavy emphasis in the earlier years on developing skills and strategies explicitly. As the spiral continues into the secondary grades, it gradually tapers off, suggesting less emphasis on direct skills and strategy instruction.

Now consider the overlapping spiral, which represents functional instruction. It begins narrowly in the elementary grades and broadens as it moves through the secondary grades. An inspection of the overlapping spirals shows that some form of direct teaching of reading should continue into the high school, but it should be superseded by functional teaching in every subject where reading is an important tool for learning. Early (1964) drew the following conclusions from her discussion of the spiral nature of the reading curriculum:

1. Content-area teachers have an important contribution to make to the reading development of their students, but they need not become a reading specialist to make it.
2. The content-area teacher should not be held responsible for direct reading instruction in remedial situations, especially if a certified reading teacher is needed to meet the specialized needs and abilities of students who are at risk in reading.
3. A high school reading program works best when reading personnel and content-area teachers respect and understand each other's roles.

When distinctions are made between direct and functional instruction, the foundation is firm for building a sturdy high school reading program.

MAKING THE READING PROGRAM INVISIBLE

The best high school reading programs are often invisible. Just as metaphysical concepts of "soul" are invisible in relation to physical concepts of "body," so it is that reading should be an invisible dynamic underlying the body of a high school curriculum — the subject-matter learning. All too often, however, high school reading programs are made highly visible, either in the form of reading classes or reading labs. Although the value of direct instruction was examined earlier, problems arise when a reading class or lab-centered curriculum becomes the primary (sometimes *the* only) rather than subsidiary vehicle for reading instruction in the high school.

Often so-called effective high school reading programs are mistakenly measured by the amount of highly visible, specialized equipment or materials used to "teach reading." In some cases, equipment (controlled readers, tachistoscopes, and the like) and materials (kits, workbooks, and so forth) are housed in a reading lab that becomes the centerpiece of the "reading program." When inquiries are made about the high school reading program, an administrator is apt to show the inquirer the reading lab, which, like a well-stocked bar, may be greeted with a nod of approval, if not unbridled enthusiasm. The problem, all too often, is that the reading lab and the reading class become *the* high school reading program. This is unfortunate. By its very design, the reading lab or class, at best, provides direct instructional services for a limited number of students.

When high school reading programs are invisible, the centerpiece for instruction is the content-area classroom. Ideally, it may not even be appropriate to think in terms of a high school reading program, but rather a series of programs, as many as there are content-area classrooms, with each differing somewhat from the other and each reflecting the diversity of the content area and the demands inherent in the subject matter under study. A casual high school observer might visit content-area classrooms and not discern any appreciable differences between reading instruction and content-area instruction. Instead, the effective use of textbooks as tools for learning would be indistinguishable from what might be commonly thought of as effective teaching strategies and practices.

Earlier, our trip back to the future showed us that Hometown High's reading curriculum committee was headed in the right direction, philosophically speaking. The curricular dilemma facing Hometown High then and high schools today is a similar one—that of translating a functional concept of reading into practice.

Getting a high school reading program, one that is essentially invisible, off the drawing board and into content-area classrooms is no easy matter. The task requires teacher change and development. Whenever change is involved, at least three important variables must be taken into account: time, ownership, and response. Content-area teachers need time to acquire, use, and adapt text comprehension strategies. Program development and staff development go hand-in-hand. Staff development must be a long-term effort, perhaps requiring as long as four years for teachers to grasp and actively incorporate strategies into content-area lessons (Vacca & Gove, 1984). In addition, classroom teachers must participate in a change process that develops ownership for the reading program. They must see themselves as being in charge of curricular decisions that affect what they will do instructionally and how they will approach content-area reading and learning situations. Finally, throughout program building, teachers need response. To put it another way, they need support, coaching, and encouragement if they are to embrace instructional change.

PROGRAM DEVELOPMENT

Since the matter of staff development is addressed in another chapter, let's explore some of the more salient issues related to program development.

Hometown High's reading curriculum committee produced a curriculum course of study, a blueprint for what ought to be, and then in all likelihood went the way of most curriculum committees, disbanding once its task was completed. Making a high school reading program work, however, necessitates the creation of an ongoing group — a reading committee — to guide, steer, and watch over program development (Anders, 1981; Sargent, 1969). This committee will have many functions and responsibilities, no doubt, but one of its most important may very well be to insure that teachers develop and maintain ownership in the reading program. The committee serves as a collective agent for change in the school. As Anders (1981) put it, "The reading committee opens both classroom doors and content-area teachers' minds to the concept of an all-school, content-area-based, developmental secondary reading program" (p. 316).

The reading committee, sometimes called a reading council, should be comprised of advocates for text comprehension and learning. Often a reading specialist serves as a resource to the committee, whose members primarily represent the various content areas. The committee representatives may be formed by content-area departmental election, appointment, or volunteers. Whatever the case may be, one factor is essential: Committee members must be respected by their colleagues as knowledgeable content-area specialists and effective instructional leaders. Each committee person is a voice for her or his content area and serves as a communication link to colleagues.

Following the establishment of a reading committee responsible for guiding the program, planning and development activities might best follow steps similar to those discussed in the remainder of this section and depicted in Figure 6.2.

Assessing Teachers' Beliefs About Reading and Reading to Learn

The first step in planning a high school reading program is an often neglected but crucial one: Find out what teachers think and believe about reading and reading to learn. The tendency in program development has often been to address *how* to solve problems before thoroughly understanding *what* the problems are. Tapping into teachers' perceptions (and misperceptions) about the reading process and its relationship to content-area learning is a necessary first step in identifying and solving problems. Teachers' views need to be articulated and linked to a discussion and for-

Figure 6.2   Steps in Program Development

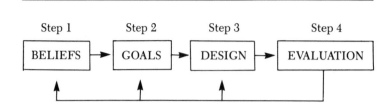

mulation of program goals and objectives. What is reading? What is the role of background knowledge in text comprehension? What does it mean to interact with the language of a content area? What does it mean to read like a scientist? a mathematician? a sociologist? a literary critic? an electrician? Questions such as these need to be aired and debated, not only within the reading committee but also in content-area departmental units.

One approach to linking reading to learn with the way content-area teachers think about reading is to determine what kinds of instructional activities and strategies make sense to teachers, within their respective fields of study. Criscuolo, Vacca, and LaVorgna (1980) developed a survey to determine what kinds of instructional strategies made sense to various content teachers. The survey consisted of twenty-nine classroom situations, each employing a reading/learning strategy for content acquisition. Technical terms were omitted whenever possible. The situations revolved around five instructional areas: decoding, vocabulary, comprehension, study/reference skill behavior, and diagnostic evaluation. For example, a situation under the instructional area of comprehension included the following:

> You are teaching a topic that involves a definite order of events. For example, it could be the results of certain activities, the outcomes of an experiment, or the steps in computing a word problem. You mix the order of these events and then ask the students to place the events in a logical order or sequence. [p. 266]

A second example from the survey included the following study situation:

> You notice that whenever you introduce a new chapter in class or give a reading assignment, students open their books and "wade" through the material. So you decide to show the students how to get a general idea of the material by reading the title, the subtitles and skimming the assignment. [p. 266]

The directions for the survey stated that the teachers were to read these "situations," each of which described a particular aspect of teaching reading in content areas. As they were reading, they were to place themselves in the position of the classroom teacher involved in the situation. Next, they were required to circle a number (on a scale from one to five) that indicated how much sense the teaching strategy made to them.

Interestingly, the content-area teachers in the study rated those situations requiring the least specialized training as the ones that made the most sense. Most of the comprehension and study strategies, for example, were supported as effective teaching practices which made sense and were within the teachers' instructional grasp.

Developing Program Goals

From an examination of the professional staff's beliefs about reading and reading to learn, the reading committee will be in a position to develop program goals. These will undoubtedly cluster around reading as a functional, meaning-making activity. Thomas and Moorman (1983) explained rather intricately how to translate belief statements about reading into program goals. Essentially, they suggested parsing teachers' beliefs into a series of "We believe" statements that could be clustered into meaningful categories according to basic instructional issues. Once a basic issue is aligned with a set of belief statements, the groundwork is set for establishing program goals, as shown in Figure 6.3.

Figure 6.3   Aligning Teacher Beliefs with Program Goals

Basic Issue: What is reading?

"We believe" statements:

- Reading involves making meaning.
- Comprehension involves connecting what a reader already knows to unfamiliar ideas.
- Reading is a language-learning activity.

    Program goals:

    - The reading program will assist students in acquiring the processes involved in learning from text material.
    - The reading program will help students comprehend materials of increasing difficulty.
    - The reading program will provide students with integrated language-learning activities.

Designing the Program

If the high school reading program is based on a premise of invisibility, then it stands to reason that the major program efforts should be reflected in what happens in content-area classrooms. In order to be effective and successful, the content-area reading component will, as suggested earlier, necessitate carefully planned, ongoing staff development.

Reading centers also can play an important role in the functional nature of high school reading programs. Unlike a reading lab, a reading center serves as an adjunct to content-area learning. It functions much like a school's writing center, where students go to work on problems they are having with writing assignments, or just to write. The reading center is staffed with a certified reading teacher, who serves as a coach for students and a resource for faculty. The reading teacher can assist students who are struggling with reading assignments, library research, and report-making projects. Instruction in the center is informative, designed to help students become *aware* of reading strategies and to *engage* in their use. Peer tutors can be trained to assist the reading teacher in the center.

Evaluating the Program

Program evaluation should be ongoing and inextricably linked to staff development efforts. Sometimes a school district will jump the gun in the evaluation of its program and wind up confusing process evaluation with product evaluation. When this occurs, the district is apt to assess student achievement in reading prematurely. Careful program evaluation requires at least three levels of assessment, as indicated in Figure 6.4.

Level 1 places the spotlight on an evaluation of teachers' thinking and attitudes related to the use of functional reading strategies. What are the teachers' attitudes toward functional instruction? What are their views of reading and reading to learn, in light of staff development activities? Are teachers committed to instructional change? How do they plan to incorporate content-area reading strategies into daily lessons?

Level 2 is closely related to level 1 but requires more of an ecological evaluation. In level 2, the focus of the evaluation is an examination of the teacher in the context of the classroom. To what extent and under what conditions are teachers attempting to use, adapt, refine, fine-tune, and experiment with content-area reading strategies? What degree of classroom interaction is there among students, teacher, and texts? Are classrooms discussion-centered or lecture-centered? Questions such as these attempt to evaluate the dynamics of the classroom instruction.

Level 3 considers the effect of the program on its ultimate goal—improving student attitudes toward and performance in content-area learning situations. Are students performing better on content-area exami-

Figure 6.4   Levels of Program Evaluation

Level 1	Teacher		
Level 2	Teacher	Classroom	
Level 3	Teacher	Classroom	Student

Source: Vacca, R. T., & Vacca, J. L. (1986). *Content Area Reading*, (2nd ed.). Boston: Little, Brown, p. 412. Reprinted with permission.

nations? Do they contribute effectively to text discussions? Has their level of reading achievement in content areas improved?

FORWARD TO THE FUTURE

Our trip back to the future helped us to recognize that the general aims and goals of high school reading programs have not changed appreciably in the past twenty-five years or so. What has changed is the knowledge base by which we can better understand issues and problems related to the reading process, text comprehension, and functional instruction. Rather than go back to the future, let us resolve to move boldly forward into a future where texts play an important role in students' learning and where teachers know not only *how* to use reading as a tool for learning but also *why* and *when* to use reading strategies effectively.

REFERENCES

Anders, P. L. (1981). Dream of a secondary reading program? People are the key. *Journal of Reading, 24,* 316–320.

Criscuolo, N. P., Vacca, R. T., & LaVorgna, J. L. (1980). What reading strategies make sense to content area teachers? *Reading World, 19*(3), 265–271.

Early, M. (1964). The meaning of reading instruction in secondary schools. *Journal of Reading, 8,* 25–29.

Herber, H. L. (1978). *Reading in content areas* (2nd ed.). Englewood Cliffs, NJ: Prentice-Hall.

Sargent, E. (1969). Integrating reading skills in the content areas. In H. A. Robinson & E. L. Thomas (Eds.), *Fusing reading skills and content* (pp. 17–25). Newark, DE: International Reading Association.

Thomas, K., & Moorman, G. (1983). *Designing reading programs.* Dubuque, IA: Kendall-Hunt.

Vacca, R. T., & Gove, M. K. (1984). *Improving the staff development process* (Occasional Paper #10). Chicago: National Staff Development Council.

Part III

PROGRAM IMPLEMENTATION AND EVALUATION

As discussed in the preceding part, goals and objectives that reflect our current understanding of reading education are essential for helping to develop skilled or strategic readers at any grade level. In most instances, teachers' and administrators' interpretations of these goals and objectives are reflected in the type of materials used, the kind of teaching strategies modeled, the degree of professional and community communication encouraged, and the nature of the learning outcomes evaluated. The district's professional actions reveal how well the district understands how to translate current theoretical understanding about reading into workable reading practices. This part of the book provides specific guidelines for five critical areas of program implementation: material selection and use, teacher observations and conferences, staff development, program evaluation, and community outreach.

Chapter 7 helps administrators to select systematically and use effectively a variety of reading materials. Specific guidelines are given for improving a districtwide adoption process for selected materials. Chapter 8 provides a detailed description of clinical supervision as well as variations in clinical supervision, including a discussion of different observational techniques for encouraging productive supervisor-teacher relationships. Chapter 9 helps supervisors to plan and conduct staff development so that supervisory leadership is felt by all those involved. Chapter 10 helps to connect all facets of the district's reading program through an innovative, thorough, and dynamic evaluation plan. Chapter 11, the last chapter in this part, encourages supervisors to reach out to the community in explaining the district's materials, staff, and evaluation efforts. Clear guidelines are provided for reaching out to those who help make the difference in whether or not students appreciate the value of reading as a lifelong pursuit.

This part of the book helps administrators to fine-tune previous programmatic efforts and move forward to initiating needed changes in specific program areas.

7 Evaluation, Selection, and Use of Reading Materials

JANICE A. DOLE
University of Utah

JEAN OSBORN
University of Illinois

Cathy A. Labate © 1988

For better or for worse, commercially developed materials determine the reading curriculum and the mode of reading instruction in the classroom of many American schools. A number of classroom observation studies (Duffy & McIntyre, 1982; Hodges, 1980; Jackson, 1981; Woodward, 1986) reveal that classroom reading programs, from the primary grades through high school, are dominated by commercially developed reading materials. Some of these studies also reveal that, as teachers present these materials to their students, they follow to a greater or lesser degree the directions that appear in the teacher's guides that accompany the materials. In addition, classroom observations (and our own discussions with teachers) remind us that the content of the student textbooks, workbooks, and other student materials associated with commercially developed materials often comprises the bulk, if not the total, of what many students *read*, both in and out of school. We also point out the strong connection between what is taught in these programs and the tests that are used to evaluate reading instruction as well as the students getting the instruction.

Along with others in the field (Brophy, 1982; Resnick & Resnick, 1985), we have come to believe that, because published reading materials are used so extensively by so many teachers and students, it makes sense to assume that the success of school reading programs will depend in part upon the quality and suitability of the materials selected for use in school districts. It also makes sense to assume that the success of school reading programs will depend to some degree upon how well and to what extent teachers and students use these materials.

This chapter contains information that will help school administrators and the supervisors of reading programs evaluate and select commercially developed reading materials, as well as support the successful use of these materials in the classrooms of the schools in their districts. We are concerned with the evaluation and selection of reading materials for use in classroom reading programs and with the appropriate use of these materials in elementary, middle, and secondary schools. We conclude the chapter with summarized guidelines for the selection and use of materials.

Much of our discussion focuses on the selection and use of what Shannon (1987) labels "commercial reading materials." This category includes basal reading programs and their many components, for example, teacher's guides, student readers, workbooks, skillbooks, and management systems. It also includes those workbooks and skillbooks not associated with basal reading programs but which have been developed as supplemental activities. To this already rather large category we can easily add the reading laboratories, multilevel kits on specific skills, and other types of programmed kits that students work through — for the most part — on their own. We concentrate on these materials because they are, and will probably continue to be, the major media for the teaching of reading in American classrooms.

The primary goal of this chapter is to help administrators and supervisors deal with the reality of the reading materials that are used on a day-to-day basis in their school districts. This emphasis does not mean that we promote the *exclusive* use of such materials. In fact, we believe that the use of other types of reading materials should be a part of every school reading program. Certainly trade books (fiction and nonfiction) should be on the shelves of every classroom, and in fact these books should spend a good part of their time off the shelves and in the hands of the students. In addition, students should have easy access to appropriate reference books and to a variety of books from school libraries. What students read should also include teacher- and student-made materials, for example, student-created books, student story charts, and teacher-made practice materials. We will also discuss these materials briefly.

OVERVIEW

From the McGuffey readers of the nineteenth century to the many and varied reading materials of the present, commercially developed reading programs have played an important role in American schools. Shannon (1987) notes that Nila Banton Smith, in her 1965 book on the history of reading instruction in American schools, devoted half of the book to a discussion of the development of commercial reading materials. It is only in the past decade, however, that the evaluation and selection of these materials have been topics of interest to researchers. The materials themselves, however, have long been of interest to two groups: the people who use them and the people who produce them.

Anyone who walks through an exhibit of commercially developed reading materials at a national or regional convention of the International Reading Association is likely to be fascinated by the number, variety, and beauty of the materials on display. Each publisher has an assortment of reading materials. There are materials for young children, elementary school students, and middle and high school students; in addition, there are materials for fast-learning students and slow-learning students and for students who have not learned much and are to be taught remedially. Each of these programs contains a number of components, including some practice exercises and management systems that flash on and off the computers that are a part of the display in the exhibit booth. Especially notable are the student textbooks. They are sturdily bound, use high-quality paper, are printed in type sizes that vary with the grade level, and are illustrated with colorful and stylish pictures. In fact, the graphics and layout of most of these programs are in keeping with the style of the glitzy magazines and gorgeous coffee-table books to which our modern eyes have become accustomed.

Visitors to these exhibits usually leave the exhibit hall carrying shopping bags full of the glossy brochures and informational booklets handed out by the publisher's representatives. How do teachers and school administrators deal with such an array of materials? To our knowledge, the selection of reading materials rarely takes place in an exhibit hall but rather begins someplace else, usually by means of a process labeled, aptly enough, "textbook adoption." Where that process begins, however, depends upon the state in which the members of the adoption committee live.

In some states, called adoption states, commercially developed reading materials are first examined by a statewide adoption committee which selects the materials that will appear on the state-approved list of programs. Then the adoption committees of local school districts (and sometimes schools within districts) determine which of the state-approved programs will be used in their districts. In other states, known by publishers as "open territory," commercially developed reading materials are selected by entire school districts or by individual schools within a district. Because there is no state list, these committees can select from any program on the market.

A discussion of how state adoption committees work and the advantages and disadvantages of a state adoption process is not within the scope of this chapter. Instead, we focus on the school- and district-level adoption of commercially developed reading programs. This focus will be relevant to people who live in either adoption states or open-territory states, as commercially developed reading materials are selected at the school or district level in all states.

Although districtwide adoption is common — and a district can be a city, a county, or a specially organized public or church-related school entity — some districts permit each school within the district to choose its reading materials. In such cases, schools only a few blocks from each other may have completely different reading materials. But, because district adoption is the more common policy, and because the repetition of the phrase *school or district* becomes awkward, we refer only to *district* in the rest of this chapter. Depending upon the unit our readers typically deal with, however, *district* can be read as *district* or *school*.

Most districts take the task of selecting commercially developed reading materials very seriously and create special textbook adoption committees to evaluate and then select the materials for the entire district. How do committees go about evaluating and selecting materials? What do the leaders of the committees do? How do the committees organize to review materials, make decisions, and help teachers become knowledgeable about the newly selected materials? To discuss these questions we will draw from a small but growing body of research on the textbook selection process and from the practical experience of people who have led adoption committees. The research we discuss focuses on the evaluation and selection of basal reading programs, not materials for older students. The concerns addressed, however, are probably of some relevance to most commercially developed reading materials.

BASAL PROGRAM MATERIALS

Ideally, it would seem that adoption committees should examine and evaluate each program on the market. Then, using objective criteria, committees would reach agreement about which materials were of the highest instructional quality and most suitable for the particular needs of the teachers and students in their district. That program would then be adopted. The reality, however, seems far from the ideal.

Problems in Adoption Practices

In a series of studies, Farr and his colleagues examined the process used in the selection of basal reading programs (Courtland, Farr, Harris, Tarr, & Treece, 1983; Farr & Tulley, 1985; Farr, Tulley, & Rayford, 1987; Powell, 1985; Tulley, 1985). These and other studies (Dole, Rogers, & Osborn, 1987b; Marshall, 1987) indicate that numerous factors can adversely affect the selection of textbooks. Some of these are *outside* pressures, such as the presentation of publishers' representatives and the influence of particular vocal groups of citizens. Other factors are *inside*, such as inadequate criteria for evaluating textbooks, inadequately trained committees, and inadequate evaluation tools.

Several of these researchers have commented on a tool adoption committees frequently use to examine materials — the checklist. Checklists containing criteria that have to do with a number of aspects of the materials (for example, content of student books, quality of illustrations, amount of comprehension instruction) are often devised by committees. The criteria on the checklists are what committee members consider as they examine the materials; the checklists are also the forms on which information about each publisher's materials is recorded.

Farr and Tulley (1985) pointed out that checklists encourage committee members to check off the listing of skills or topics in scope-and-sequence charts rather than encouraging them to examine the instructional quality of those skills or topics in the teacher and student materials. We would like to expand on this point. A checklist might, for example, include an item such as "develops higher-level comprehension skills at the literal, inferential, and applied levels." We believe such items tend to promote a superficial look at programs. The first problem is the vagueness of the item: What should "higher-level comprehension skills" look like in a basal reading program? All basal programs claim to develop higher-level comprehension skills. How can such vague language help evaluators differentiate one program from another? Committee members can easily look up "higher-level comprehension skills" in the scope-and-sequence charts, find these skills "covered" on many pages in the program, and conclude that the program develops these skills. What is being evaluated, though, is the *appearance* of topics and *not* how well they are translated into instruction or other learning experiences. Comas (1983) found another aspect of checklists disturbing. She reviewed checklists from a number of school districts and found them to be inadequate for evaluating the *instructional quality* of basal textbooks. She found, for example, that although 71 percent of the checklists she examined included references to racial or sexual stereotyping, only 34 percent of the items referred to criteria about instructional quality.

Perhaps it is because of the inadequacy of the checklists, the insufficient amount of time allocated to the task, and in some cases the lack of preparation of the committee members that caused one researcher to conclude that committee members often end up making subjective evaluations or choosing the basal textbooks that most closely resemble the materials they currently are using (Powell, 1986). Powell (1986) concluded that the selection of basal programs was based more on peripheral than important issues.

Given the problems that have been identified by research on the adoption process, how can the process be made more effective? We have been involved with adoption committees in several school districts in several states. This work was done in conjunction with the tryout of a set of booklets developed to provide both research information and evaluation procedures for committees examining basal reading programs. The booklets and the work with these committees are described elsewhere (Dole, Rogers, & Osborn, 1987a); we will, however, offer some general advice for the improvement of the adoption process that derives from our experiences with the committees, our conversations with school administrators concerned with the adoption process, and our review of the literature on adoption.

Background Questions

We begin by discussing three questions frequently raised by teachers and administrators: Aren't all published reading materials more or less the same? Should our district adopt one set of materials, or do we need a multiple adoption? How many components of commercially developed materials do we really need?

Associated with the first question is usually the subliminal belief (and sometimes quite obvious hope) that the materials are all more or less the same and that there is therefore little point to expending school personnel effort and spending school district money on a time-consuming adoption process. Follett (1985) and Winograd (1987) report that many teachers feel that the major basal reading programs are all alike. That belief is not unique to the teachers in that study. We have heard similar statements many times. On the other hand—and quite predictably—publishers of these programs argue strongly that programs are *not* all alike. A perfunctory look at several programs easily affirms that most basal reading programs have certain physical similarities such as teacher's guides, student textbooks, workbooks, ancillary materials, and full-color art; and a perusal of their scope-and-sequence charts confirms that most of them cover a similar-sounding set of topics such as word identification, vocabulary development, comprehension instruction, and higher-order thinking skills.

We suggest, however, that a more careful analysis of the *content* of the materials reveals that there are significant differences among programs. The most obvious differences are in the varying approaches taken to the teaching of beginning reading. In addition, the content of the student readers and workbooks also varies considerably from program to program and, increasingly, so do the kind and amount of direction given for comprehension instruction and vocabulary development. The committees we worked with found that it often took careful examination to reveal some of the sometimes subtle, but often important, differences among basal reading programs. We also suggest that the new editions of the late 1980s contain, at least for some publishers, significant departures from previous editions. So, our answer to the question, Aren't they all the same? is that basal reading programs of different publishers vary significantly. We suspect the same is true of other types of commercially developed reading materials. We therefore suggest that school district administrators support a meaningful effort to evaluate the materials available to them in order to determine which publishers' materials will most positively affect the quality of instruction in the classrooms of their district.

This advice brings up the question about a single or multiple adoption. Should every school in the district use the program of a single publisher? Or should a "multiple-basal" strategy be utilized, in which teachers have available to them different materials to use with different groups of students? We know of no research that supports or refutes the value of using a single basal reading program in a district, as compared to two or more programs. We observe, however, that some district administrators and supervisors are often adamant that a single series be adopted. Their argument is usually that consistency of materials across schools is vital, particularly in districts that have a lot of students who move from school to school during the school year. On the other hand, administrators and supervisors who support the use of more than one publisher's materials argue that it is unreasonable to expect that one published program will meet the needs of all of the students in a district and that multiple adoption provides for a better match of students with materials.

Since there is no definitive research on this question, we suggest that the decision to adopt a single basal reading program or several be based upon the experiences and beliefs of the teachers and administrators within a district, the size and diversity of the district, the number of students who move from school to school within the year, the instructional needs of the students, and the features of the materials being considered.

The final question concerns how many of the numerous available components of a basal reading program are really needed for their effective use in classrooms. Again, we know of no compelling research on this topic, but we observe that most districts begin a new adoption with a core of materials that includes student textbooks, teacher's manuals, student workbooks, and placement and assessment instructions. We echo the warnings of a lot of classroom observers (e.g., *Becoming a Nation of Readers,* 1985) and caution against the all-too-frequent heavy reliance upon workbooks. We also suggest, as discussed earlier in this chapter, that trade books and other kinds of printed materials be purchased as valuable supplements to basal reading programs; perhaps these may be more valuable than many of the supplemental components of basal reading programs.

Adoption Procedures

We next discuss the heart of the adoption process—what the committee members do and how the work gets done. Although the procedures, membership, and policies of adoption committees differ from district to district, most committees are similar in their ultimate purpose: They must choose the materials that will be used in the classrooms of their districts. To accomplish this task, once they are assembled and organized, most adoption committees follow some variation of these steps:

1. *Gathering information.* Most textbook adoption committees feel the need to update their own knowledge of current research and practice before they begin to evaluate reading materials. We suggest that several members of the committee be assigned to report on the implications for instruction of recent and well-documented research. Another possibility is to enlist the help of a local reading expert, such as a reading coordinator or a reading teacher particularly interested in research. Some committees hire outside experts.
2. *Developing criteria.* After committee members feel that they have enough information, they must decide what to look for as they evaluate materials. We urge that they develop criteria that emphasize research-based information about effective instruction. These criteria must be supplemented with practice-based criteria that reflect the needs of the district and the experiences of the committee members.
3. *Evaluation and selection procedures.* Once committee members decide on criteria for evaluating materials, they must develop a systematic way of organizing and recording the information they find. We urge not only that the criteria devised to analyze and record information focus

on topics of *importance*, but also that the procedures used to evaluate the correspondence between the criteria and the materials focus on the *content* of the materials and not on the appearance of labels in scope-and-sequence charts (Dole et al., 1987a; Farr, Tulley, & Powell, 1987).

Once the materials have been evaluated according to the criteria established by the committee, a basal program can be selected.. Selecting a program can proceed by rating and then ranking the overall quality of the programs or by comparing two or three series at a time and then eliminating the weakest series.

Committee Leaders

There is no substitute for an effective leader who can organize an adoption committee, develop a reasonable timeline, keep the committee on task, and help the group synthesize the information it has gathered. Our experience indicates that leaders do not necessarily have to be reading experts, as long as they can effectively organize and manage the committee and have access to people who are knowledgeable about reading. We turn to some suggestions leaders may find valuable.

Provide Expert Advice.   While the committee leader does not have to be knowledgeable about reading, there must be someone available who is. That person should assist the committee leader in answering questions committee members might have and, equally importantly, in providing information that will upgrade the committee's knowledge about effective reading instruction.

Divide the Labor.   Because examining and evaluating materials is so time-consuming, committees should divide the work among group members, sometimes by grade level, sometimes by topic, sometimes by different publishers. This division of labor avoids the overwhelming task of having every member of the committee examine every topic at every grade level in every set of materials being considered for adoption. Some researchers (Farr, Tulley, & Powell, 1987) recommend that subcommittees should not be based on usual grade-level distinctions but rather on areas of committee members' expertise or interest, for example, beginning reading instruction, comprehension instruction, content of student readers, or higher-order thinking skills. In any case, committee members should be able to provide specific evidence from the teacher's guides, student readers, and workbooks to support their conclusions. Leaders need to show committee members how to do this and periodically check to make sure they follow through.

Organize the Data.   Once the examination process comes to a close, the subcommittees will have compiled a mass of forms and data about the programs they have evaluated. The leader must find ways to organize and synthesize this information. Leaders are also instrumental in determining how final decisions will be made and insuring that the information will be delivered to the administration and the rest of the district. Committee members need to keep teachers at each school in the district informed about the evaluation and selection process, and leaders need to follow up with committee members to make sure they are doing so.

Give Committees Power.   Leaders of textbook adoption committees must see to it that adoption committees have the power to make the final selection. When committee members go through a careful evaluation process to reach a decision, their decision must not be undermined by "higher-up" administrators who decide, for whatever reasons, to ignore the committee decision. It is up to the leader of the committee to insure that statements of the administration's budgetary and other constraints are explicit. Assuming that the committee operates within these constraints, and that their evaluation process is a reasonable one, committees' recommendations must be considered as binding. When this *doesn't* happen, adoption committees will very quickly lose the motivation to expend time and effort on the adoption process.

Suggestions for Improvement

We move now to some suggestions that administrators, supervisors, and leaders of adoption committees may find useful. These suggestions are, for the most part, derived from experience, some of it from the school of hard knocks.

Know the District Personnel.   Up-to-date information about the teachers and students who will be using the materials is essential. The goal of an adoption process is for teachers to have the best materials available to them. But, if teachers are not willing to use the materials that are adopted, no matter how good, then nothing will be accomplished. Information about the attitudes and needs of the teachers who will be using the materials will inform administrators and supervisors about the kinds of materials most likely to be used successfully in the classrooms of the district. This kind of knowledge can only be gained from visits to schools, observations of classrooms, and discussions with teachers. Questionnaires can be helpful but are not always reliable. Sometimes teachers say one thing when responding to a questionnaire but do quite another thing in their classrooms.

Nothing can replace the kind of firsthand knowledge that this reading coordinator describes:

> As you move from school to school, talk with teachers about the materials they are currently using and about their satisfaction with those materials. Then talk with administrators and get their impressions as well. Before you leave each school, check out the materials storeroom. See what reading supplies and materials are being used, and, more importantly, not being used. Once I went into a materials storeroom and found several expensive and excellent boxes of language materials unopened. At the same time I found the ditto master phonics worksheets in very short supply. This type of information can tell you a lot about what teachers are likely to use and not use.*

Know the District.   A second, related kind of knowledge is accurate and realistic knowledge of the district in which the materials will be used. At the most obvious level, it is necessary to know the district's budget, as it will almost always restrict the range and quantity of materials that can be purchased. Equally important is to acknowledge the real educational needs of the district. For example, a district's ethnic and cultural diversity will affect the kinds of materials that will be adopted. A district with a high proportion of Spanish-speaking students, for example, might adopt Spanish reading materials. A district with a high proportion of at-risk primary grade students may adopt special language development materials.

Know the District's History.   Information about the history of the district is also important. Knowing about the past will make it possible to understand why, for example, the teachers in a particular school shy away from the use of trade books in the classroom. (Several years ago we had a situation where some parents adamantly objected to some books assigned for class reading.) Knowledge about a district's history will also help members understand why an adoption committee is unmotivated and negative. For example, their past decisions may have been consistently overridden by administrative changes and budgetary constraints.

Knowing the history of the district can prevent costly mistakes. We know of one school with a large number of at-risk children. That particular school was known for its reliance on a particular publisher's materials *and* for the success of those materials with its students. The district adoption committee chose another basal reading program for the rest of the district but agreed that this school should continue to use the materials they were used to. The committee could have forced that school to change

---

*Dixie Spangler (1987), personal communication.

materials; however, they knew the history of the school well enough to know that nothing would have been accomplished by such a decision and that, in fact, the teachers in that school would simply have put the new program in their closets and continued to use their old materials.

Concerns About Implementation

How will change come about, and how will reading instruction ever be improved if teachers never go beyond what they are used to? We have suggested that it is of the utmost importance to find out what teachers are using and what they want. But it is also important to realize that moving teachers from the materials they are familiar with to something new requires careful staff development. Simply purchasing new materials, no matter how good they are, is unlikely to change what teachers do. If teachers don't want the materials or don't know how to use them, the new materials will be closeted and the teachers will return to what they have used before. Regardless of the materials that are chosen, teachers will need continued staff development and support as they implement the new materials in their classrooms.

An important part of staff development is helping teachers to use basal materials appropriately. This means using them as part of a total reading program (*Becoming a Nation of Readers*, 1985; Farr & Tulley, 1985). Unfortunately, in some schools these programs are the *only* resource for reading instruction. Researchers and reading educators believe that students whose only reading is in commercial reading programs can easily draw the conclusion that reading is what you do in a reading circle when you read aloud from a basal reader. We believe members of adoption committees, as well as administrators and supervisors, should be concerned with what *else* students read in classrooms.

OTHER READING MATERIALS FOR ELEMENTARY SCHOOLS

Common sense and good teaching practice dictate that students must read from a variety of materials, not just their basal readers. Recent research (*Becoming a Nation of Readers*, 1985) has documented what many teachers have observed for years—that students often separate what they learn in a textbook from what they know in their real life. By bringing a variety of reading materials to the classroom, teachers make available to their students the real-world applications of reading. When students read "real" books, newspapers, and magazines; follow directions for making things and figure out how things work; and look up information in reference books, they learn about the functions of reading.

Another reason for including more than the content of basal readers in a reading program is that students need access to the best of children's literature. Although most basal reading programs include excerpts from children's classics, these excerpts are often shortened and adapted. Davison (1984), Bruce (1984), and Green (1984) point out some of the negative effects of these adaptations. For example, the watered-down language often actually increases the conceptual difficulty, and the removal of paragraphs and sentences often inhibits insight into characters' motives and their interpersonal conflicts. In fact, one researcher (Bruce, 1984) is so concerned about the effects of adaptations that he advises that teachers who want their students to have experience with the kinds of stories and books they will encounter as they mature *must* have them read trade books as well as the stories in their basal textbooks.

Students should also have the opportunity to read other students' writings. Materials that students write can be published, shared, and read by class members and should play an important role in what students read during the day. Graves and his colleagues (Calkins, 1986; Graves, 1983; Hansen & Graves, 1983) report success in developing reading and writing classrooms that enhance students' reading as well as writing.

Specific criteria for selecting additional reading materials are difficult to set forth. Administrators and reading specialists can be guided by experienced and knowledgeable librarians and media specialists. We make a few suggestions:

1. Choose a variety of materials from different genres.
2. Include informational and at-home reading materials (newspapers, children's magazines, "how-to" books).
3. Include reading materials that cover a wide range of reading abilities.
4. Consult published recommended book lists for suggestions of appropriate books.
5. Include classic literature to read to children as well as to have children read.
6. Display, share, and include children's written works as part of the reading materials.

MATERIALS FOR MIDDLE AND SECONDARY SCHOOL READING PROGRAMS

While reading instruction has a clear function in elementary schools, its function at the middle and secondary school levels is less clear. Most do have some kind of separate reading course (Greenlaw & Moore, 1982); however, according to Witte and Otto (1981), these courses differ in content and organization because they are designed to meet different kinds of student needs.

Types of Programs

Singer and Donlan (1980) classified nine different types of reading programs in use in middle and secondary schools. We have chosen to discuss three of their classifications.

Reading Laboratories.
One of the most popular forms for secondary reading programs is the reading laboratory. Singer and Donlan (1980) describe a typical reading laboratory as an individualized reading class filled with a variety of self-instructional commercial reading kits. Students are placed according to their current reading level and work through the materials at their own pace. The students typically read short stories or paragraphs, answer questions about what they have read, complete additional vocabulary or word recognition exercises, correct their work, and record their progress. Students work through the kits on their own, often receiving little or no direct instruction from the teacher.

Functional Reading Programs.
Singer and Donlan (1980) describe functional programs as those designed to teach students the kind of functional reading that adults do at home or at work. These programs sometimes use materials developed from real-world print, such as newspapers, telephone directories, ticket maps, and theater and sports events. Singer and Donlan also report on several prepackaged kits designed to help students develop functional reading skills. These kits simulate real print, but in the form of dittos and worksheet pages.

Three-Stage Programs.
Some schools have reading programs for low, average, and high achievers. Often a remedial class may resemble a reading clinic, with tutoring and individualized instruction. An average class often resembles a developmental program in which students are assigned to reading labs. Students in the advanced class are sometimes assigned to speed-reading classes or to advanced study skills programs.

Selection of Materials

How can appropriate materials be selected for middle and secondary reading programs? To prepare for the adoption of new materials, administrators and supervisors should determine the kind of reading courses that are in place, the instructional needs of their students, and any changes they wish to make in how reading is taught. A discussion of these issues is presented in chapter 5. We will concentrate on the selection of materials for different types of programs.

We suggest that administrators and supervisors be extremely selective when considering the purchase of commercial reading materials for the middle and secondary school levels. The tendency in many districts is to let the materials dictate both the curriculum and the form of instruction. This practice is of serious concern. Programs with little or no teacher instruction run counter to research on the value of direct teacher explanation and instruction (Brophy & Good, 1986; Rosenshine & Stevens, 1986) and the research on socially mediated learning (Brown & Campione, 1984). Findings from a substantive body of research suggest that classrooms in which teachers provide strategies, offer guided practice, and give regular feedback result in higher achievement in a number of different contexts. In addition, classrooms in which teachers interact with students in a way that gradually transfers the ownership of skills and strategies from the teachers to students increase achievement (Pearson & Dole, 1987; Pearson & Gallagher, 1983). Instruction based on these research findings is not likely to take place in reading programs in which students work individually on commercially developed kits.

Another concern is that many middle and secondary school commercial reading programs isolate specific reading skills from the context of real reading (Pearson & Dole, 1987). Students can spend countless hours filling out endless worksheet pages on identifying main ideas, drawing conclusions, and sequencing, without understanding how these skills relate to the reading process and to their daily lives. Yet another — and related — concern about the use of these materials is that of transfer. Research indicates that increases in students' reading achievement often do not transfer to their subject-matter achievement (Herber, 1984; Singer & Donlan, 1980). That is, many students who attend and make progress in special reading classes do not seem to read their content-area textbooks with any more success. This observation is not only current but also has been in evidence for decades.

What materials *should* be used in middle and secondary school reading programs? Our suggestions are that, in addition to any kits and study skill programs, classrooms should contain

1. Environmental print materials so students can relate reading to their daily lives (e.g., newspapers, magazines, and driver's license manuals)

2. Tradebooks, both classic and current, as well as a variety of popular books of varying reading difficulty
3. Content-area textbooks that students use in their subject-matter classes
4. Content-area trade books on different topics, to supplement the content textbooks used in the subject-matter courses

Our two main suggestions to supervisors and administrators are to present materials that provide for the type of reading students will do in their daily lives and to offer direct and explicit instruction for small and large groups on how to read these materials.

PUTTING READING MATERIALS TO USE

Once reading materials have been selected, how do they get used by teachers and students? This question has only very recently been addressed in the research literature. Observations by several researchers (Duffy & McIntyre, 1982; Durkin, 1984; Shannon, 1983, 1987; Woodward, 1986) on the question of how teachers actually use reading materials indicate a noticeable discrepancy between how teachers use reading materials and how those researchers think materials ought to be used.

Duffy and McIntyre (1982) found that teachers relied heavily on commercial reading materials (especially the teacher's manuals) for planning and conducting reading instruction and that their teaching followed closely the recommendations in these manuals. They observed that typical teaching routines consisted of asking the questions provided in the guides, eliciting answers from students, and assigning workbook pages. Often, establishing background, purpose-setting, and other forms of assistance were omitted. These researchers concluded that the teachers were task monitors and managers rather than active decision makers and instructors. Duffy, Roehler, and Putnam (1987) observed that, regardless of the grade level, "many teachers of reading simply follow instructional materials and make few decisions about what to teach or how to teach it" (p. 359).

Why do so many teachers use textbooks so trustingly? Perhaps it is because many of them have been told to teach "by the book." Duffy, Roehler, and Putnam (1987) found that teachers felt constrained by administrators to follow commercial reading program directives. One teacher in their study said, "We've been told to do it the way the basal says" (p. 360). Shannon (1983) reported similar findings and suggests that teachers follow the manuals closely because they believe their administrators want them to.

Another reason for teachers' heavy reliance on commercial reading materials may be their belief that the materials have been written by experts and are therefore better than anything that they, the teachers, could provide. Shannon (1983, 1987) reported that teachers and administrators believe in the scientific nature of the reading materials they use. He observes that they "treat the directives in teacher's manuals as the science of reading instruction" (1987, p. 314), and he is concerned that this type of thinking moves the focus of reading instruction away from a human undertaking and toward a scientific undertaking.

Other researchers point out that the teacher's use of commercial reading materials also has to do with the time constraints of the classroom and the complexity of designing instructional materials and making instructional decisions (Duffy et al., 1987). Time constraints mean that teachers often use what is readily available and limit the extent to which they design their own instructional programs. Experienced teachers point to the enormous amounts of time needed to create even simple worksheets and games, let alone to develop materials for a complete reading program.

Our own experiences confirm these observations and those of other researchers (Apple & Tietelbaum, 1986; Duffy & Ball, 1986; Stern & Shavelson, 1983), who point to the heavy cognitive demands placed on teachers on a day-to-day basis. Teachers face the complexities of managing an entire class, meeting schedule demands, and meeting the needs of many students, as well as of content. Some researchers claim that these heavy demands make it more likely that teachers will become technicians who simply *manage* instruction, rather than decision-makers who *actively engage in* instruction. It is not difficult to conclude that teachers have jobs that are both time and labor intensive and that their reliance on help from published materials is not unreasonable.

We acknowledge what these studies, as well as common sense, point to about the demands on teachers, but we still propose that the exclusive and indiscriminate use of commercially developed reading materials is neither advisable nor desirable. Commercial reading materials, no matter how well developed, can never fit the many situations in which they are used in classrooms. Furthermore, these materials do not represent the full range of reading experiences that schools should give students.

What can administrators and supervisors of reading programs do to help teachers use instructional materials more appropriately? First, they must help teachers recognize good instruction. The adoption of a new basal reading program is a good time for districtwide staff development. The reading specialists we talked to stressed the necessity of appropriate staff training once new materials have been adopted. Sometimes publishers' representatives provide training (as compared to sales pitches) in the use of their materials. Administrators and supervisors need to discuss with them the kind of staff training that will accompany the purchase of basal reading programs. Sometimes the district develops a training program, often with the help of outside consultants.

We believe that teachers need to think in ways that will permit them to look critically at their materials and at their instruction. The training should emphasize the importance of instructional decision-making. Teachers should understand the purpose and content of the materials and then be encouraged to make their own decisions about how to use them most appropriately. A series of meetings might begin with discussions about what's most important to teach at different grade levels. Teachers can then meet in subgroups by grade levels to discuss the kinds of instructional decisions they need to make on a day-to-day basis. Examples of the topics of such discussions are

1. The match between students and materials
2. The appropriate pacing of students through materials
3. The appropriate amount of time spent in the direct instruction of important reading skills
4. The appropriate use of teacher's guides and manuals
5. The use of materials other than the basal textbooks

Such discussions can do much to help "reskill" teachers and put them back in their role as instructional decision makers.

Commercial reading materials, when used judiciously and in combination with other reading materials, can be of great help to teachers of reading. Administrators and supervisors of reading programs have a very important role to play in the evaluation and selection of these materials, and in the selection of other supplementary materials. They also play an important role in providing a forum for the discussion of commercially developed reading materials and the function of those and other materials in the total reading program, whether that program be for elementary school, middle school, or high school.

SUMMARY

The following guidelines for the evaluation, selection, and use of materials represents a synopsis of the ideas presented in this chapter.

1. Because the differences among the materials of various publishers are often marked, the careful evaluation of these materials is warranted.

2. The decision to adopt one publisher's commercially developed reading materials for an entire district (single adoption) or several publishers' (multiple adoption) should depend upon the experiences and beliefs of the district personnel, the size and diversity of the district, the characteristics of the students, and the features of the materials.

3. The "core" materials of most programs include the student textbooks, teacher's manuals, student workbooks, and placement and assessment instruments; an over-reliance on workbooks should be avoided; committees should reserve funds for the purchase of other kinds of reading materials.

4. Members of adoption committees must review current reading research before beginning an evaluation process.

5. The criteria developed for program evaluation should include research-based information as well as the practice- and experience-based information of members of the committee.

6. An effective committee leader must organize the committee; develop and keep to reasonable timelines, divide the labor, keep committee members on task, and help the group synthesize the information it has gathered.

7. Knowledge of the district — its personnel, its history, and its context — is essential to a successful adoption.

8. The decisions of adoption committees who have worked within the constraints of a district, and who have followed a reasonable evaluation process, should be binding.

9. The selection of materials at any level should assume the classroom use of materials other than the adopted reading materials, for example, trade books, magazines, and newspapers.

10. The selection of materials for middle school and high school students should assure that the students are provided with a variety of reading materials that they will encounter in their daily lives as well as explicit instruction in how to read them.

11. The selection of materials must be accompanied by plans for inservice training in the use of the materials and in teacher decision making.

REFERENCES

Apple, M. W., & Tietelbaum, K. (1986). Are teachers losing control of their curriculum? *Journal of Curriculum Studies, 18,* 177–184.

Becoming a nation of readers: The report of the Commission on Reading. (1985). Washington, DC: National Institute of Education.

Brophy, J. E. (1982). How teachers influence what is taught and learned in class-rooms. *The Elementary School Journal, 83,* 1–13.

Brophy, J. E., & Good, T. L. (1986). Teacher behavior and student achievement. In M. C. Wittrock (Ed.), *Handbook of research on teaching* (pp. 328–375). New York: Macmillan.

Brown, A. L., & Campione, J. C. (1984). Three faces of transfer: Implications for early competence, individual differences and instruction. In M. E. Lamb, A. L. Brown, & B. Rogoff (Eds.), *Advances in developmental psychology* (pp. 143–192). Hillsdale, NJ: Lawrence Erlbaum Associates.

Bruce, B. (1984). A new point of view of children's stories. In R. C. Anderson, J. Osborn, & R. J. Tierney (Eds.), *Learning to read in American schools: Basal readers and content texts* (pp. 153–174). Hillsdale, NJ: Lawrence Erlbaum Associates.

Calkins, L. (1986). *The art of teaching writing.* Portsmouth, NH: Heinemann Press.

Comas, J. (1983). *Item analysis: Basal reading evaluation forms.* Unpublished manuscript, Indiana University.

Courtland, M. C., Farr, R., Harris, P., Tarr, J. R., & Treece, L. J. (1983). *A case study of the Indiana state reading textbook adoption process.* Bloomington, IN: Center for Reading and Language Studies.

Davison, A. (1984). Readability-appraising text difficulty. In R. C. Anderson, J. Osborn, & R. J. Tierney (Eds.), *Learning to read in American schools: Basal readers and content texts* (pp. 121–140). Hillsdale, NJ: Lawrence Erlbaum Associates.

Dole, J. A., Rogers, T., & Osborn, J. (1987a). Improving the selection of basal reading programs: A report of the Textbook Adoption Guidelines Project. *Elementary School Journal, 87,* 283–298.

Dole, J. A., Rogers, T., & Osborn, J. (1987b, April). *Improving the textbook selection process: Case studies of the Textbook Adoption Guidelines Project.* Paper presented at the American Educational Research Association, Washington, DC.

Duffy, G., & Ball, D. (1986). Instructional decision making and reading teacher effectiveness. In J. Hoffman (Ed.), *Effective teaching of reading: Research and practice* (pp. 163–179). Newark, DE: International Reading Association.

Duffy, G., & McIntyre, L. (1982). A naturalistic study of instructional assistance in primary-grade reading. *Elementary School Journal, 83,* 15–23.

Duffy, G., Roehler, L., & Putnam, J. (1987). Putting the teacher in control: Basal reading textbooks and instructional decision making. *Elementary School Journal, 87,* 357–366.

Duffy, G., Roehler, L., & Wesselman, R. (1985). Disentangling the complexities of instructional effectiveness: A line of research on classroom reading instruction. In J. Niles & R. Lalik (Eds.), *Issues on literacy: A research perspective* (pp. 244–250). (Thirty-fourth yearbook of the National Reading Conference.) Rochester, NY: National Reading Conference.

Durkin, D. (1984). Is there a match between what elementary teachers do and what elementary manuals recommend? *The Reading Teacher, 37,* 734–744.

Farr, R., & Tulley, M. A. (1985). Do adoption committees perpetuate mediocre textbooks? *Phi Delta Kappan, 66,* 467–471.

Farr, R., Tulley, M. A., & Powell, D. (1987). The evaluation and selection of basal readers. *Elementary School Journal, 87,* 267–282.

Farr, R., Tulley, M. A., & Rayford, L. (1987). Selecting basal readers: A comparison of school districts in adoption and nonadoption states. *Journal of Research and Development in Education, 20,* 59–72.

Follett, R. (1985). The school textbook adoption process. *Book Research Quarterly, 1,* 19–23.

Graves, D. (1983). *Writing: Teachers and children at work.* Portsmouth, NH: Heinemann.

Green, G. M. (1984). On the appropriateness of adaptations in primary-level basal readers: Reaction to remarks by Bertram Bruce. In R. C. Anderson, J. Osborn, & R. J. Tierney (Eds.), *Learning to read in American schools: Basal readers and content texts* (pp. 175–192). Hillsdale, NJ: Lawrence Erlbaum Associates.

Greenlaw, M. J., & Moore, D. (1982). What kinds of reading courses are taught in junior and senior high school? *Journal of Reading, 25,* 534–536.

Hansen, J., & Graves, D. (1983). The author's chair. *Language Arts, 60,* 176–183.

Herber, H. L. (1984). Subject matter texts — Reading to learn: Response to a paper by Thomas H. Anderson and Bonnie B. Armbruster. In R. C. Anderson, J. Osborn, & R. J. Tierney, (Eds.), *Learning to read in American schools: Basal readers and content texts* (pp. 227–234). Hillsdale, NJ: Lawrence Erlbaum Associates.

Hodges, C. A. (1980). Reading comprehension instruction in the fourth grade: Three data-gathering methods. In M. K. Kamil & A. J. Moe (Eds.), *Perspectives on reading research and instruction* (pp. 110–116). Washington, DC: National Reading Conference.

Jackson, S. A. (1981). About publishers, teachers and reading achievement. In J. H. Cole & T. C. Sticht (Eds.), *The textbook in American society.* Washington, DC: The Library of Congress.

Marshall, J. D. (1987, April). *State-level textbook decision-making: The way things were in Texas.* Paper presented at the American Educational Research Association, Washington, DC.

Pearson, P. D., & Dole, J. A. (1987). Explicit comprehension instruction: The research, the concerns and a new conceptualization of instruction. *Elementary School Journal, 88,* 151–165.

Pearson, P. D., & Gallagher, M. C. (1983). The instruction of reading comprehension. *Contemporary Educational Psychology, 76,* 1239–1252.

Powell, D. A. (1985). Selection of reading textbooks at the district level: Is this a rational process? *Book Research Quarterly, 1,* 23–35.

Powell, D. A. (1986). *Retrospective case studies of individual and group decision making in district-level elementary reading textbook selection.* Unpublished doctoral dissertation, Indiana University, Bloomington, IN.

Resnick, D. P., & Resnick, L. B. (1985). Standards, curriculum and performance: A historical and comparative perspective. *Educational Researcher, 14*(4), 5–20.

Rosenshine, B., & Stevens, R. (1986). Teaching functions. In M. C. Wittrock (Ed.), *Handbook of research on teaching* (pp. 376–391). New York: Macmillan.

Shannon, P. (1983). The use of commercial reading materials in American elementary schools. *Reading Research Quarterly, 19*, 68–85.

Shannon, P. (1987). Commercial reading materials, a technology, an ideology and the deskilling of teachers. *Elementary School Journal, 87*, 307–329.

Singer, H., & Donlan, D. (1980). *Reading and learning from text*. Boston, MA: Little, Brown.

Stern, P., & Shavelson, R. J. (1983). Reading teachers' judgments, plans and decision-making. *The Reading Teacher, 37*, 280–286.

Tulley, M. A. (1985). A descriptive study of the intents of selected state level textbook adoption processes. *Educational Evaluation and Policy Analysis, 7*, 289–308.

Winograd, P. (1987, April). *Adopting textbooks in Kentucky: A retrospective*. Paper presented to the American Educational Research Association, Washington, DC.

Witte, P. L., & Otto, W. (1981). Reading instruction at the postelementary level: Review and comments. *Journal of Educational Research, 74*, 148–158.

Woodward, A. (1986). Over-programmed materials: Taking the teacher out of the teaching. *American Education, 10*, 26–31.

8 Teacher Observations and Conferences

MAURICE KAUFMAN
Northeastern University

A reading teacher, whom I shall call Ms. Jones, related the following incident: "The junior high school supervisor, Ms. Smith, arrived to conduct her formal observation of my teaching. The children were working in several groups. One group was working in the adjoining cloakroom. The remaining groups were working here." (She indicated the small room in which we were seated.) "I was working with one group when Ms. Smith arrived. After a few minutes Ms. Smith said, 'Ms. Jones, I cannot supervise this lesson.' And she left."

I was once supervising student teachers in elementary schools. When I arrived to observe a Ms. Johnson in a first-grade classroom, she informed me that the class followed an "open education" program. The children were distributed in different places throughout a large room. The classroom teacher and an aide were occupied with the children in separate locations in the classroom. Ms. Johnson was with one child for about twenty minutes. During this time the little girl used materials in one place, then moved to another center, then another. Ms. Johnson followed the child. She provided no direction to the child. There was no verbal exchange at all. I wanted to say, "Ms. Johnson, I cannot supervise this lesson."

TEACHING ACTIVITIES AND THE SUPERVISORY PROCESS

These two incidents point to several problems in the relation of supervisor to teacher. In both cases the supervisor and teacher lacked a common frame of reference with regard to acceptable instructional practice. Moreover, the supervisor and teacher in each situation needed a shared understanding of the goals and organization of curriculum. Preparation for the observation should have included discussion of these matters and of the teacher's plan for the session.

In the first situation, the supervisor possibly entered the room expecting to see whole-class instruction following some standard format. She was not ready for grouping practices, with different children working toward several goals during the same class session. In the second situation the student teacher's role when teaching needed to be clarified for the supervisor, and perhaps for the student teacher as well. Prior discussion might have focused on justifying the arrangement of the learning materials provided for the child and on explaining the sequence of activities in which the child was expected to engage. The student teacher could then have explained her expected role during the planned learning activity. Was it merely to monitor the child? Was there to be any verbal exchange? If so, to what end?

Costa and Garmston (1985) identify four categories of teaching activity: planning, teaching per se, analyzing/evaluating (in which the teacher compares planned and actual outcomes), and applying (planning of future teaching strategies). An effective supervisory process should address these several teaching activities. Corresponding to the four categories of teaching activity are four supervisory activities: auditing of the planning phase, monitoring teaching (i.e., observing), validating, and consulting (Costa & Garmston, 1985). Both teacher and supervisor must prepare adequately for each supervisory activity.

Planning and teaching reflect the choice of curriculum goals and the selection of teaching strategies designed to attain these goals. There is no single model of teaching that is appropriate under all circumstances or for all purposes. For example, the lesson outline described by Hunter (1984), consisting of (1) anticipatory set, (2) objective or purpose, (3) input, (4) modeling, (5) check for understanding, (6) guided practice, and (7) independent practice, may be appropriate for planning direct instruction that leads to the acquisition of a skill, such as finding the main ideas of paragraphs. It would be a difficult guide, however, for planning a directed reading-thinking activity with a literature selection or for planning a discussion about a historical incident.

A supervisor's insistence that one teaching model be used to the exclusion of others may lead to a lack of innovation in teaching (Slavin, 1987) and to boredom on the part of the students. Moreover, it may lead to defensive teaching, that is, teaching that is designed to satisfy the supervisor's demands but not the learner's needs.

THE CLINICAL SUPERVISION CYCLE

One supervisory model that enables the teacher and the supervisor to address the several aspects of teaching is called *clinical supervision*. This has been defined as "face-to-face contact with teachers with the intent of improving instruction and increasing professional growth" (Sergiovanni & Starratt, 1979, p. 286). It also encourages teacher and supervisor to prepare adequately for each supervisory activity.

Clinical supervision, according to Cogan (1973), follows an eight-step supervisory cycle:

1. The supervisor establishes the relationship between teacher and supervisor.
2. The teacher and the supervisor jointly plan the lesson, series of lessons, or units.
3. The supervisor and the teacher plan the observation procedures.
4. The supervisor observes instruction.
5. The teacher and the supervisor analyze the teaching-learning process.
6. The supervisor plans the conference.
7. The supervisor and the teacher confer.
8. The teacher and the supervisor renew the planning of the next lesson.

Clinical supervision encourages a consulting role for the supervisor, rather than an inspectional role. A criticism of clinical supervision is that it does not address curriculum improvement. An alternative model has been proposed as a cooperative problem-solving process for curriculum improvement (Tanner & Tanner, 1987). Called *developmental supervision*, it recognizes that the teacher is equal in status to other educators. "The working relationships are democratic-participatory" (p. 200).

For our purposes, developmental supervision will be considered one of several modifications of clinical supervision. Developmental supervision does not provide an analog to the eight-step cycle of clinical supervision. To implement a program of supervision it will be simpler to work with the cycle of clinical supervision, enhancing it, especially at step 2 (planning), so as to incorporate procedures for curriculum development. Additional modifications will also be proposed.

Establishing the Teacher-Supervisor Relationship

Usually an initial meeting between teacher and supervisor is held to help establish a mutually supportive relationship. During this meeting the supervisor helps the teacher to explore the teacher's goals, problems, strengths, and limitations. The teacher and supervisor inform one another of their criteria for successful teaching and identify where they are in agreement. Also, each makes a commitment for future action; they state what each will do in preparation for subsequent sessions of the supervision process (Cogan, 1973).

The supervisor can sometimes facilitate a discussion of instructional goals and problems by providing the teacher with reference materials. Simple outlines of reading skill areas and scope-and-sequence charts are good examples. Teachers of high school subjects, especially if they have had little preparation for teaching reading skills, find that the references quickly provide an overview of the skills. Longer reference materials, such as curriculum bulletins and professional books, may be given to the teacher for consideration before the next meeting. Curriculum bulletins in the teacher's subject area should be included when they provide some discussion of reading and writing skills, however cursory. The presence of this discussion in subject-area curriculum guides helps to encourage subject-area teachers to accept some responsibility for the development of reading skills and for their systematic application in their classrooms.

Planning Instruction

Joint planning by teacher and supervisor helps to establish their relationship as colleagues. Planning is to be conceived of as a joint attack on shared problems (Cogan, 1973). What is the best way to formulate teaching objectives? What resources can be used to help students attain these objectives? What teaching strategies are consistent with the objectives? How can student achievement be evaluated? Are the objectives and procedures that are planned for the day's lesson consistent with the more general and long-range goals of a larger unit of work? These are some of the questions that may be addressed when planning instruction.

Teachers have generally contributed to curriculum planning in two ways. First, they have served on curriculum committees that develop curricula in particular areas. A curriculum committee, for example, may be responsible for developing a new language arts curriculum for a school system. The committee's charge may be further delimited by specification of grade levels to which the curriculum applies. The curriculum would specify goals and objectives, teaching strategies and learning activities, units of instruction, and resources. This aspect of curriculum development lies outside the bounds of clinical supervision.

The second way teachers contribute to curriculum development is the selection and planning of teaching units for specific classes. This entails a study of the characteristics of a particular group of students, the selection of appropriate goals and objectives for this group, the planning of teaching strategies and learning activities, and the identification of resources. The teacher in this instance draws upon the curriculum guide and resource units already developed by a curriculum committee and adopted by the school district. The clinical supervisor can play a significant role in helping the teacher to plan and implement a curriculum for a specific class. The clinical supervision process enables supervisor and teacher to plan teaching units jointly and to translate these into a series of plans for day-to-day instruction.

Planning the Observation

During the preobservation meeting the teacher and supervisor may select aspects of teaching strategies, teacher behavior, student behavior, or other features of classroom instruction for later analysis. Having made this selection, the supervisor may suggest a procedure for gathering data during the observation, in order to expedite later analysis of the lesson. The data-gathering procedure may be one requiring joint analysis by supervisor and teacher, or it may permit the teacher to work alone in interpreting the information.

For example, the supervisor can prepare a simple tally of types of questions used in a directed reading activity; this tally can then be interpreted by the teacher. Likewise, the supervisor can monitor how oral questions are distributed among students in a group or classroom by tallying on a seating chart the way the questions are allocated; this tally can readily be interpreted by the teacher.

Certain observational procedures used to collect data would need to be interpreted by the supervisor, who has special skills. Specific observation techniques will be presented later in this chapter.

Planning for observation, then, reflects the decision making by teacher and supervisor, working collaboratively. The selection and use of observational procedures are intended to help the teacher adopt a reflective and analytic approach to his or her own teaching.

Observation of Teaching

At this juncture in the clinical supervision cycle, teacher and supervisor perform very different tasks. The teacher is now teaching — implementing the plan that was jointly developed with the supervisor. The supervisor observes the teaching, records the observations in written form, perhaps supplementing written recording with audio or video recording, and uses any specialized data-gathering procedure that may have been selected during the preobservation meeting.

Analysis of the Teaching-Learning Process

Analysis of the instructional process includes a comparison of planned and actual outcomes. The teacher now examines the lesson plan and compares it to any recorded chronology of the actual lesson and to her or his own recollection of it. In addition, the teacher examines any products of the lesson, especially the written work of the students, for evidence that learning objectives were attained. The teacher may write down any questions to be discussed with the supervisor.

In addition, the teacher may identify any critical incidents that occurred when teaching and write detailed descriptions of them, followed by interpretations of them. This activity encourages analytic and reflective attitudes toward teaching (Posner, 1985).

The supervisor prepares the data obtained from any specialized instrument, such as a tally sheet of verbal interaction patterns, for later interpretation with the teacher. Preparations are made for subsequent discussion with the teacher of any written records that were made during the observation.

Teacher and supervisor may work jointly on aspects of the analysis. The focus is likely to be the "identification of patterns of teacher behavior that exist over time" (Sergiovanni & Starratt, 1979, p. 311), descriptions and evidence of teacher behavior, and critical incidents that affect classroom activity.

Planning the Conference

It is the supervisor's responsibility to plan the conference. Based on the previous steps in the cycle, the supervisor establishes conference objectives, procedures to be followed, and a time frame. The supervisor also collects relevant materials, including the observational records. Objectives for the conference may include the evaluation of the teaching strategy and its success in meeting the teaching objectives, the evaluation of previously selected aspects of instruction or behavior to which the observation had been directed, the interpretation of the analysis of instruction undertaken separately or jointly by teacher and supervisor, and the identification of patterns or incidents that suggest new directions for ongoing supervision. A further objective for the conference is to plan the next lesson.

Conducting the Conference

Cogan (1973) describes several conference strategies that might be applied at this stage. One is to use the clinical cycle itself to structure the conference. This strategy starts with a brief review of the analyses performed by the teacher and supervisor. Aspects of teaching that are suitable for future work with the supervisor are selected. Then planning the next cycle is undertaken.

A second strategy is the chronological inventory of events. According to Cogan (1973), describing the series of events in the classroom may help to identify a weakness in teaching.

Another strategy is to analyze students' behavior in detail. Teaching is "treated as method, materials of instruction, etc., in relation to students' behavior" (Cogan, 1973, p. 213).

Finally, in the didactic strategy, the supervisor directly interprets the results of the observation. The strategy is helpful to a teacher who is motivated to improve her or his teaching and wishes to learn the techniques of the clinical supervision conference (Cogan, 1973). Additional strategies include encouraging the teacher to talk freely and using role playing.

Renewing the Planning

During the conference, the teacher and supervisor plan to make the changes in teaching that they agree should be made. The teacher should make a commitment to effect the changes (Cogan, 1973). The next lesson is planned so as to incorporate these changes. The subsequent steps in the clinical supervision cycle are repeated for the next lesson.

VARIATIONS IN CLINICAL SUPERVISION

Harris (1976) proposes intervisitations and demonstrations to supplement clinical supervision. He also recommends that the supervisor and teacher use training and practice sessions to augment the planning process. The basic sequence that he describes is similar to the clinical supervision cycle: (1) teach, (2) observe, (3) analyze, (4) interpret, (5) replan. He would insert the supplementary activities, as required, in the second or third turn of the cycle. For example, he would add (2a) secure other related data, and (4a) seek special training experience. Also, he suggests the omission of the observation step when no new information is expected.

Demonstration Lessons

In the basic clinical supervision cycle, a demonstration lesson can be added between steps 1 (establishing the teacher-supervisor relationship) and 2 (jointly planning the lesson). Demonstration lessons by a consultant are systematically incorporated in a program of inservice training described by Umans (1963) and Burg, Kaufman, Korngold, & Kovner (1978). Umans (1963) implemented this program in the junior high schools of New York City. She describes a six-week training cycle during which a reading consultant worked with a group of teachers in various content areas. The first week was devoted to orientation and included observations and group conferences. For each of the next five weeks the basic pattern of activities consisted of

1. A demonstration lesson by the reading consultant in one of the participating teacher's classes, with the teacher observing
2. A conference between the consultant and teacher, to discuss the demonstration, explain the skill that was taught, and plan the follow-up lesson
3. The follow-up lesson, taught by the teacher while the consultant observed
4. A conference to discuss the lesson's effectiveness and choose the next demonstration

My experience with the same program came after some modifications had been introduced. For one, the program was applied to team teaching as well as individual teacher training. The basic pattern used a single weekly conference with the teacher, after the initial week. The pattern followed was

1. Orientation activities, including an initial conference and observation

2. Demonstration by consultant
3. Conference
4. Follow-up lesson by teacher

Steps 2, 3, and 4 were repeated in subsequent cycles. The conference had to serve double duty in that it was necessary both to plan the next follow-up, based on the most recent demonstration, and discuss the previous follow-up lesson (Burg et al., 1978).

Another modification of clinical supervision is working with teachers in groups, which Sergiovanni and Starratt (1979) consider feasible. In one junior high school, the entire English department faculty attended the consultant's demonstration lessons and participated in group conferences (Burg et al., 1978).

Demonstration lessons, if added to the cycle of clinical supervision, may be conducted by the supervisor or by an expert teacher working with the participating teacher's class. An alternative is for the participating teacher to observe an expert teacher's class.

An Alternative Approach to the Conference

The conference in the clinical supervision cycle may be adapted to special circumstances. Hunter (1980) suggests the supervisor may wish to plan and conduct a different type of conference, depending on the teacher's level of ability and degree of security when supervised, and the stage of the supervision process that has been reached. She identifies five "instructional" types of conferences, according to their purpose:

1. To identify and explain the teacher's effective instructional behaviors
2. To propose alternatives to already effective behaviors, in order to expand the teacher's repertoire of effective teaching practices
3. To identify parts of the lesson with which the teacher was dissatisfied and suggest alternative procedures
4. To identify less effective parts of the lesson that were not evident to the teacher and develop alternative procedures
5. To enable an already excellent teacher to develop professionally

She describes a sixth conference type, the evaluative conference, which sums up the results of the instructional conferences.

When first supervising a teacher, the supervisor may wish to start with the first conference type and then gradually move, in order, to the second, third, and fourth types during several cycles of supervision (Hunter, 1980). An initially secure teacher could be encouraged to address, in a single conference, aspects of the lesson that fall into more than one category.

OBSERVATION TECHNIQUES

When the supervisor arrives to observe a lesson, he or she should take a seat in an unobtrusive place, yet near enough to see and hear what is happening. The teacher should provide the supervisor with a copy of the lesson plan, a seating chart, and a set of the reading matter the students will use.

Supervisors may employ any of several observation recording techniques during a lesson. These include informal notes, verbatim or paraphrased records of classroom dialogue, checklists, rating scales, tallies of behaviors observed, and interaction analysis systems such as the Flanders Interaction Analysis System (Amidon & Flanders, 1963). The particular technique should be selected during the preobservation conference.

Occasionally a supervisor may prefer to write informal notes about a lesson during or immediately following the observation. Informal notes can help to recall later what transpired during the lesson. Informal notes should include major themes and critical incidents. Absent is the wealth of detail that can be captured by verbatim or paraphrased records.

Verbatim or Paraphrased Records

Some supervisors prefer to prepare a verbatim or paraphrased record of classroom dialogue. Sometimes this is supplemented with a description of nonverbal behavior and the context, such as the content of a chart or page the class is reading or discussing. Of all the recording techniques, the verbatim or paraphrased record is richest in detail. In addition, statements within this record can be analyzed further, using one of the other systems to be described. For example, the supervisor and teacher can later classify the questions that were asked during the lesson and tally the number of correct and incorrect responses to each question type, in order to evaluate the teacher's questioning procedures and to diagnose the students' comprehension difficulties.

One variation, illustrated in Figure 8.1, is to use a two-column format, recording teacher talk to the left and student talk to the right. This makes obvious to the teacher how much time is taken for providing information, giving directions, and asking questions, in contrast to the opportunities for students to respond, question, and discuss.

Checklists and Rating Scales

Sometimes a supervisor may wish to use a checklist or rating scale to supplement or replace a verbatim record. These alert the supervisor to note specific aspects of the lesson. A checklist enables the supervisor to note

Figure 8.1   Two-Column Format for Recording Classroom Dialogue

Six children are seated around the table with T. They have read pages 128–129. In the story, the circus has left town; Billy is looking at a poster.

TEACHER TALK	STUDENT TALK
T: Where is the circus now?	(All children raise their hands.)
T: Susan?	*Susan:* The circus is far away.
T: What did Billy do each day? Bob.	*Bob:* He looked at pictures of the circus.
T: What does he want to do? Mike?	*Mike:* He wants to work for the circus.

whether something occurs at any time during a lesson or during a particular time interval within the lesson. Three types of checklists are shown in Figure 8.2. One limitation of a checklist is that an item is checked if it occurs even once; therefore it is best to restrict it to items that would, in fact, appear only once during the lesson. Examples of such items are (1) "establishes the purpose of the lesson," and (2) "presents a final summary." Some activities can be expected to occur more than once, even repeatedly. A variant of the checklist can be used if the supervisor wishes to track the frequency of these activities. Examples of these frequency counts are presented in a later section.

A rating scale is constructed so that items can be marked on a scale of value or frequency. Often the judgment of frequency is not based on an actual count of occurrences but is reached subjectively. Figure 8.3 shows two sample rating scales; whether an assigned rating is represented by a numeral, as in example A, or by a mark on a line, as in example B, the formats are equivalent.

A criticism of rating scales is that the assigned ratings are subjective. This easily prevents the teacher from accepting the supervisor's judgment. To support judgments reflected in a rating, specific events in the lesson related to the item should be noted. The supervisor can write the rating-scale item number next to the events recorded in the verbatim record. If a verbatim record is not prepared, the supervisor can record events in a "comments" section of the rating scale worksheet (see Figure 8.4). It should be possible for teacher and supervisor to note that a judgment was based on a trend reflected in the specific occurrences.

Frequency Counts or Tallies

To overcome the problem of subjective judgments associated with rating scales, the supervisor can use simple frequency counts. In preparation for this, behavior categories must be established. To use frequency

Figure 8.2   Three Examples of Checklists

EXAMPLE A.   In this example, items are checked if they occur at any time during the lesson.

	Check if observed
Checklist items	
1. Stated the objective of the lesson	_____
2. Modified teaching to meet individual needs	_____
3. Encouraged student participation	_____

(and so forth)

EXAMPLE B.   Sometimes a checklist includes items that are to be checked only if judged satisfactory overall.

	Satisfactory
Checklist items	
1. Used appropriate materials	_____
2. Teaching was effectively paced	_____

(and so forth)

EXAMPLE C.   In this example, items are checked if they occur within certain time intervals.

	Start	*Middle*	*End*
Checklist items			
1. Modified teaching to meet individual needs	_____	_____	_____
2. Encouraged student participation	_____	_____	_____

(and so forth)

counts, the supervisor observes the behavior, mentally assigns it to one of the several preestablished categories, and records a tally mark in that category. Following the observation, the supervisor counts the tallies in each category, to arrive at the frequency count. The procedure is objective and reliable. The supervisor avoids having to make subjective judgments at a high-inference level, provided only that low-inference-level categories are used, that is, categories that are close to the direct behavior.

The difference between low- and high-inference-level categories can be illustrated by the following situation: The supervisor is to tally the children's responses to the teacher's questions. Two low-inference-level categories of response are (1) correct responses and (2) incorrect responses. In contrast, three high-inference-level categories are (1) response shows boredom and apathy, (2) response shows inattentiveness, and (3) response

Figure 8.3   Two Examples of Rating Scales

EXAMPLE A.   Record: 5 if very effective
                                                       4 if effective
                                                       3 if just adequate
                                                       2 if needs improvement
                                                       1 if very ineffective

1. Focusing event   _____

2. Pacing   _____

3. Distribution of questioning   _____

4. Monitoring and adjusting   _____

                                                      (and so forth)

EXAMPLE B.

	All of the time	*Most of the time*	*Some of the time*	*Never*
1. Used simple explanations	_____	_____	_____	_____
2. Used appropriate language	_____	_____	_____	_____
3. Gave sufficient time for students to respond	_____	_____	_____	_____

                                                      (and so forth)

Figure 8.4   Rating Scale with Section for Comments

	Check if observed
Checklist items	
1. Pacing	_____
Comments:	
2. Distribution of questioning	_____
Comments:	

                                                      (and so forth)

shows passive-aggressiveness. There would likely be poor reliability in classifying responses into the latter three categories.

Figure 8.5 gives examples of situations in which behavior is tallied according to preestablished categories. In example A the categories are the children's names. In example B the categories are the teacher's verbal behaviors. Example C illustrates the use of a single category — a verbal mannerism — and the use of time intervals, while example D uses three categories of student behavior. Example E collapses the category of children's names (coded) and the categories of student behavior. The chief value of these simple procedures is that the supervisor and teacher can select categories that are specific to the problem needing solution. Frequency counts can be adapted to quantify what occurs during verbal interactions between teacher and student or between student and student. For example, the supervisor can tally student responses to the teacher's questions, or teacher responses to students' statements, in several response categories (Amidon & Flanders, 1963; Amidon & Hunter, 1966; Guszak, 1967; Ober, Bentley, & Miller, 1971).

The Flanders Interaction Analysis System (Amidon & Flanders, 1963) contains ten categories of "talk" by teacher or student. The supervisor records the category number of the observed verbal behavior at three-second intervals. The supervisor later constructs an interaction matrix from the list of numbers recorded during a twenty-minute duration. The interaction matrix is constructed by pairing each category number (i.e., verbal behavior) with the category number immediately following it. Each pair is recorded as a tally mark in the matrix.

The interaction matrix can be analyzed and interpreted by supervisor and teacher. For example, tallies in one cell of the matrix represent the number of times student responses were followed by teacher encouragement or praise. This desirable interaction can be identified during the teacher-supervisor conference.

SUMMARY

This chapter has centered around the supervisory model called clinical supervision. The cycle of clinical supervision encourages teacher and supervisor to identify areas of agreement regarding curriculum emphasis, classroom management, and teaching procedures. This common frame of reference is a prerequisite for successful supervision. Clinical supervision provides for joint planning, observation of teaching, analysis, and consultation. It can be adapted to include teacher observation of demonstration teaching and to provide group or individual supervision. Several types of

Figure 8.5   Examples of Frequency Counts or Tallies

EXAMPLE A.   The supervisor has the impression that the teacher calls on some children much more often than others. To verify this impression, the supervisor makes a tally mark near the child's name on a seating chart or name list, each time the child is called on.

EXAMPLE B.   The supervisor tallies ways that the teacher acknowledges children's responses to questions.

Categories	Frequency
Correct response is confirmed or praised.	/ / /
Correct response not acknowledged.	——
Incorrect response is corrected.	/ / / /
T. guides child who responded incorrectly to a better response.	/
After incorrect response, T. calls on another child.	/ / /

EXAMPLE C.   To help the teacher overcome a verbal mannerism, the supervisor tallies the instances of saying "Okay" during ten-minute intervals.

10:00 _____

10:10 _____

10:20 _____

EXAMPLE D.   This example is based on a technique described by Glickman (1981) for monitoring the attentiveness of particular students. In this example, the supervisor monitors time on task, in order to detect patterns and causes of inattentiveness. She observes a random sample of students in the class during a class period. At five-minute intervals she places a tally for each student in one of three categories. The supervisor may also record the time on a verbatim record of the lesson or may state, alongside the tallies, significant occurrences at that point in the lesson, to permit later correlation of events to changes in behavior.

	Attentive to task	Inattentive/ not disruptive	Inattentive/ disruptive	Comments
11:00	/ / / /	/		
11:05	/ /	/ /	/	

EXAMPLE E.   If it is desired to monitor certain children who have shown inattention in the past, these children can be identified individually and noted according to the categories shown in example D.

Bob = A; Mary = B; Jim = C.

11:00	A B C			
11:05	A	B C		

teacher-supervisor conferences can be incorporated into the cycle, depending on the particular needs of the teacher. The supervisor may employ any of several observation techniques, the selection of which is a process of collaboration between supervisor and teacher.

REFERENCES

Amidon, E., & Flanders, N. A. (1963). *The role of the teacher in the classroom*. Minneapolis: Paul Amidon and Associates.

Amidon, E., & Hunter E. (1966). *Improving teaching: The analysis of classroom verbal interaction*. New York: Holt, Rinehart and Winston.

Burg, L. A., Kaufman, M., Korngold, B., & Kovner, A. (1978). *The complete reading supervisor: Tasks and roles*. Columbus, OH: Charles E. Merrill.

Cogan, M. L. (1973). *Clinical supervision*. Boston: Houghton Mifflin.

Costa, A. L., & Garmston, R. (1985). Supervision for intelligent teaching. *Educational Leadership, 42*(5), 70–80.

Glickman, C. D. (1981). *Developmental supervision: Alternative practices for helping teachers improve instruction*. Alexandria, VA: Association for Supervision and Curriculum Development.

Guszak, F. J. (1967). Teacher questioning and reading. *The Reading Teacher, 21*, 227–234.

Harris, B. M. (1976). Limits and supplements to formal clinical procedures. *Journal of Research and Development in Education, 9*(2), 85–89.

Hunter, M. (1980). Six types of supervisory conferences. *Educational Leadership, 37*(5), 408–412.

Hunter, M. (1984). Knowing, teaching and supervising. In P. L. Hosford (Ed.), *Yearbook of the Association for Supervision and Curriculum Development: Using what we know about teaching* (pp. 169–192). Alexandria, VA: Association for Supervision and Curriculum Development.

Ober, R. L., Bentley, E. L., & Miller, E. (1971). *Systematic observation of teaching: An interaction analysis-instructional strategy approach*. Englewood Cliffs, NJ: Prentice-Hall.

Posner, G. J. (1985). *Field experience: A guide to reflective teaching*. New York: Longman.

Sergiovanni, T. J., & Starratt, R. J. (1979). *Supervision: Human perspectives* (2nd ed.). New York: McGraw-Hill.

Slavin, R. (1987). Hunterization of America's schools: Part 1. *Instructor, 46*(8), 56–58.

Tanner, D., & Tanner, L. (1987). *Supervision in education: Problems and practices*. New York: Macmillan.

Umans, S. (1963). *New trends in reading instruction*. New York: Teachers College Press.

9   Staff Development

JOANNE L. VACCA
Kent State University

Cathy A. Labate © 1988

Planning and conducting successful staff development is similar to providing effective leadership to the reading program itself. Several ingredients are essential if supervisors are to orchestrate staff development programs competently:

- An adequate and current knowledge base in reading, writing, and language theory and practice
- A concept of a total language arts curriculum and a systematic view of the reading program
- Interpersonal skills with which to communicate well with teachers and principals, to establish rapport in group and individual settings, and to engage in problem solving

- An understanding of students' developmental needs as a base for matching curricular practices, materials, and strategies with students' abilities.

In addition, an understanding of teachers and their workplace is necessary to the task of matching staff development goals and activities with participants' needs. The following vignette illustrates this point.

One late afternoon about 5:30, Kay, a K–12 reading supervisor in a suburban school district, was driving home, mulling over the day's events. Remembering her morning conversation with Tina, a first-grade teacher, Kay visualized the teachers' lounge at J.F.K. Elementary School. As they drank coffee, Tina was animated as she explained to Kay and another teacher in the room how she had come to understand that reading does indeed begin at home. This year, her third in teaching, at least half of Tina's children already knew how to read in September. She said, "It really does seem that some children learn to read naturally; someone should study how they learn this at home." Kay smiled as she thought about the conversation, because, frequently during the past year, she had made efforts to talk about and provide reading materials for the teachers in Tina's school, on the importance of creating conditions for learning in the classroom. Kay had promoted the goal that each child would receive individual instruction in learning how to read and write; early readers would need easy access to reading materials in the classroom. Just as the home environment is responsive to what the child is learning, so the school environment should allow each child the *opportunity* to learn when she or he is ready. Then Kay's thoughts wandered to the staff development series that she would be conducting beginning next month at J.F.K. She asked herself, "How can I capitalize on this situation with Tina and her first graders, using it to the advantage of the entire group of teachers in the building?"

Kay is an example of a reading supervisor who has the ingredients necessary for planning effective staff development. Her knowledge of the reading process, her work experience with the district's language arts curriculum, her understanding of early literacy in relation to the children now attending J.F.K. school, and her skill in listening to what teachers are really saying will all be useful in the upcoming staff development series. Kay's awareness that, in many ways, working with teachers is akin to recognizing individual differences in children is equally important. "You need only observe teachers of reading in action or talk to them about instructional concerns to recognize that every teacher operates in the class-room with what we call an implicit theory of reading" (Vacca, Vacca, & Gove, 1987, p. 5).

Hence, reading supervisors can capitalize on their "inside" position to plan for effective staff development. They, like Kay, are in the enviable position of learning firsthand what teachers do, in the course of planning and teaching reading, that influences children's ideas and attitudes about reading. The key is to use that same information about teachers and their teaching to create an environment conducive to effective staff development.

It should be obvious by now that *staff development*, even when geared specifically for reading and language instruction, is a rather amorphous term. On one hand, it "consists of any activities designed to influence the knowledge, attitudes, or skills of educational personnel so that the quality of learning is improved" (*Staff Development Leadership*, 1983, p. v.). Such a global definition may seem too comprehensive at first; however, it represents a gradual change in thinking, from the 1960s' and 1970s' notion of "inservicing teachers" to the more contemporary perspective that "teachers are only one part of a complex and often misunderstood system of interaction" (Griffin, 1983, p. 2).

On the other hand, staff development also deals with the personal and professional needs of the individual adult participants, who are at various stages in their careers, and the circumstances in their home lives. It stands to reason that, although Kay and other reading supervisors shouldn't be expected to diagnose and provide for every individual personal/professional need of teachers, they should take them into consideration when planning to implement staff development. How she and her colleagues deliver staff development can be improved with an understanding of how adults learn and how they progress through their careers. Furthermore, there is "a growing body of evidence to suggest that certain approaches to professional development are more potentially powerful than others" (Griffin, 1983, p. 3). The principles, planning, and implementation segments in this chapter will assist reading supervisors in applying those approaches to staff development at each educational level.

PRINCIPLES

There are many principles available to guide the planning of effective staff development programs. Some come from research, others from writings of professionals who have been engaged in staff development, and still others from experience in the professional development of teachers. The seven major principles that follow hold true for each educational level: pre-elementary, elementary, middle/junior high, and high school.

1. *The most critical unit for staff development is at the building level.*

This calls for an "ecological" perspective, one that takes into account the context or the environment in which teachers work on a daily basis. According to Goodlad (1983), the school building is the largest and smallest unit for school improvement. If staff development is to be participatory, teachers who have common interests and problems can share as they develop strategies for instruction or participate in mutual problem solving.

One of the key factors in teacher satisfaction is the principal/teacher relationship. Teachers need to have principals whom they regard as competent and independent professionals, possessing their own professional autonomy. The relationship between teachers and the building principal is an important one in the quality-of-life factors for the workplace. Marsh and McLaughlin (1979) argue that staff development is most effective when viewed as a part of the program-building activities within a school.

2. *There are different purposes for staff development.*

Some programs are very clearly structured to impact directly on the improvement of instruction and students' performance on tests and other measures. Others take into account more of what we know now about the development of teachers as they progress through their induction and become experienced teachers. As Figure 9.1 illustrates, there is a range of purposes for staff development (Vacca & Vacca, 1986). At one end is the institutional goal, in which increased student achievement is the priority; in the center is instructional improvement, entailing work on implementation strategies and professional collaboration; and on the other end is the personal goal, with an emphasis on collegiality and increased self-esteem for the participants.

Staff development programs do not have to be one-dimensional. Working toward staff collegiality in the school environment and developing reading strategies to improve student learning are not mutually exclusive goals; we need to recognize the complexity of a teacher's professional growth in setting the purposes for staff development.

Staff cannot work on everything at once; therefore, it is critical that priorities are identified very early in the planning of a staff development program. These priorities take shape on the microlevel and the macrolevel. On a microlevel, within a school building site, an intervention model might be used toward the improvement of instruction. The reading supervisor can conduct needs assessment and help teachers engage in problem solving as they introduce and work with an instructional innovation. At

Figure 9.1   Continuum of Staff Development Goals

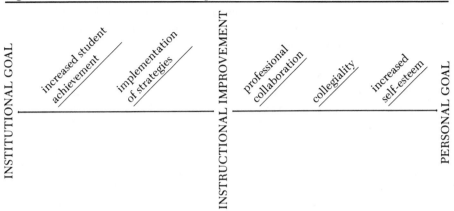

Source: Vacca, R. T., & Vacca, J. L. (1986). *Content Area Reading* (2nd ed.). Boston: Little, Brown, p. 383. Reprinted with permission.

the macrolevel, a priority item would be similar to one suggested by Goodlad: quality of life in the workplace. The focus here would be on its assessment and subsequent continuing improvement. Creating a satisfying place of work for individuals who inhabit schools is an item that always needs to be on the agenda.

3. *The importance of teachers sharing with the colleagues with whom they work on a daily basis cannot be overemphasized.*
Teaching remains an isolated profession in which teachers still close their classroom doors, with autonomy to teach the way they prefer. Often this means that they will continue with the way that they have been taught to teach and that insures the maintenance of discipline in the classroom. In a study conducted by Pac-Urar and Vacca (1984), teachers cited advice and delivery of help by colleagues as one of the most important aspects in the improvement of their instruction. When given a choice of activities for an all-day staff development session, teachers will frequently choose visitation as their favored means of involvement; that is, they would like to visit the classroom of another teacher and have the opportunity to observe and then talk with the teacher about the activities and reading instruction within that classroom.

4. *It has been said that good research confirms common sense.*
This applies as well to good staff development practice. In other words, common-sense solutions and practical ideas are often the most useful,

relevant, and well received by any group of teachers. Handouts and other materials tend to be viewed more positively in all staff development activities if they describe local situations and examples (Patton & Anglin, 1982). Teachers want staff development sessions in which relevant ideas, strategies, and materials are presented.

In a recent U.S. Department of Education publication called *What Works* (1986), some very basic principles about teaching and learning were highlighted. While it has been criticized as being too simplistic by presenting watered-down research findings, a reading supervisor could capitalize on this very clearly written publication by using the findings to verify good practices and then to illustrate how they can be extended and elaborated on. Also, teachers could analyze ways in which present practice in their classrooms in school is or is not meeting the suggestions for good teaching. For example, one finding is that "children improve their reading ability by reading a lot. Reading achievement is directly related to the amount of reading children do in school and outside" (p. 11). In our earlier vignette, Kay might build on Tina's discovery about young readers to include teachers at higher grade levels by using this statement as a catalyst in small-group discussions.

5. *Time remains a major problem in creating and delivering staff development.*
There is too little time in the day and week for both teachers and reading supervisors to do their regular jobs; they simply have too much to do. In *News for Administrators* (1987), a column in the IRA newspaper, one busy reading specialist was described as working with sixty or seventy students each day. A more flexible schedule was proposed as a more productive alternative, in terms of working with other teachers. For example, doing some individual testing, talking with teachers, making classroom observations, working on a schoolwide reading incentive program, attending a workshop, and spending an hour reading a journal are all valuable activities that a supervisor locked into a rigid schedule cannot do.

Classroom teachers also find that time is a very critical element. For example, teachers in Goodlad's (1983) study who expressed the most satisfaction with their workplace perceived themselves as spending more time on instruction and less time on routines and discipline in the classroom.

Another consideration is the time chosen for the staff development session. While it is obvious that time devoted to an improvement activity at the end of a long day is not going to be very productive, when given a choice, teachers are very reluctant to give up any time on a weekend or in the evening.

6. *There is a recognizable process of change involved in any long-term staff development project.*

When an instructional innovation is instituted, there are many changes that take place, in the teaching that occurs, with the innovation itself, with the teachers who try out the innovation, and probably with the reading supervisor or staff developer who is working with the group. Teachers, it seems, go through different levels of use when they are piloting an instructional innovation during long-term staff development. As developed by Hall, Loucks, Rutherford, and Newlove (1975), there are eight levels, as outlined in Table 9.1.

7. *Engaging in staff development is a continuing process that needs to be planned and conducted over time.*

Staff development entails individual and professional growth and the making of connections. Again, the most satisfying schools in the Goodlad (1983) sample were those in which there was some capability for coping

Table 9.1   Levels of Use in Teacher Adoption of Innovative Reading Strategies

	LEVEL OF USE	TEACHER RESPONSE IN READING INSTRUCTION
0	Nonuse	Is not doing anything in relation to teaching reading
I	Orientation	Is oriented to change; has not decided to use new reading strategies, but is thinking about how they differ from present practices
II	Preparation	Has decided to use several new reading strategies and is planning how to incorporate them
III	Mechanical Use	Has begun new reading strategies, but in a mechanical way
IVa	Routine	Has established a level of routine in using new reading strategies
IVb	Refinement	Is refining use of the innovation; making adaptations within the classroom to increase impact
V	Integration	Is working with others in using new strategies so that coordination of efforts will increase impact
VI	Renewal	Is moving into using additional new innovations related to reading instruction

Source: Adapted from Hall, G., Loucks, S., Rutherford, W., & Newlove, B. (1975). Levels of use of an innovation: A Framework for Analyzing Innovation Adoption. *The Journal of Teacher Education, 34,* 226–233.

with problems. Greater awareness of the processes through which such capability is acquired and channeled into schoolwide study and action is important. Collaboration with colleges and universities in combining preservice education and inservice school improvement activities is suggested by Goodlad. Encouraged by the Holmes report, *Tomorrow's Teachers* (Holmes Group, 1986), colleges of teacher education and local school districts are collaborating to make professional development schools a reality.

The foregoing principles should be useful guidelines in working with today's public school teacher, who is "better educated, has more experience and works harder and is putting in longer hours than ever before," reports National Education Association President Mary Hatwood Futrell, in the *Education Daily* ("Teachers Have More Experience," 1987, p. 2). According to recent statistics, today's teacher averages fifteen years of experience, an increase of three years since 1981. The average teacher spends more than ten hours per week on school-related activities without financial compensation; and a majority of teachers hold one or more advanced degrees. Thus, as reading supervisors prepare to implement staff development for today's teachers, careful and systematic planning is a must.

PLANNING

In order to make staff development successful, supervisors need information about the current situation; they need to base decisions on data that are collected in this context. Next, they need to *work with participants* in setting goals. A recent study by Rycik (1986) confirmed the importance of including teachers in every phase of the staff development program. Teachers who were knowledgeable about reading instruction preferred supervisors who provided them with the freedom to put their knowledge into practice, rather than insisting that they conform to a preexisting program. Furthermore, Rycik concluded, teachers would be amenable to a collaborative relationship in which they would have a say in targeting goals for improvement.

Probably the most efficient and effective way for the reading supervisor/staff developer to engage in planning is to follow a model that is both systematic and participatory. In other words, it should be orderly and flexible and depend on input from those most directly involved. Depicted in Figure 9.2 is a model suggested by Siedow (1985), which fits well with the basic principles for effective staff development. Above all, the cyclical design allows for interaction among and involvement of teachers, administrators, coordinators, and committees. A plan such as this virtually guar-

Figure 9.2 Staff Development Planning Model

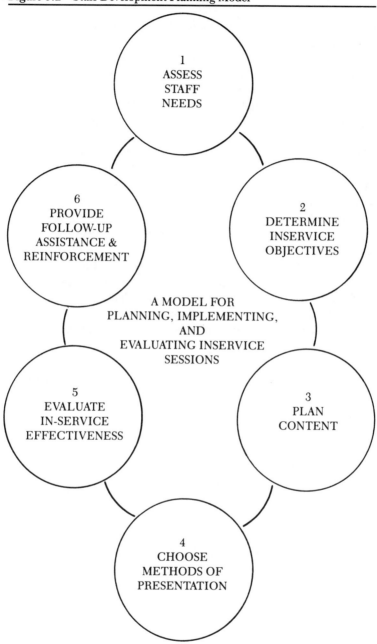

Figure content (circles, clockwise from top):

1
ASSESS
STAFF
NEEDS

2
DETERMINE
INSERVICE
OBJECTIVES

3
PLAN
CONTENT

4
CHOOSE
METHODS OF
PRESENTATION

5
EVALUATE
IN-SERVICE
EFFECTIVENESS

6
PROVIDE
FOLLOW-UP
ASSISTANCE &
REINFORCEMENT

A MODEL FOR
PLANNING, IMPLEMENTING,
AND
EVALUATING INSERVICE
SESSIONS

Source: Siedow, M. D. (1985). Inservice Education for Content Area Teachers: Some Basic Principles. In M. Siedow, D. Memory, & P. Bristow (Eds.), *In-service Education for Content Area Teachers.* Newark, DE: International Reading Association, p. 6. Reprinted with permission of the International Reading Association.

antees the reading supervisor that staff development will be well designed and tailored to meet participants' needs.

Another way to assist a committee in planning is to focus on three major questions in designing the staff development program: what, why, and how? What is the current situation? What needs to be improved? What is the baseline? What exists right now? Why do we want improvement in a particular area? Why are teachers and administrators doing what they are doing in the classroom; in the building? How can we begin to make some changes in the status quo? How should we initiate the staff development, and how do we proceed?

As a rule of thumb, planning proceeds in phases, beginning with a proposal to initiate change in the school's reading program. This phase of planning (which corresponds to steps 1 and 2 in Figure 9.2) should rely on information and ideas from several sources, especially the group for whom staff development is intended. Needs assessment enables the reading supervisor and planning committee to identify needs, attitudes, interests, and potential resources. Kay, the reading supervisor in our earlier vignette, designed two types of assessment surveys to collect information from the teaching staff of 21 at J.F.K. Elementary. Portions of the one for intermediate grade teachers are shown in Figure 9.3 while Figure 9.4 excerpts the one for primary grade teachers.

At this juncture in the planning process, basic goals and objectives can be set by the committee. The next phase—actual implementation of content and process—is under way.

IMPLEMENTATION

The implementation of staff development involves delivery of the program. It should occur over a series of planned activities, lasting anywhere from a month to a year or two. To work effectively with teachers, the reading supervisor/staff developer needs to be open to new ideas and demonstrate identified strategies and techniques for improving instruction. Interpersonal skills, as well as one's basic delivery and knowledge base, are particularly important. Following are some personal characteristics that are associated with effective presenters at staff development sessions (Vacca & Vacca, 1986):

- Demonstrates enthusiasm and interest in the topic
- Stimulates excitement
- Relates in open, honest, and friendly manner
- Answers questions patiently

- Doesn't talk down to participants
- Displays sense of humor

As reading supervisors take on the role of staff developer, they need to be confident and collaborate with teachers on ways to work with each other. They need a tolerance for ambiguity and a realization that participants are involved in a learning effort, with no one having the "right" answer.

One of the most practical ways to implement a staff development project is to follow a four-stage model based on the process of change (Lewin, 1948). Essentially, adults go through a change process beginning with unfreezing or readiness, then moving forward and gaining experience, then refreezing and, finally, incorporating changes into the environment. Figure 9.5 shows how this four-stage model was applied recently in

Figure 9.3   Survey of Competency Needs for Intermediate Grade Teachers

Directions: Indicate whether or not you would like assistance in each area of competency related to reading comprehension in the intermediate grades:

	NEEDS		
COMPETENCY	I feel confident in this area.	I would like a little more help here.	I would like lots of help here.
1. Building background activities to develop a frame of reference			
2. Showing students how to generate their own questions			
3. Involving students in process of predicting and verifying			
4. Getting students involved in group discussions			
5. Sensitizing readers to sources of information where answers to questions can be found			

Figure 9.4 Survey of Needs and Concerns for Primary Grade Teachers

Directions: Please number in order of importance (1=most important; 5=least important) the areas in which you feel you need additional help in order to teach reading in the primary grades. Then, answer each question as completely as possible.

_____ Using conversation to encourage individual or group language experience stories

_____ Linking singing, dancing, and other rhythmic activities to reading and writing instruction

_____ Creating a dress-up area for dramatic activities

_____ Using evaluation procedures that are developmentally appropriate for the children

_____ Using the language children bring to school as a base for language activities

1. What is your area of greatest concern about teaching reading?

2. What is your area of least concern?

Figure 9.5 Four-Stage Staff Development Implementation Model

Stage 1: Stimulation and Motivation

Create relaxed setting to discuss problems and felt needs; lessen feelings of discomfort and/or hostility; establish a feeling of open-mindedness toward what is to follow; engage in writing and responding to one another as writers.

Stage 2: Simulations and Explanations

Introduce participating teachers to new approaches, concepts, strategies for instruction; demonstrate strategies; increase willingness and ability to incorporate new knowledge into writing instruction; model process strategies by engaging teachers in writing activity.

Stage 3: Planning and Organization

Provide time for lesson planning; create writing activities to be used in classroom situations.

Stage 4: Coaching

Coach and support the efforts of teachers who are now applying new ideas in their classrooms.

a suburban Ohio school district (middle and high school buildings), over the course of one academic year. The project's overall goal was to develop teachers' knowledge of the writing process and their ability to plan and implement writing instruction. Ten workshops, each two hours long, were held during the first half of the year; five workshop sessions and six all-day coaching sessions were held during the second half. Figure 9.6 reviews the operational chronology developed by the planning committee.

Figure 9.6   Staff Development for Process Writing: Operational Chronology

Stage 1: Workshop Sessions

September	Introduction and overview; writer's workshop
	Issues in middle school and secondary writing instruction; process vs. product; writer's workshop
Early October	Writing as development
	Writer's blocks
	Writer's workshop

Stage 2: Workshop Sessions

Mid-October	Helping students find topics for writing
	Stages of writing
	Prewriting strategies
	Coaching in classrooms
November	Strategies for writing and rewriting
	Receiving, responding, evaluating
	Coaching in classrooms
December	Conducting conferences, revising, editing
	Valuing finished products: publishing and sharing writing
	Coaching

Stage 3: Workshop Sessions

January	Create an environment
	Develop writing activity lessons
	Coaching
February	Develop writing activity lessons
	Coaching

Stage 4: Coaching for Application

| March | Coaching for application |
| April | Coaching for application |

Implementing staff development with this four-stage model allows reading supervisors and staff developers to introduce a range of action-oriented instructional options to participating teachers. The key to effective delivery is involvement, through "hands-on" activities such as role playing, demonstration teaching, observations, interviewing, and problem-solving groups. As the teachers sense the process of reading by playing the role of reader and experiencing new strategies and materials, the leader explains the how and why of selecting techniques to use in delivering a workshop series. The leader will need to sustain the rapport that was established in the beginning and will need to vary the choice of activities, remembering that no single technique will be effective in all situations.

Frequent and informal evaluation by participants can help keep the staff development program on track. Simple rating scales to provide information on the perceived value and usefulness of a workshop session should help the leader decide on modification in planned implementation. Feedback at the end of each coaching session might be a two-way street, with both staff developer and teacher exchanging suggestions for improvement. This in turn would result in follow-up at the next whole-group workshop session. Evaluation in this context, then, becomes an integral and responsive part of the staff development implementation.

CONCLUSION

Creating an environment conducive to successful staff development is not an easy task—even for an astute reading supervisor like Kay. She, too, will probably have to do what the teachers in J.F.K. Elementary will do during their staff development: experience firsthand and risk getting involved in opportunities to learn and change.

In addition to the basic principles for staff development, the process of planning, and the stages of implementation, there are some less tangible but powerful ingredients that are needed for staff developers and teachers to work and learn together (Vacca, Shanklin, & Vacca, 1987). These include

- Mutual caring revolving around a common interest in children's learning and the topic at hand
- Consultants' (or supervisors') experience as and empathy for teachers with many roles and responsibilities
- A sense of consultants' genuine support of teachers, *before* any constructive criticism is offered
- Mutual desire for greater and shared understanding, to open the way to constructive disagreement

- Mutual respect and commitment to level with each other, solve problems, and move toward constructive, nonthreatening change, by teachers *and* consultants

Cultivating these is a continuous process.

REFERENCES

Goodlad, J. (1983). *A place called school*. New York: McGraw-Hill.

Griffin, G. (Ed.). (1983). *Staff development*. 82nd Yearbook of the National Society for the Study of Education. Chicago: University of Chicago Press.

Hall, G., Loucks, S., Rutherford, W., & Newlove, B. (1975). Levels of use of an innovation: A framework for analyzing innovation adoption. *The Journal of Teacher Education, 34*, 226–233.

Holmes Group Executive Board. (1986). *Tomorrow's teachers: A report of the Holmes Group*. East Lansing, MI: Holmes Group.

Lewin, K. (1948). *Resolving social conflicts*. New York: Harper & Row.

Marsh, D., & McLaughlin, M. (1979). Staff development and school settings. In A. Lieberman & L. Miller (Eds.), *Staff development: New demands, new realities, new perspectives*. New York: Teachers College Press.

News for administrators. (1987, June/July). *Reading Today, 4*, 11.

Pac-Urar, I., & Vacca, J. L. (1984, May). Working toward collegiality: If at first you don't succeed. *Thresholds in Education, 10*(2), 36–38.

Patton, W., & Anglin, L. (1982). Characteristics of success in high school inservice education. *The High School Journal, 65*, 163–168.

Rycik, J. (1986). *Teachers' perceptions of supervision of reading instruction*. Unpublished manuscript, Kent State University, Kent, OH.

Siedow, M. D. (1985). Inservice education for content area teachers: Some basic principles. In M. Siedow, D. Memory, & P. Bristow (Eds.), *In-service education for content area teachers* (pp. 1–7). Newark, DE: International Reading Association.

Staff development leadership: A resource book. (1983). Columbus, OH: Ohio Department of Education.

Teachers have more experience and education than ever before, NEA finds. (1987, July 2). *Education Daily*, pp. 1–2.

Vacca, J. L., Shanklin, N. L., & Vacca, R. T. (1987). Learning about writing process instruction: Some principles to guide teacher change. *The Reading Instruction Journal, 31*(1), 6–9.

Vacca, J. L., Vacca, R. T., & Gove, M. K. (1987). *Reading and learning to read*. Boston: Little, Brown.

Vacca, R. T., & Vacca, J. L. (1986). *Content area reading* (2nd ed.). Boston: Little, Brown.

What works: Research about teaching and learning. (1986). Washington, DC: U.S. Department of Education.

10 Evaluation of District Reading Programs

ROGER FARR
Indiana University

ROBERT H. PRITCHARD
California State University, Fresno

The focus of any reading program evaluation should be the improvement of instruction. It is wasteful of time and resources to evaluate merely to determine if a program is successful or unsuccessful. The basic premise of this chapter, then, is that evaluation needs to be focused on *program considerations*, particularly on those things that can be done to make instruction more effective.

Evaluation studies often attempt to determine the worth of a program by answering such questions as, Is this a good program? While the answers may make administrators or teachers feel better or worse, depending on the outcome, they are of little value in improving a program. If a program is to improve, evaluation must, from the start, concentrate on things that can be changed (Farr & Carey, 1986). The following are a few examples of constructive questions:

- Is enough time being devoted to the teaching of reading?
- Is the reading program providing students with instruction in the reading skills needed for success in content-area classes?
- Does the library have adequate reading materials for a wide range of student reading abilities?

In addition to concentrating on decisions, a worthwhile reading program evaluation must plan for the collection of a wide variety of information. This is needed because the outcomes of a reading program cannot be understood by just collecting test scores to determine how well students read (Tyler & White, 1979). A more complete understanding of students' reading abilities, including their reading habits and attitudes, is needed. Moreover, information about the program activities, as well as program outcomes, is vital if decisions to change program activities are being considered.

Too often, evaluation is nothing more than administering a set of tests, analyzing the results, and filing a report (Farr & Wolf, 1984). In more elaborate evaluations, questionnaires may be completed by teachers or parents, open meetings may be held, and pronouncements about the quality of the reading program may be made. But do such evaluations lead to program improvement?

Traditional reading program evaluations have been excessively goal and objective oriented, primarily concerned with the match between objectives and outcomes. The focus has almost always been on finding areas of weakness to be corrected. Seldom has the focus been on areas of strength that can be used to build a more vital program.

It is no simple matter to understand the complex variables that intertwine in a typical reading program, yet traditional evaluations nearly always attempt to reduce the process to listing objectives, matching objectives with test scores, and proclaiming whether a program is effective or ineffective (Scriven, 1973). Often, based on little more information than that, programs can be labeled ineffective and faced with a mandate for change.

The perspective of this chapter is that the administrator who views evaluation as a process of collecting information to make decisions about program improvement must avoid the search for simple solutions and be prepared to deal with complexity. When evaluating a reading program, a conscientious effort is needed to identify the factors that shape the program, the needs of the program participants, and the impediments to making the program even more successful — as well as those things that have brought it success.

It is not the purpose of this chapter to provide a set of guidelines for a successful reading program; rather, it is our intent to provide a framework from which a school administrator can plan and conduct an evaluation that will result in action rather than in another report that gathers dust on a shelf.

USING QUESTIONS TO FOCUS THE EVALUATION

Formulation of clear and explicit evaluation questions is the most important step in planning and implementing effective assessment of the reading program. Decision making is the goal of the evaluation, and the success of an evaluation should be the extent to which it provides valid, reliable, and useful information for making decisions (Stufflebeam et al., 1971).

What Constitutes a Good Evaluation Question?

A good question should suggest at least two possible courses of action. For example, one might ask whether or not a special reading class should be started for all middle school students. More typically, however, the courses of action being considered are more complex than this example. It may be that a pilot program may be initiated with less able readers, or that the course may be started as an elective rather than a required course. *All* of the possible courses of action cannot be specified at the outset. A variety of alternatives, besides the basic decision to have the course or not, will emerge as the evaluation proceeds.

It is important to recognize that an evaluation has little potential for success if the basic question is a general, unfocused query such as, What can be done to improve the reading program? Such a question does not pose alternative courses to be considered. Such a general question could, however, serve as the key to soliciting specific action alternatives from teachers, administrators, and board members. Without these, however, the question would not help to focus an evaluation.

How Are Good Evaluation Questions Formulated?

The list of questions should be formulated by soliciting input from those who are implementing the reading program (usually teachers and curriculum specialists), as well as from those who are responsible for managing the program (usually administrators and board members). One approach to gathering this list of considerations is to organize an evaluation steering committee, as discussed in the next section, and ask that committee to solicit potential questions from various groups. The steering committee will need to work with the list of potential issues, to organize them, to determine exactly what is meant by each concern, and to select the final list of appropriate questions that will form the focus for the evaluation. In short, this group's function is to conduct the evaluation and to provide information to those who are charged with making the final decisions.

Care should be taken that the solicitation include all staff members as well as representatives of parent groups. It should contain a statement explaining that an evaluation is being planned that will focus on making decisions for the improvement of the reading program, and it should ask for ideas from the various program constituencies regarding such improvement. These might include increasing the time devoted to teaching reading, adding classroom libraries, adding teacher's aides to help with the reading program, or increasing the emphasis on teaching higher-level reading/thinking skills.

Each of these suggestions for improvement can be recast into evaluation questions such as, Should we increase the time devoted to the teaching of reading? Obviously, grouping and organizing the list of suggestions will shorten it, as many questions will overlap. Refining the list should be carried out by the steering committee. After a final list of potential questions has been developed, it can be sent to teachers and administrators, who can be asked to comment on and prioritize its items.

This process emphasizes the importance of teachers, administrators, and parents having a strong voice in selecting the list of evaluation questions and describing the potential courses of action. It should not be expected that "what to do" will somehow grow automatically out of the evaluation. Evaluation can provide information for choosing a particular course of action, and the evaluation may provoke people to think about alternatives; however, it cannot conclude that a certain action should be taken if the alternatives are not part of the decision-making process.

Questions Should Be Flexible

Finally, it should be remembered that a good evaluation is one that is responsive to the needs of those involved with the program. To be responsive, an evaluation must be flexible. Flexibility must be extended to the questions that form the focus of the evaluation, permitting additional considerations to emerge as the evaluation is undertaken, other decisions to be clarified by information that is collected, and the prioritizing of issues to be changed as needed.

Also, there must be flexibility as to when answers to the evaluation questions are provided. The evaluation process rarely results in all courses of action being chosen and all decisions being made all at once, at the end. Some decisions may be made early in the process because adequate information may have been collected at that point. Others may require more information.

THE WORK OF THE EVALUATION COMMITTEE

Planning and carrying out the evaluation is the responsibility of the evaluation committee. Since decision making is the key to the evaluation process, it must be clear who the decision makers are. Moreover, a successful evaluation is one that is open and public. The effort should not be carried out privately by an evaluator who assumes the position of an all-knowing investigator.

In order to develop an open and public evaluation, it is necessary to establish an evaluation committee that includes representatives from all groups concerned with the school district reading program, including teachers, administrators, parents, librarians, and board members. Each person should be a respected member of the school community and have the ability to communicate and the willingness to listen, rather than just talk. Special expertise in evaluation methodology, testing, and measurement are not necessary; however, the committee needs to know where to get such expert help when it is needed.

The evaluation committee has four major functions:

1. Determining the issues and questions that will focus the evaluation
2. Ascertaining the kinds of information needed for arriving at decisions
3. Organizing and assimilating the collected information
4. Reporting information to the appropriate decision makers

As the planning for the evaluation gets under way, committee members' names should be made public. The initial announcement should also explain the decision-making focus of the evaluation and encourage people to contact the committee to learn more about the process. Moreover, people should feel free to contact committee members to discuss the concerns they feel should be the focus for the evaluation.

Collecting and Selecting Evaluation Questions

A previous section discussed the determination of the structure of a good evaluation question. There are no specific guidelines, however, as to which issues should be the particular focus of an evaluation in any given year. It may be that the committee will decide to select those questions that seem of most concern to the greatest number of people, or they may decide to focus on considerations that pose the possibility of implementation. Regardless of the criteria the committee uses to select the final questions that will become the focus of the evaluation, the process must be open; everyone involved must recognize that their concerns are being considered.

It is also often the case that all the important questions are not known prior to the information-gathering stage of evaluation. The known issues serve as the initial focus, but, as the evaluation evolves, the need to address other questions may become obvious. Evaluation conducted with a focus on issues that are stated before the evaluation begins is referred to as *preordinate evaluation*. When it focuses on decisions that evolve as the evaluation progresses, it is referred to as *responsive evaluation* (Farr & Wolf, 1974). Both types are legitimate and useful (Stufflebeam, 1983).

Determining Information Needs

When the final list of questions that will form the initial focus of the evaluation has been determined, it should be made public, along with a request for information that might help to answer them. In addition to soliciting information from the school staff in general, the evaluation committee should, at this point, consult with school staff experts in reading curriculum and evaluation/measurement. Their special knowledge about the reading curriculum and about the collection of information (including information that may already be available) will be critical.

The committee must also consult with those who are ultimately responsible for implementing the various decisions, to determine what information they feel is essential to making good decisions. From this list of suggestions, the committee can begin to determine the specific information that can be collected efficiently and considered reliable and valid. Quite often it will be the case that the same information needed for addressing one question will be useful for another.

Because the questions that focus the evaluation will be concerned with improving the program's activities, it is natural that both process and product information will need to be collected (Farr & Wolf, 1984). Process information has to do with those things that are going on in a program, including the time devoted to teaching reading, the use of various teaching methods, and the availability of a variety of reading materials. Product information has to do with the outcomes of instruction, both intended and unintended.

In recent years, a misunderstanding has evolved that there are two different kinds of evaluation, process and product, each of which calls for the collection of different kinds of information (Stufflebeam, 1983).

Hence, product evaluation (or summative evaluation) has come to be seen as the final or definitive program evaluation, the one that determines the value or worth of a program. Its conduct has been typified by the use of norm-referenced tests and a final report to a funding agency or a superintendent.

Process evaluation (or formative evaluation) has been defined as ongoing evaluation that is used to identify problems with program activities and to change them. Thus, it is characterized by the collection of descriptions of program activities and the analysis of program problems, sometimes with little attention given to program outcomes. Process evaluation thus results in reports to program implementors, regarding possible program changes.

We think it is incorrect to conceive of process and product as two different kinds of evaluation. The superintendent is surely interested in the factors that make the program function successfully (process), and those who are implementing the program are concerned with gathering information about students' reading achievements (product). When we separate product from process, we tear interdependent program components apart. Evaluation must link process to product; it must inform decision makers about the processes that result in a better program. In short, if evaluation is to lead to systematic program improvement, it must consider all aspects of instruction, as well as include a broader consideration of student outcome variables, of which student achievement might be only one dimension. For example, it is as important to learn about students' reading habits, attitudes about reading, and use of reading to solve problems as it is to determine how well students read.

Collecting and Summarizing Information

Collecting specific information should be the shared task of the committee and the school specialists assigned to these tasks. For example, the committee may want to take on the task of interviewing teachers to gather certain kinds of information. On the other hand, the committee may want to leave the design and implementation of a community questionnaire to staff members with expertise in that field. As information is collected, it should be returned to the committee for review and consideration. The committee should be responsible for summarizing the information.

The summary developed by the committee should include a restatement of each question that formed the basis for the evaluation. After each question the sources of information and the results should be listed. The summary should not obfuscate any information. The range of viewpoints represented in the data must be reflected as must be the frequency of each viewpoint. The summary is by necessity a reduction of information, but the summary should be written so that it reflects as completely as possible the full range of information.

Reporting to Decision Makers

The committee should make its final data available in coherent form to the appropriate decision makers. It is *not* the task of the evaluation committee to make decisions. Each question and its corresponding data will be placed in the hands of some authorized person or group.

Reporting information must be done tactfully. The evaluation committee must not appear to be providing a report that dictates decisions to be made. That is the province of the decision maker. On the other hand the evaluation committee does have the responsibility to provide decision makers with complete information for each issue.

The evaluation committee must also consider the confidentiality of the information that was collected. Some of the information the evaluation committee will have received will be confidential and the sources of that information should not be part of the evaluation report. Moreover, the evaluation committee should carefully consider the harm that some of the information may cause. Because of this concern, the evaluation committee may wish to make some of the information available to decision makers in a confidential addendum to the full report.

COLLECTING INFORMATION FOR
VARIOUS EVALUATION QUESTIONS

The primary concern in collecting information is that it relate specifically to the questions that are the focus of the evaluation. Success is likely when those who are providing the information understand that

- It will be used for making decisions to improve the reading program.
- It will not be used to judge the staff or the faculty.
- It is to be as closely related to what is actually happening in the program as it can be.
- If it concerns individuals, it will be kept confidential, as the focus is on program improvement.

Beyond these basic principles, the information must be valid and reliable and must be collected efficiently. This sounds like a tall order, but the issues are fairly straightforward.

- *Validity is truthfulness.* If the data are to be true, they must be collected from a variety of viewpoints and through a variety of means, and they must reflect as accurately as possible the real behaviors or information needed for making a decision.
- *Reliability is consistency.* Information is generally more consistent if we have more of it and if it is collected under a variety of conditions, rather than just one.
- *Efficiency* means that the information must not be more difficult to collect than its value to decision making.

The application of these three criteria to the data-collection process for two examples follows.

Example 1

Evaluation Question.   Do content-area teachers have the skills and knowledge to help students learn to apply reading skills in a variety of contexts?

Information Needed.   (1) A list of skills considered essential to teaching content-area reading in a variety of contexts; (2) a list of actual skills of classroom teachers in the school, as they go about teaching content-area subjects.

How To Collect.   A listing of the skills needed for teaching content-area reading could be collected from reviewing professional publications, from interviewing classroom teachers and reading specialists, and from reviewing the content-area textbooks. Once the list of skills has been assembled, teachers' use of the skills could be determined by (1) developing a checklist of the skills and asking teachers to evaluate themselves in relation to the skills, (2) conducting follow-up interviews with a selected sample of teachers, (3) developing an observation checklist so that some teachers could observe each other and discuss which content-area skills they did and did not observe teachers using. It is also possible to develop a short test for teachers and ask questions about certain content-area teaching skills, such as the use of study techniques and story maps.

The list of data-collection approaches is only suggestive and should not necessarily be considered the best approaches that could be devised. However, for the data to be as valid as possible, at least two or three data-collection procedures should be used. Reliability will be enhanced if the data are collected at different times and under differing conditions. For example, it would not be wise to collect all of the interview data on the same day, as that may be a day when, for example, teachers are upset because of a decision by the board regarding teacher salaries.

Data collection should also be efficient. A particular school system may not be at a stage where teachers feel comfortable observing in each others' classrooms. Or, the development of a test may be too time-consuming to make that an efficient data-collection procedure.

Example 2

Evaluation Question.   Do students have adequate time each day just to read, so they can apply and develop their reading?

Information Needed.   (1) How much time per day is considered adequate; (2) amount of reading time students have during the day to engage in some kind of sustained reading, regardless of whether or not they are assigned this time to read or they find time in their schedule.

How to Collect.   Reading specialists, classroom teachers, and professional publications can be consulted regarding the recommended amount of time per day. Students could keep reading logs regarding the amount of time they spend reading in and out of school each day; this could be linked to a math project on record keeping and charting; a random sample of the students could be interviewed about their reading; teachers could make systematic observations of certain randomly selected students, to determine how much time they spend reading during certain class periods; questionnaires could be developed to distribute to students so they could list the number of different selections and times they read during the day.

In all of the data collection for this particular question, it would be important to determine both whether the students have the time and whether they choose to use it for reading, as well as if they just do not have the time. If it is determined that they have the time but don't read, then another question will emerge, namely, What needs to be done to alter the program so that students use the time they have for reading during the school day?

REPORTING THE FINAL RECOMMENDATIONS OF
THE DECISION MAKERS

The guidelines for reporting the final results of the evaluation are straightforward. First, the results should be presented in a format that describes the questions that the evaluation sought to answer, the data that were collected to inform the decision, and the decisions or recommendations that were made.

Thus, the decision-makers' report might state that the school district was interested in deciding whether or not adequate time was provided during the school day for students to read. The information that was collected indicated that students don't often read during the day. The report may suggest that the reasons seem to be related to classroom organization and the fact that teachers believe that "just reading" is not an appropriate use of class time. The report might recommend that the school engage in a program to help teachers understand the importance of giving students class time to increase their reading skills through independent reading. Classrooms could also be made more conducive to reading by providing a more relaxed environment.

The primary audience to be served by the decision-makers' report is, of course, the person or group responsible for implementing a particular decision. Beyond that audience, others should be informed of the decision and its implementation; however, they do not need to be informed of all of the details of the evaluation process itself.

One of the major problems in most evaluations is that information is collected without specific questions to be answered. That information then gets used inappropriately, to answer questions for which its use is neither valid nor reliable (Madaus, 1983). That situation can be avoided in the kind of evaluation we have described in this chapter by always relating information to the specific use for which it was intended, and by never releasing information without including the context of its intended use.

EVALUATION PROCESS CASE HISTORY

The decision-making evaluation process described in this chapter was carried out with an elementary school district in the Midwest. The evaluation came about because everyone in the district was dissatisfied with the traditional evaluation system that had been used in the school district for a number of years. Board of education members, administrators, and teachers had felt for some time that their "test-only" evaluations had not provided adequate information for improving the school district reading program.

The following description is a brief overview of what happened in a two-year decision-making evaluation that involved almost every teacher, administrator, and board member in the district, at some point in the process. The stages in the process included determining the goals for the evaluation, determining the information to be collected, assigning specific tasks to various people, and finally evaluating the information and determining future directions for the reading program.

Goals for the Evaluation

The goals for the evaluation evolved from a series of discussions, meetings, interviews, and reviews of various information. A steering committee of twelve people—including a board member, several administrators, teachers, and parents—actually directed this phase of the process. Effort was made to allow everyone to supply the committee with information and to participate in focusing the evaluation.

An initial task for the committee was to develop a working definition of exactly what was meant by "the reading program." The committee felt that they needed to have a clear focus on what they were trying to understand. Without such a basis, the formulation of questions aimed at improving the reading program would have been impossible.

After considerable effort the committee established the following major goal for the evaluation: The evaluation is to determine the degree to which a comprehensive reading program is being provided to meet the needs of all students and to determine what modifications should be made to improve the program. More specifically, the evaluation is designed around four decisions [evaluation questions] which are sub-topics for the overall goal:

1. Do any modifications need to be made so the district will have a comprehensive reading program?
2. Does the professional staff have the skills and knowledge to implement a comprehensive reading program?
3. Are sufficient and appropriate materials available to implement a comprehensive reading program?
4. Should greater emphasis be placed on student achievement of the four major goals of the district reading program? These goals are that students will:
   understand what has been read;
   read orally for specific purposes;
   obtain and use information gained from reading; and
   use reading as part of everyday activities.

Information to Be Collected

After the four evaluation questions had been determined, the steering committee began to consider the kinds of information that needed to be collected to answer them. The criteria for this process included the traditional factors of reliability and validity; however, the committee also wanted to collect information that was comprehensive and open-ended and would be acceptable to the school community.

It would be impossible in this brief review to describe completely all of the information that was collected for each of the four issues, but the following list of strategies gives some idea of the scope of the data collection:

- Interviews with students, parents, teachers, and administrators
- Questionnaire studies with selected groups
- Observations of classroom instruction by district teachers and by educators from outside the district
- Interviews with students as they visited the school and the community library
- Interviews with students as they left school each day, to determine the kinds of reading materials they were taking home to read; interviews with students about what they did read outside of school
- Analyses of classroom and school libraries
- Reviews of the instructional materials available — and used — to teach reading
- Visits to other school districts to learn about alternative reading programs

The information was, of course, not collected from every teacher, parent, or student. Random selection procedures were used and implemented when it was not feasible to collect information from everyone in a particular group. The information was always collected with a clear focus on the evaluation question that it was to serve. When the information revealed the need for related information, that was added to the data collection.

Everyone in the school and community was informed about the evaluation and its goals and was encouraged to submit any information that they felt might be helpful in making a decision. The focus on the four evaluation questions kept attention from shifting to the issue of determining the worth of the reading program, and kept it solidly on determining what was needed in order to make it better. This emphasis was the key to its success, for, had there been a focus on judgment, there would have been little openness among the various groups who provided sensitive information.

Assignment of Tasks

In assigning data-collection tasks, the committee made a review of who knew most about a certain area and then determined if that person(s) could collect the information in a reliable and valid manner. Often the steering committee decided to collect the same information in two or more different ways; for example, using classroom observations, interviews, and questionnaires to learn about areas in which teachers felt they did not have the skills to carry out a good reading program. The committee felt not only that multiple data collection increased the validity and reliability of the data, but that more information provided a broader and more in-depth understanding of particular issues.

Evaluating the Information and Making Decisions

The actual decision-making process was easier than anyone had thought it would be when the evaluation started. At the beginning, there was a concern that the evaluation would end up blaming the lack of an adequate reading program on the administration, for lack of leadership, or on the teachers, for lack of teaching skills, or on the board and community, for not supplying adequate resources. That never happened. The focus on action-oriented decisions that could make the program better seemed to overcome the emphasis on placing blame. Indeed, few people asked at the end of the evaluation whether the school district had a "good" reading program. Almost everyone was too interested in moving ahead, using the information that had been collected. One teacher stated it rather succinctly: "I don't know for sure how good we are, but I do know that any group of people that takes the time and effort that we have to learn how to improve is good — and is going to be better."

The evaluation did result in several important decisions and a great deal of action. The general results included the establishment of inservice programs to help teachers learn more about two areas: (1) the teaching of word recognition skills in context and (2) the informal diagnosis of reading. The teachers and administrators also determined that the district reading program was too narrowly conceived as just a single class period during the day. Efforts were started to extend the teaching of reading throughout the school day. The school library materials were found to be adequate, but they were not readily accessible to the students for independent reading; therefore, classroom libraries were established. Finally, a parents' reading program was established, to get the total community more involved in supporting reading outside of school.

SUMMARY

In this chapter we presented a framework that school administrators can use to plan and conduct evaluations of district reading programs. The evaluation process we described is based on two assumptions: first, that the focus of a reading program evaluation should be the improvement of instruction and, second, that the way to maintain that focus is through the formulation of clear and explicit questions to be answered. We believe that the implementation of this framework will lead to more meaningful evaluations and ultimately to more effective reading programs.

REFERENCES

Farr, R., & Carey, R. F. (1986). *Reading: What can be measured* (2nd ed.). Newark, DE: International Reading Association.

Farr, R., & Wolf, R. L. (1974). *A plan for the development of preordinate and responsive evaluation to study the USMES curriculum project.* Bloomington, IN: Division of Teacher Education, Indiana University.

Farr, R., & Wolf, R. L. (1984). Evaluation and secondary reading programs. In A. Purves & O. Niles (Eds.), *Becoming readers in a complex society* (pp. 271–292). Chicago: University of Chicago Press.

Madaus, G. F. (1983, April). *Test scores: What do they really mean in educational policy?* Address presented to the National Consortium on Testing, Washington, DC.

Scriven, M. (1973). Goal free evaluation. In E. R. House (Ed.), *School evaluation: The politics and the process* (pp. 319–328). Berkeley, CA: McCutchan.

Stufflebeam, D. L. (1983). The CIPP model for program evaluation. In G. F. Madaus, M. Scriven, & D. L. Stufflebeam (Eds.), *Evaluation models: Viewpoints in educational and human services evaluation* (pp. 149–163). Boston: Kluwer-Nijoff.

Stufflebeam, D. L., Foley, W. J., Gephart, W. J., Guba, E. G., Hammond, R. L., Merriman, H. O., & Provus, M. M. (1971). *Educational evaluation and decision making.* Itasca, IL: E. E. Peacock.

Tyler, R. W., & White, S. H. (1979). *Testing, teaching, and learning.* Washington, DC: U.S. Department of Health, Education and Welfare and National Institute of Education.

11 Community Outreach

ANTHONY D. FREDERICKS
York College

School personnel seeking to establish effective reading programs need to be cognizant of many factors that impact on the development and maintenance of those programs. Current research suggests that dynamic reading programs emanate from strong leadership within the school as well as from sincere efforts by school personnel to reach out and involve all members of the family and community (Ervin, 1982; Fredericks & Taylor, 1985; Rich, Van Dien, & Mattox, 1979). In fact, reading programs that seek to establish a strong and positive partnership with parents and other community members are those that promote reading as more than just a school-related subject; rather, students are provided with innumerable opportunities to make reading a very natural part of their everyday lifestyles.

BACKGROUND ON COMMUNITY OUTREACH

The need to involve all family members in scholastic affairs is sup-ported by both logic and a growing body of research that underscores the impact parents and others have on children's literacy development (Gor-don, 1979; Mason & Au, 1986; Vukelich, 1984). While involving the entire family in a school's reading program would seem to be a naturally valuable extension of that program, past practices have not always subscribed to this notion. During the early part of this century, parents were admonished not to get involved in the scholastic affairs of their offspring. Many school personnel felt that the education of students should be left entirely to those formally trained to undertake such a task. In a sense, parents were system-atically excluded from any and all educational matters (Vukelich, 1984). Some educators believed that parents would create unneeded conflict for youngsters by imposing inappropriate values or using unsophisticated "teaching" methods. Unfortunately, this isolationist policy persisted for many years, creating a "we-versus-them" attitude that, in many cases, threatened the fundamental tenets of American education.

Fortunately, the accumulation of a significant body of data in recent years has resulted in some rethinking for many school personnel. Gordon (1979), in reviewing eighteen studies dealing with the impact of the family on children's learning, concluded that "programs dealing directly with the family . . . affect in a positive fashion the learning and development of the child" (p. 16). This thesis is further supported by the successful outreach programs of the Home and School Institute and their "nondeficit" ap-proach to family participation in the education of children (Rich et al., 1979). Located at Washington, DC, the Home and School Institute's philos-ophy subscribes to the notion that "(1) home environments, no matter how poor, are a citadel of care and concern for children; (2) all parents intrinsi-cally possess the abilities to help their child succeed in school; and (3) schools should start with what the family has instead of worrying about what it doesn't have" (p. 32). We also know that, when parents are provid-ed with significant opportunities to contribute to the overall reading devel-opment of their children, positive reading achievement can result (Burgess, 1982; Henderson, 1981; Siders & Sledjeski, 1978).

URBAN–SUBURBAN DIFFERENCES

Although many schools are utilizing the power of parent participation within and throughout their reading programs, large numbers lack suffi-cient projects, most noticeably those in urban or economically deprived neighborhoods. Lightfoot (1978) has noted that poor families are "excluded from life inside schools, and the extent of their participation reflects their social class, race, and ethnicity" (p. 38). She goes on to state that, for too many economically deprived families, the school exists as a "frightening monolith, not only in the sense that the power of knowledge makes them feel inadequate . . . but because every bit of communication from the school comes as a negative appraisal of their child, a destructive comment about their lives" (Lightfoot, 1978, p. 36). Jenkins (1981) suggests that this distancing of poor families from the doors of the school is then perceived by educators to be a lack of parental interest—a factor that may contribute to the tacit assumption that poor families should not or cannot participate in school activities. This attitude is substantiated, in part, by data gathered from 3,698 elementary teachers in Maryland, which indicated that teachers frequently perceive less-educated parents as unable or unwilling to carry out activities related to children's schoolwork at home (Becker & Epstein, 1982).

There are significant differences between suburban schools, which are typified by highly involved community outreach efforts and high levels of student achievement, and urban schools, typically characterized by low levels of participation and similarly low levels of achievement. These facts represent a considerable challenge for educators. In fact, many urban administrators are realizing that they may be neglecting a potent force for their reading program if they systematically exclude parents and the community at large. To be sure, urban parents, beset by a host of social and economic restraints, compounded by years of benign neglect, offer urban reading supervisors challenges not faced by their suburban counterparts. What surfaces, therefore, is the need for an interactive model that respects the pressures of urban life and attempts to enjoin parents in supportive roles throughout their youngster's reading growth.

One model designed by Edwards (1987) specifically to facilitate communication between teachers and diverse parent populations, has undergone rigorous evaluation in several inner-city schools. Initiated by the classroom teacher, this model provides for the many needs extant in a highly diverse classroom population. First, the teacher analyzes a child's reading needs, through either classroom performance or standardized tests. The teacher then determines individual parent reading involvement capabilities, which are assessed through survey questionnaires, informal needs assessment, personal interviews, telephone calls, and home visits by a home/school coordinator, a teacher's aide, Chapter 1 personnel, or a community helper. With the child's reading needs as a focus, the teacher then makes a judgment as to whether or not the parent is able to assist.

If the parent is able to participate actively, the teacher then provides strategies for helping the parent assist the child. These can include, but are not limited to, parent/teacher conferences, parent workshops, reading skills modeling for parents, and communications with parents (e.g., newsletters, calls, notes). Crucial to each step is the fact that the teacher praises the parent for assisting the child.

If the parent is unable to assist, the teacher informs the parent of others who can offer assistance, including Chapter 1 parents, tutors, and school volunteers. The teacher provides the parent with continuous updates on the child's reading progress and attempts to solicit parental feedback on efforts to improve the child's reading skills. Periodically, the teacher encourages the parent to continue in supporting the child's reading program.

What distinguishes this model is that all parents, irrespective of economic or social constraints, can share in the reading program. Parent involvement is not based on ability to assist directly; rather, it involves a concerted attempt to keep parents actively engaged in and informed of their child's reading progress. Parents are not penalized for noninvolvement; rather they are provided with a means of supporting their child's academic achievement continuously throughout the year. This is in contrast to traditional urban programs, which assume an all-or-nothing attitude concerning parents' desires to contribute to the reading curriculum. Suffice it to say, Edwards's (1987) model holds the promise of narrowing the gap between the participatory practices traditionally associated with suburban schools and the exclusionary beliefs that typify many urban schools.

It also seems that the perceptions concerning the urban poor and their involvement in the reading program reflect (1) ineffective administrative leadership, (2) the entrenchment of class bias and racism in the public schools, and (3) a bureaucratic hierarchy that excludes parents (Jenkins, 1981). While these factors are particularly significant for urban schools, they may also "bubble up" to suburban and rural schools, too, creating a perception in the minds of some school personnel that parent and community involvement is more a panacea than a process.

In addressing the issue of involving parents and other community members in the dynamics of the classroom or school reading program, two questions surface: What materials, models, and methods seem to be most effective in stimulating and maintaining parent participation? What factors are important in insuring the success of those outreach efforts? These issues will be the focus of the remainder of this chapter.

EFFECTIVE STRATEGIES

Perhaps the most significant concern of administrators and reading supervisors deals with the methods and models proven effective in stimulating, promoting, and maintaining parent and community involvement.

This section will address those methods educators have traditionally used, the data educators need to establish a viable home/school connection, and an effective model that insures positive parent participation.

Assessing Traditional Methods

Over the years teachers have communicated with parents through a few established and universal methods. Becker and Epstein (1982) reported that almost 95 percent of the 3,698 teachers in their survey typically engaged in three types of parent contacts: sending notices home, talking with parents during open-school evenings, and making occasional telephone calls. It also appears that this pattern of interaction is present in almost every school across the country. Vukelich (1984) has reported other media that teachers employ to establish an open dialogue with parents concerning their children's reading growth. Included in her list are booklets and handbooks, brochures or pamphlets, activity sheets, progress letters, notes and conferences, reading and shopping lists, courses and workshops, "calendars" of activities, and home learning kits. What is apparent in reviewing these parental contact methods is the fact that educators have a multiplicity of ways to reach out to parents and involve them in the dynamics of the reading program.

Just as the methods of sharing are diverse, so too, are the types of information typically disseminated to parents. Vukelich's (1984) study, which involved a search of thirty-seven references on parent involvement in reading, listed the following suggestions as those most frequently made to parents (listed in order of frequency): read to your child, be a good literate model, provide books and magazines for your child to read, build a reading atmosphere at home, talk and listen to your child, exemplify a positive attitude toward reading, provide a variety of experiences for your child, read environmental signs, provide children with paper and pencil, be aware of your child's interests, and point out similarities and differences in the environment. Various other kinds of information were shared with parents, but less frequently. It is interesting to note that, while most educators would logically support these suggestions for parents, only one — "read to your child" — has been supported by any empirical research data (Vukelich, 1984).

Gathering Needed Information

Although we are aware of a plethora of ways to communicate with parents and the types of information traditionally suggested to parents, one major concern still remains: What kinds of information do educators need in order to plan, develop, and implement an effective outreach program? A study conducted among seventy-five reading educators (Freder-icks & Taylor, 1984–1985) found that teachers and administrators are pri-marily interested in learning about (1) examples of materials for parent use, (2) parent participation in the home, (3) various models of parent involvement, and (4) methods of involving "absentee" parents. This study also found that most reading professionals are aware of the variety of ideas, suggestions, and information that could be shared with parents, but need an operational framework upon which to build a successful outreach pro-gram. While most educators have had little or no formal training in how to work with parents, they do, for the most part, have an intuitive knowledge of some communication methods and materials. What is lacking from their repertoire, however, is a systematic and easy-to-use network that facilitates outreach efforts and promotes family involvement as a positive extension of the school reading program.

Creating a New Model

Unfortunately, there appears to be a dearth of available models for those seeking to establish successful family participation programs. Edwards's (1987) two-phase model and Gordon's (1979) four-tiered model are two of the few that offer educators structures to use in engaging parents in their children's learning. I have been involved in the design of a cyclical paradigm which provides an efficient and workable model for engaging parents in their youngsters' reading development (Fredericks & Taylor, 1985). We point out that most parent involvement programs in reading suffer because sufficient care was not taken in setting up a plan of action that takes into account community types, resources, needs, or long-term projections. Our model, known as the Parent Reading Engagement Profile (PREP), provides a methodical approach to designing a successful involve-ment project. The four stages of the PREP model are as follows:

1. Needs assessment
2. Planning
3. Program implementation
4. Evaluation

We will discuss each in turn.

Needs Assessment.   Most outreach programs fail because parental needs were not assessed prior to initiating the project. In other words, there is an overwhelming necessity for educators to determine parental desires within and throughout a reading program. Quite often, educators make the mistake of assuming that they know what parents need, instead of taking time to assess their needs and develop an appropriate program (Gardner & O'Loughlin-Snyder, 1981). Outreach efforts risk failure whenever they are predicated on ease of delivery rather than assessed needs. Parents will be more willing to participate in an outreach program when they know that the project is addressing their identified needs, more so than when the program is being set up at the convenience of the school or teachers.

PREP needs assessment procedures typically take two forms — formal and informal. Included within the formal method are questionnaires, attitude scales, checklists, inventories, and self-evaluative scales. Informal methods can include individual conferences, small-group discussions, telephone conferences, brainstorming sessions, and informal interviews (Fredericks & Taylor, 1985). It is crucial that a variety of assessment methods be utilized so that appropriate opportunities exist for parents and the community members to voice their opinions.

Planning.   After parental needs have been assessed, it is vitally important that both educators and parents take sufficient time to analyze the results. In this way, necessary program goals can be established. While many concerns usually surface through the needs assessment procedure, any outreach effort must be careful to address only a limited number of needs, rather than tackle too many. The PREP model (Fredericks & Taylor, 1985) suggests that the planning group consider the following sequence of activities:

1. Determine a few areas of greatest need.
2. Establish priorities for those needs.
3. Analyze the highest-ranked needs.
4. Project a long-range plan (establish goals).
5. Brainstorm for action.
6. Outline a plan of action.
7. Develop details for the plan of action.
8. Develop a timeline.

Program Implementation.   Putting a program or project into place requires coordination of time and personnel tasks. While many outreach efforts may be simple in design, focusing on one class over a brief period of time, others may involve many elements of the school throughout the school year. Whatever programs are developed to reach into the community, it is vitally important that the individuals involved (educators, parents, students) all understand their roles and responsibilities. A program cannot exist on the whims or desires of a single individual; rather, it must be predicated on the combined efforts of all concerned.

Also, in timing the outreach program, administrators must consider the hectic schedules of both parents and teachers. In short, programs need to be built so that parents and teachers have a multiplicity of options by which to participate, in line with schedules that are constantly changing and evolving. Such decisions are not always easy but demand that a flexible schedule of activities be designed to allow for the ebb and flow of time responsibilities for parents, educators, and students. We (Fredericks & Taylor, 1985) note, in using the PREP model, that implementation procedures must also insure that both parents and educators are *aware* of program benefits, are *motivated* to participate in the project, are *involved* throughout the duration of the proposed activities, and are *recognized* for their efforts to participate in and promote the program. With teacher and parent schedules often oversubscribed, it becomes necessary for the planning team to consider a multitude of scheduling options that maintain and preserve the program throughout its projected timeline.

Evaluation. Designing and implementing a parent involvement project is one thing; knowing whether the project has made an impact on its intended audience is quite another. Unfortunately, some outreach efforts are developed with the simple goal of "making it to the end." The PREP model advises the effective administrator or reading supervisor to collect evaluative data that can lead to modifications or revisions during the course of the project and/or at its conclusion. This data collection must be both systematic and comprehensive (Williams, Kahn, & Coyle, 1981), so that intelligent decisions can be made as a project is in progress or is being considered for a "second round." As in the needs assessment stage of this model a variety of evaluation techniques can be implemented (both formal and informal) which will provide the needed information. Of course, evaluation becomes particularly useful whenever it is keyed to the program goals established during the planning phase.

In sum, the PREP model provides a workable framework for any reading supervisor or administrator interested in soliciting parent support and participation within the school or district reading program. Its influence lies in the fact that it underscores the cooperative effort needed by both educators and community members to work together for the benefit of all students. Of course, as a model, PREP does allow for necessary modifications according to the dynamics of individual schools or communities. Suffice it to say, however, that working with parents is not a hit-or-miss proposition; rather, it requires an investment of time, talent, and energy on the part of many individuals, in order to guarantee success.

GUIDELINES FOR SUCCESS AND SOME SUGGESTED PROJECTS

Without question, there is a wide diversity of outreach projects and programs that can be incorporated into the reading curriculum. The range of community outreach efforts is limited only by imagination and the dynamics of a specific community. Yet, regardless of the type of outreach program planned by administrators and/or reading supervisors, there are several guidelines against which a proposed project should be measured, in terms of its potential impact. These guidelines (Rasinski & Fredericks, 1988), generated from an exhaustive survey of successful outreach projects, offer reading educators some practical considerations in planning effective parent/community involvement efforts. Included with each of the following guidelines are some suggested parent involvement possibilities for the classroom, school, or district. These ideas are designed not only to foster positive reading achievement but also to provide rational and realistic learning opportunities for students, within the context of parent/child interactions.

1. *Parents and children must have regular daily opportunities to share, discuss, and read together.*
Establish "Reading Contracts" with school families. Encourage families to read together on a regular basis every day. Ask parents to sign a contract that pledges them to make this a regular family practice. Special calendars can be prepared and distributed so that parents can check off appropriate reading times for all family members. Families who read together for a specified number of minutes each month can be awarded special certificates obtained from a local teacher supply store.

Community and neighborhood newspapers are always on the lookout for newsworthy items to put into their pages. Consider drafting a regular column on tips and ideas parents can use in promoting the reading habit at home. This space can also be used to describe literacy-related events happening at school or list recommended children's books.

2. *Purposeful activities need to be at the heart of the program.*
Children must be able to understand the relevance of reading-related activities (reading recipes, assembling a model, and so on) to their own growth as readers.

Develop and design a series of orientation programs for parents new to the school or district. It would be valuable to develop a slide program, a series of brochures, family guides, or other appropriate orientation materials to assist new families in learning as much as they can about the purposeful activities in the reading curriculum.

Work with a group of parents to prepare a notebook of vacation home/community activities. Games, reading activities, places to visit, and sites to see in the community could all be included. These notebooks could be distributed to all families prior to a vacation period, especially summer.

3. *Children must be provided with regular opportunities to interact with good literature and well-written stories.*
Establish a lending library of resource materials and books for parents to check out and utilize at home. These materials can be purchased with school funds or by the local home and school organization. Also, include a selection of educational games and activities for families to check out.

Periodically provide parents with various lists of recommended books. Work with the school librarian in distributing lists such as "The Supervisor's Hot Hits" throughout the year. Consider disseminating a list of books on child-rearing practices, as well as those containing reading-related activities. If possible, plan a few "share-and-discuss" sessions with groups of parents to talk over selected books.

Promulgate the benefits of public library membership to all families. Plan to work closely with the local public library to share information on the wealth of resources and information available to families in the community.

Ask parents and community people to list some of their favorite children's books, either those they read as children or those they are currently reading to their own children. Publish this list on a frequent basis and distribute it to all families.

4. *Projects should take into account not only specific needs of parents but the day-to-day needs of youngsters as well.*
Students' interests, hobbies, and free-time activities can be utilized in promoting the reading habit.

Distribute lists of recommended books to parents based on students' interests. Suggested readings on popular hobbies, arts and crafts projects, and playtime activities would be welcomed by parents. For example, families can be provided with book lists on how to create or practice a project or activity along with names of books covering important personalities or discoveries in those particular areas. Encouraging families to bring and/or share their experiences with other students would also be appropriate.

5. *An outreach program should not attempt to turn parents into surrogate teachers, but rather should promote and extend the natural relationship between parent and child.*
Parenthood is not the easiest of "jobs." It's one in which tolerance levels

may be low and frustration ever present. As such, any outreach effort must not place any undue pressure on parents, but rather should subscribe to the notion that parent/child interaction time should be unhurried, pleasant for all parties, and tolerant of everyone's feelings.

Set up an exhibit in the local shopping mall, church, or synagogue that includes photos of parents and children reading together, tips for parent participation, and other reading-related activities. Engage children in designing and creating these displays, including their ideas for sharing the reading experience with the entire community.

Ask parents to keep special diaries or scrapbooks of family-related reading activities. For example, include books they have read and stories discussed, as well as photos of family members reading together. These can then be brought to school by students for special sharing.

6. *Parents should be provided with a variety of opportunities to support and encourage their children's growth as readers.*
Utilize the local media in disseminating information on how parents can and should become involved in their school's reading program. Public service announcements distributed to local television and radio stations, letters to the editor of the local newspaper on the value of community and parent involvement in the reading curriculum, or a monthly advice column in the Sunday newspaper can all be effective.

Invite parents and community people to join a "reading curriculum council" to assist in the selection of new reading materials or to help establish guidelines and directions for the reading program throughout the year.

Establish an "open-door" policy with the community, early in the school year. Parents need to feel comfortable in visiting their children's classrooms or schools. Frequent invitations from the administrator or reading supervisor are an important way of transmitting this philosophy. Also, invite parents and other community leaders to demonstrate their hobbies or favorite reading materials to groups of children. This reinforces the idea that all community members can and should enjoy reading as a lifetime pursuit.

Involve the community in establishing homework policies and practices. Homework continues to be the most traditional method of contact between home and school. By encouraging parental input in the design of an all-inclusive homework policy, schools can insure the support they need.

7. *Although sufficient planning is the key to any effective program, informality needs to be the watchword.*
Offer parents and other community people a series of informal workshops

throughout the year which focus on various aspects of the reading curriculum. The workshops can address specific components of the school's reading program as well as ways and methods that parents can help support teachers' instructional efforts.

Establish regularly scheduled informal meetings with parents throughout the year. These can be set up as brown-bag lunches with the building principal, a meeting over tea and coffee with the reading supervisor, or a "bring-your-own-dessert" gathering in the evening. The intent of these meetings should not be to provide instruction, but rather to give educators and community people an opportunity to meet informally and discuss common goals and objectives. If these meetings can be held in a neutral location, such as a church or YMCA, parents will be more inclined to come, particularly if the meeting is planned for the convenience of their schedules.

8. *A spirit of shared responsibility needs to be built into any outreach effort.*
That is, parents and children need to have a plethora of opportunities to interact with one another, sharing ideas, thoughts, and a host of learning opportunities.

Gather a coalition of parents, community workers, local businesspeople, and educators together to write a series of newsletters on suggested parent involvement ideas. Plan to have these distributed throughout the community in workplaces, office buildings, factories, and community centers.

Don't neglect grandparents and other senior citizens. Many effective volunteer programs have relied on older people to provide innumerable reading services to the school. These can include listening to children read aloud, sharing childhood experiences with reading, and reading popular stories to classes of students.

Undoubtedly, no list can ever provide all the ideas or projects possible for a single community. It is hoped that a list such as this will stimulate the creation of programs that reach far beyond the classroom walls and encompass the needs and desires of a particular community. The ideas just presented are only suggestions; what is needed is the creative vision generated when parents, community members, and educators come together for the mutual benefit of all students. Only then will a project or set of projects validate the positive relationship necessary for effective reading development.

What these guidelines suggest is that effective and dynamic parent/ community outreach programs that support the reading curriculum are not one-shot endeavors. Typical public relations efforts such as "Meet the

Teacher Night," an open house, and the like have proven to be ineffective in terms of overall reading achievement of children (Gillum, 1977). What surfaces is the fact that effective programs — those that impact directly on student achievement and attitude formation — are those that are comprehensive, well planned, and long lasting (Henderson, 1981). Added to this list should be the following considerations (Rich et al., 1979):

1. Outreach efforts need to be a viable and vital part of the overall reading curriculum, not an "add-on" to appease certain factions.
2. Parents and community members must understand that their involvement will have a direct bearing on the overall progress of youngsters.
3. Any parent participation effort must have the support of the entire school community if it is to be both functional and sustaining.

CONCLUSION

To the administrator or supervisor seeking to develop or implement a truly effective reading program, parent and community involvement holds the promise of maximizing the school's efforts in literacy instruction. A viable partnership between home and school promotes reading as a pleasurable, lifetime activity enjoyed by all members of society. Engaging those outside the schoolroom walls in the reading curriculum can be a positive dimension to any youngster's development as a reader.

REFERENCES

Becker, H. J., & Epstein, J. L. (1982). Parent involvement: A survey of teacher practices. *Elementary School Journal, 83*, 85–102.

Burgess, J. (1982). The effects of a training program for parents of preschoolers on the children's school readiness. *Reading Improvement, 19*, 313–318.

Edwards, P. (1987). *Establishing a model for communicating with diverse parent populations*. Unpublished chart.

Ervin, J. (1982). *How to have a successful parents and reading program: A practical guide*. Boston: Allyn and Bacon.

Fredericks, A. D., & Taylor, D. (1984–1985). Parent involvement in reading: What educators want to know. *The Reading Instruction Journal, 31*(2), 17–20.

Fredericks, A. D., & Taylor, D. (1985). *Parent programs in reading: Guidelines for success*. Newark, DE: International Reading Association.

Gardner, E., & O'Loughlin-Snyder, C. (1981, May). *Parent participation: The foundation of a successful reading program*. Paper presented at the annual convention of the International Reading Association, New Orleans.

Gillum, R. M. (1977). *The effects of parent involvement on student achievement in three Michigan performance contracting programs*. Paper presented at the annual meeting of the American Educational Research Association, New York.

Gordon, I. J. (1979). The effects of parent involvement on schooling. In R. Brandt (Ed.), *Partners: Parents and schools* (pp. 4–25). Alexandria, VA: Association for Supervision and Curriculum Development.

Henderson, A. (1981). *Parent participation — student achievement: The evidence grows*. Columbia, MD: National Committee for Citizens in Education.

Jenkins, P. W. (1981). Building parent participation in urban schools. *Principal, 61*(2), 21–23.

Lightfoot, S. L. (1978). *Worlds apart: Relationships between families and schools*. New York: Basic Books.

Mason, J. M., & Au, K. (1986). *Reading instruction for today*. Glenview, IL: Scott, Foresman.

Rasinski, T. V., & Fredericks, A. D. (1988). School sharing literacy: Guiding principles and practices for parent involvement. *The Reading Teacher, 41*, 508–512.

Rich, D., Van Dien, J., & Mattox, B. (1979). Families as educators of their own children. In R. Brandt (Ed.), *Partners: Parents and schools* (pp. 26–40). Alexandria, VA: Association for Supervision and Curriculum Development.

Siders, M., & Sledjeski, S. (1978). *How to grow a happy reader: Report on a study of parental involvement as it relates to a child's reading skills* (Research Monograph No. 27). Gainesville, FL: Florida State University.

Vukelich, C. (1984). Parent's role in the reading process: A review of practical suggestions and ways to communicate with parents. *The Reading Teacher, 37*, 472–477.

Williams, R., Kahn, L., & Coyle, D. (1981). *Program improvement evaluation*. Durham, NC: NTS Research Corporation.

Part IV

INTERCONNECTIONS

The reading program should not stand alone. Rather, it should be linked to other school programs that are concerned with literacy. First and foremost, current research has established that reading and writing are both active, constructive processes; Chapter 12 shows how the teaching of reading and writing can be intertwined in the instructional program. Computers, our valuable new teaching resource and communication tool, should not be "taught" as a separate subject; Chapter 13 demonstrates how they can be integrated into the teaching of reading and writing.

The reading program must not be just for the developmentally "average" child; it must provide for all children, including those who speak differently and come from other cultures and those who operate at the extreme ends of the academic scale, from the slow learner to the intellectually gifted. Chapter 14 will help supervisors and administrators to deal with these special populations.

Last, the reading program must have as its ultimate goal the cultivation of lifetime readers who not only know how to read but who also seek out literature and informational reading to enrich their lives; this goal calls for close bonds between the reading program and library/ media centers. Chapter 15 will provide practical guidelines for the establishment of recreational reading programs. Because this part deals with these important links that must be made between and among reading and other school programs, we have titled it "Interconnections."

12 Writing in the Reading Program: The Process Approach

JOAN T. FEELEY
William Paterson College of New Jersey

Cathy A. Labate © 1988

Six-year-old Natasha puts the finishing touches on the draft of her first book. She draws a sign with a very definite message, "The door is loct." The book, entitled *Me and My Sister*, is about Tasha and her big sister, Tara. In it Tasha tells about the times she likes Tara and the times she doesn't, especially when Tara has friends over and puts *the sign* on the door. This six-page book, including dedication and about-the-author pages, is eventually typed out by her teacher, illustrated by Tasha, and published in their first-grade writing-as-process classroom.

Craig, who is in a third-grade writing-as-process classroom in a northern New Jersey suburb, wrote the following poem after much thinking, conferring, revising, and playing around with line arrangement:

A Parking Lot

A parking lot
    is like
a candy machine
a car
    goes in
        another
            comes out.
A gumball goes
    bobbling around
in the machine looking
    for the spot to get out.

As part of her study of Colonial America, second-grader Mitzi writes a letter to an imaginary seven-year-old living in the 1700s. She writes,

Dear Abigail,
    What do you do in school? Do they spank you if you are bad? What games do you play? What do you do at home?
    Please write me your answers.

                        Your friend in 1987,
                              Mitzi

Mitzi next uses the collection of trade books and texts on Colonial America to find the answers to her questions. Then she writes back, as Abigail, answering the questions.

Over the past decade, some exciting innovations have been taking place in the teaching of writing, and the effects are being carried over to the reading program. The three young writers in the real-life scenarios just presented are in classrooms in which writing and reading are taught as processes, through the use of whole, meaningful texts, rather than as a series of isolated skills taught in short, unrelated drill exercises.

The writing-as-process movement (Calkins, 1986; Graves, 1983; Murray, 1985; Zinsser, 1985) has spawned a cadre of teachers who are committed to having students write on a daily basis, read over their work with peers to revise for better communication, and, finally, edit carefully to produce a "publishable" piece for a specific audience. Writing in this process approach requires much reading and rereading of one's own writing and that of others. Process teachers quickly realize that writers don't grow in a vacuum; they need to be exposed to good literature and well-written expository texts in order to become better writers.

The writing-as-process movement has also led to the use of writing across all curriculum areas (Fulwiler, 1987; Young & Fulwiler, 1986); that is, teachers are encouraged to have students write to learn in all content areas. Again, increased writing generally leads to more reading as students read to become knowledgeable (Calkins, 1986) in self-selected content topics in social studies or science, like Mitzi in her study of Colonial America. In math, they write out problems for others to solve, thus becoming sensitive to reader/writer concerns. They write logs in order to track science experiments and journals to record their reactions to what they read in literature and social studies.

Applebee, Langer, and Mullis (1987), in a recent report for the National Assessment of Educational Progress (NAEP) entitled *Learning to Be Literate in America*, say that most children and young adults can read and write, with *surface understanding*, a range of materials appropriate for their age. But, only a small percentage can *reason effectively* about what they are reading and writing. On an encouraging note, however, the authors go on to say that, with more years of schooling, students' reading and writing performance levels, especially those that are at a surface level of understanding, will rise. Still, even with more schooling, the percentages of those who read at higher levels of thinking and write reasoned papers for a particular purpose remain small. The schools have a long way to go toward producing a fully literate society.

The current attention being given to reading/writing should positively affect general literacy levels, since students in process programs are encouraged to *think* about what they are reading and writing, keeping the focus on making sense and communicating through print. The purpose of this chapter is to describe the writing-as-process and writing-across-the-curriculum movements and then to suggest how administrators and supervisors can encourage their staff to join the movement, thus adding to the nation's growth in higher-level literacy.

A PROCESS APPROACH: WHAT IS IT?

In the 1970s, projects such as the Bay Area Writing Project (BAWP) in California (Camp, 1982) and Janet Emig's (1983) research in New Jersey brought about a new way of looking at how writers write and how to teach writing. Now termed the National Writing Project, James Moffett (1981a, 1981b) calls the resulting curriculum changes the most positive development in English education since the time of World War II. Prior to these changes, writing had been judged mainly by the end product and teaching had focused on helping students produce compositions relatively free of grammatical and mechanical errors. There had been much talk of "bleeding" papers, as teachers wielded the red pen to correct spelling, mechanics, and sentence structure. Many times the message had become lost in the pursuit for perfection in form.

The researchers of the past two decades who studied writers in action described writing as a recursive process of prewriting activities such as brainstorming, inner speech, and reading/reflecting; followed by drafting, reading, and revising; and concluding with editing to standard form. The implications for teaching writing became clear: Take the focus off the product and place it on the process; teaching writing by having students go through the process, writing frequently and getting feedback from teachers and peers, thus learning mechanics within the context of real writing endeavors.

The first impact came at the high school and college levels, as English instructors began to introduce journal writing, a kind of free response to readings, lectures, or everyday happenings that is not graded but usually responded to in marginal notes. Journal entries then became the source for topics to be developed more fully in a process approach to composing, proceeding from prewriting to finished piece. This approach began to replace the old formula of having students write on assigned topics, correcting their papers for mechanics, and having them write final drafts.

In the 1980s, the process approach has been brought to the elementary school level, largely through the research and practical applications of people like Don Graves (1983) at the University of New Hampshire and Lucy Calkins (1983, 1986) at Teachers College, Columbia University. Both have written veritable handbooks on how to implement writing as process in the elementary school. Their approaches stress having children write daily on important topics generated from their own lives. These compositions are kept in writing folders so that children can have ready access to works in progress. A workshop atmosphere, similar to one used by artists learning to paint or sculpt, is suggested for the writing period. Students compose from their own lists of topics, read their pieces to the teacher in a conference or to others in impromptu "peer" conferences, revise their work (adding, deleting, moving text around) based on its reception by readers or listeners, and then edit with teacher help if the work is to be "published."

Publication can mean many things, such as placing an article in a class collection or creating a separate, hand-printed, and illustrated bound book. What will be published remains the decision of the young writers. Usually they are asked to select one piece, from three or four pieces in progress, to work up into publishable form. Students begin to see themselves as authors and add about-the-author and dedication pages to their publications. Writing is celebrated when parents are invited to class to hear their children read their pieces aloud.

Writing across the curriculum was a natural outgrowth of writing as process, as English teachers in the secondary schools and colleges encouraged their colleagues to promote writing as a valuable approach to learning in all the content areas. Moffett (1981a) led the way with a handbook, *Active Voice: A Writing Program Across the Curriculum*. While Tchudi and Huerta (1983) wrote a resource for the middle school and junior high and Tchudi and Yates (1983) produced a guide for high school teachers, Young and Fulwiler (1986) compiled a book of readings useful for college instructors. Ways of bringing writing into every area of learning were offered. Content-area teachers were urged to have students write journals, logs, problems, explanations, interview findings, letters, editorials, how-to pieces, and a myriad of innovative composing activities related to their specific fields.

In the elementary school, process teachers soon found themselves using the workshop approach in the content areas as well as in language arts. Children wrote math problems for each other to solve, kept science logs and diaries, and researched specialty reports for social studies. Tchudi and Tchudi (1983) and Thaiss (1986) wrote books addressed to teachers at this level. From a forgotten child, writing has come rapidly to the forefront as a major component in the learning cycle.

THE READING/WRITING CONNECTION

While reading has always occupied a prominent place in the school curriculum, until recently writing has generally taken a back seat. In fact, Moffett (1981b) says that writing from grade one through graduate school has served mainly to test reading. In the elementary school, children have composed answers to questions about their reading and written belabored book reports. In high school and college, the book reports of earlier days have become research or critical papers. Moffett says, "We have always been more interested in reading than in writing, so much so that writing in schools has hardly existed except as a means to demonstrate either reading comprehension or the comprehensiveness of one's reading" (p. 86).

Actually, there should be no quarrel about which is more important or which should receive more attention, because research from the Center for the Study of Reading supports the notion that reading and writing are similar in many ways and therefore of equal value. Tierney and Pearson (1984) have described both as constructive, composing processes. As they interact with text, both readers and writers go through planning, drafting, revising, and monitoring processes. The planning stage (like prewriting) involves purpose setting and knowledge mobilization: Why am I reading/

writing, and what do I already know? Just as a writer begins to draft his first thoughts, a reader tentatively scans a text to get the overall plan, going back later to fill in details. Just as writers revise their work upon reading, readers often change their interpretations as they go through a text, rereading to make sense of ideas within the context of their own prior knowledge and experiences. Both are constantly monitoring their impressions, asking questions of themselves as they go along.

Giacobbe (1981) says the relationship between reading and writing is not linear; that is, learning to do one should not necessarily precede the other. Children are more willing to write much earlier than was previously thought. Since children come to school in control of their own experiences and can illustrate those experiences through drawing and labeling (albeit with their own "invented" or phonetic spelling), it is much easier for them to start with writing. On the other hand, reading involves a response to others' ideas and a learning of a printed symbolic system of communication devised by others. Giacobbe believes that reading instruction and opportunities for writing should begin at the same time.

Shanahan (1986) evaluated three models of learning to read and write. The *reading-to-writing* model theorizes that reading knowledge can influence writing but that writing would not be useful or influential to reading. Shanahan, like Moffett (1981a), notes that traditional school reading programs have been characterized by this model, with reading and literature instruction preceding the formal teaching of writing. The *writing-to-read* model, on the other hand, posits that writing will affect reading but does not expect reading to affect writing. Shanahan found a third alternative, the *interactive* model, in which influence goes from reading to writing and back again, to be the most successful. Learning word analysis in reading is seen as positively affecting the spelling and vocabulary diversity needed for writing. Exposure to a variety of sentence structures and story organizations in reading and frequent writing of a variety of pieces is seen to affect comprehension in reading and the ability to compose writing that can be read by others. This interactive model would seem to be consistent with the aligned processes model suggested by Tierney and Pearson (1984).

To learn about how the writing/reading process works within the child, Boutwell (1983) focused on one child, eight-year-old Marta, who was in a writing-as-process class in Atkinson, New Hampshire. Marta tape-recorded answers to three questions about her writing: What was she doing? What was she wrestling with? What did she plan to do next? It was found that Marta became a strategic reader of her own writing. She wrote, read, made changes, and reread her own written work. She began to approach reading the work of others with the same questions she had for her own writing. Marta constantly monitored her reading by asking if it made sense. She made a reciprocal agreement between herself as writer and herself as reader. While Boutwell had begun by trying to learn about the process, Marta herself seemed to internalize the process and take control of her own reading and writing.

In any case, since reading and writing are reciprocal processes, it appears that reading programs that do not include a full-blown writing component and writing programs that are devoid of a rich reading/literature component are missing these obvious and natural connections.

HELPING SCHOOLS MOVE TOWARD A PROCESS APPROACH

To learn how administrators can move their schools toward a process approach, we interviewed key staff members in New Jersey and New York schools cited as having exemplary reading/writing programs by the following sources: the nationally validated program, Project WR.I.T.&E.; the Reading/Language Arts Coordinator for the State of New Jersey; and the National Council of Teachers of English (NCTE). In all, we spoke to representatives from seven school districts (Banks & Feeley, 1987).

One of the first questions we asked our sample participants was, How did your program start? Calkins (1986) says that most process-approach programs are begun by key teachers who assume leadership roles by starting their own classroom programs; helping other colleagues get started; and acting as liaisons among classrooms, supervisors, and outside consultants. While this certainly is the case in many districts, all of our respondents cited supervisors and administrators as the initiators of their programs, a significant message for this chapter.

Interestingly, three suburban school districts credited the research from national writing projects as the inspiration for the start of their programs. Specifically mentioned were the New Jersey research (Emig, 1983) and the Bay Area Writing Project (Camp, 1982). Montclair Kimberley Academy (MKA), a private K–12 coeducational system in Montclair, New Jersey, said that they responded to these same research findings, as disseminated through NCTE publications. Montclair Kimberley also credited the results of the NAEP studies (Applebee et al., 1987), which found schools were doing a good job of teaching lower-level literacy skills but were doing less well in moving beyond the basics. These findings motivated them toward investigating a process approach in which reading and writing would be taught together through the use of whole, interesting, meaningful texts.

A mid-sized urban school district in northern New Jersey cited as their entrée the poor showing of students on standardized tests, especially in writing. This led them to attend workshops on Writing as Process (WAP) and holistic scoring of writing samples. Once involved, they knew that curriculum change that was focused on writing and its connections with reading was necessary. After the initial "winds of change" started, committees were formed to implement new programs.

In a southern New Jersey suburban district of about 2,500 students (Glassboro), a writing committee led by an administrator who was director of educational media and himself a playwright developed a K–12 curriculum over a two-year period. Based on the work of Emig (1983), Graves (1983), Murray (1985), Britton (1970), and others, the program that emerged is now called Project WR.I.T.&E. (The letters stand for Writing Is Thorough & Efficient.) Reporting very significant positive changes in writing achievement in the 1981–1982 school year, Project WR.I.T.&E. has since become a part of the National Diffusion Network (NDN), offering consulting services to school districts across the country (New York, Georgia, Washington, Oregon, and others). While the original administrator who developed the project remains as director, a district reading specialist now serves as project coordinator and main teacher trainer. (See resources at the end of this chapter.)

The reading supervisor in another southern New Jersey suburban district had worked in Project WR.I.T.&E. and so was a natural to initiate a similar approach in her district. Wantagh Public Schools, a suburban system with approximately 3,000 students located on Long Island in New York State, also participated in Project WR.I.T.&E. training. The key person to initiate and implement the program was the district reading coordinator. Here, teachers were released to work with project consultants, who conducted workshops and spent time in classrooms to help teachers with planning and management problems.

To start their program, the reading supervisor at MKA sought the help of experts such as Morton Botel from the University of Pennsylvania, Don Graves from the University of New Hampshire, and Don Holdaway from New Zealand (on leave in the United States). While the emerging curriculum was based mainly on Botel's Pennsylvania Comprehensive Reading/Language Arts Plan (PCRP), it now reflects contributions from Graves, Holdaway, and others. The PCRP includes four critical experiences: responding to literature, self-selected reading, composing, and the study of language patterns. Graves's workshop approach to writing forms the basis for the composing and reading/literature areas, and Holdaway's (1979) influence may be seen in the "big books" used to introduce kindergarten children to print (Green & Parker, 1985).

Aided by a team of reading specialists and librarians, the K–6 teachers piloted a number of these new ideas in the 1981–1982 school year. After 1982, the entire K–6 reading/language arts curriculum was restructured to maintain and extend the program. It is presently being extended further into grades seven through twelve, through an integrated, cross-disciplinary humanities approach in which students read and write in thematic units that involve literature, social studies, art, and music.

Selected as an NCTE Center of Excellence in 1985, the MKA program was initiated by Av Green when she was the school's reading coordinator. After becoming assistant principal, she continued to work closely with the reading specialist who assumed responsibility for ongoing implementation.

A language arts staff member who spends half her time supervising writing workshop classrooms has been responsible for the development of the K–12 language arts curriculum in her northern New Jersey suburban district. Change there began in the high school, with a committee headed by the English department chairperson. After attending workshops and conferences and reading the work of experts such as Moffett (1981a, 1981b) and Graves (1983), the committee members in this district decided to go with the process approach, developing their own model for implementing a writing workshop. An original committee member, the language arts teacher/supervisor, helped to extend the process approach from the high school, down through the middle school, and into the elementary level, through inservice work and demonstrations. Outstanding fourth- and fifth-grade teachers who were very interested in process teaching were given special advanced training to help bridge the gap between the upper and lower grades.

Several districts reported that they started out by focusing on the process approach through inservice training and having curriculum committee members attend area workshops and conferences on the teaching of writing and reading/writing connections. Eventually these activities led to the development of new language arts curricula reflecting the process approach.

WHAT ACTIVITIES CHARACTERIZE A PROCESS APPROACH?

To get a general idea of what might be going on in these schools to make them especially "process" oriented, we asked our respondents to describe some of the outstanding components of their programs. While all mentioned scheduling writing and reading every day, journal writing where appropriate, and writing across the curriculum, the respondents from Glassboro and MKA gave in-depth information on special features of their programs, which is summarized as follows.

Glassboro's Project WR.I.T.&E. is underscored by several general themes:

- *Climate.* Teachers model writing by sharing their own writing with their students. Students learn to write, share, and respond to others' writing, working cooperatively with partners or groups. There is much oral and written interaction.
- *Fluency.* Journal writing by teachers and students is a daily activity. Some journals are used to record ideas and learnings in subject areas (grades three through twelve); others, from which pieces are chosen for further development, are used for free writing. Journals are examined by teachers but never graded.
- *Audience.* Students always write with an audience in mind: self, peers, parents, friends, community leaders, celebrities, government figures, or any real readers. Each year, a young authors' conference is scheduled in which students share their writing with a real audience.
- *Writing as process.* Through teacher modeling, students are introduced to the process: prewrite, compose, revise, and edit for publication. They are encouraged to keep a flow chart to monitor their progress. During conferences, students read their work to the teacher and peers, revising as needed; they always have a piece of writing in progress.
- *Writing as learning.* Writing is used for learning in all subject areas. Besides keeping journals, students write essays and reports using the writing process stages. Audiences other than the teacher are provided, and pieces are published in a variety of ways.
- *Literacy skills.* Starting in grade three, skills such as spelling, capitalization, usage, and punctuation are taught, in the context of the writing process. A lesson, such as in the use of quotation marks, is introduced in a large class session, then reinforced in conferences. (This supplements traditional spelling and handwriting programs.)
- *Evaluation.* Writing folders are kept for longitudinal evaluation. Teachers and students evaluate their own writing through sharing and conferences. Selected pieces are graded when grades are necessary.

While MKA's general four-part framework (PCRP) has already been described, the following are special highlights of their program:

- *Big books.* In kindergarten and grade one, children sit around the teacher as a "big book" (an enlarged version of a trade book, usually with a predictable story line) is read to them every day for about a week. After the initial reading, children chime in, and the teacher points out sight words and print conventions such as punctuation. Then they write a class big book, with each child illustrating a page to which the child and teacher add a simple text. In a similar way, songs, poems, and plays are charted and displayed, to introduce reading and writing through whole text.

• *Writing workshop.* Beginning with a brief mini-lesson on topics or a specific skill, the workshop is a time for writing. Students are encouraged to start with personal narrative before moving on to writing other genres. They begin with planning (rehearsing), engaging in prewriting activities such as drawing, free writing, or telling their story to a partner. Then they draft their story and revise it after conferences. Editing takes place when writers are satisfied that their work is finished. In grade one, editing is done by student and teacher working together, and final copies are produced by volunteer parent typists. The book is published in conventional form and added to the class library. The workshop ends with a sharing time in which students read their work to the class.

• *Reading workshop.* Modeled on the writing workshop, the reading workshop begins with a tune-in time, during which the teacher reads to the class, and a mini-lesson. The mini-lesson is a short, focused, direct instruction time in which some aspect of reading/writing is taught, from a sight word like *said* in grade one to how to punctuate and read direct discourse in grade four.

During reading time, students read books of their own choosing (from preselected groups offered by the teacher). They read to themselves, to the teacher, or to a partner. Then they write responses to their reading, in notebooks. During sharing time, they read or tell a favorite part of their book or read from their response notebooks.

• *Whole-class reading books.* Whole-class reading books, of which each student has a copy, are read in a number of different ways, which usually includes the teacher reading a chapter aloud, followed by students reading in pairs, students taking parts and reading dialogue, the whole class taking turns reading aloud, and/or students reading to the teacher or to themselves. After reading, the students write personal reactions, answers to questions, and plays and puppet shows, and engage in numerous other response activities like designing advertisements for the book and writing original stories in the same genre. Vocabulary lists are developed from the books, and specific skills about such areas as affixes, sentence construction, and grammar are taught through the text. Students also begin to examine authors' styles and writing techniques. All books are chosen for reader interest and literary merit, and some are selected to correlate with the social studies curriculum.

• *Junior Great Books.* Teachers are trained to lead discussions over books selected from the Junior Great Books series. Students are encouraged to read for deeper meaning and to support conclusions with examples from the text.

• *Language arts phonics.* In grades one through three, phonics instruction is offered through a program called *Language Arts Phonics* (Botel & Seaver, 1986). This program teaches sound and linguistic patterns through songs, chants, poems, and word- and sentence-making activities. Sounds are not isolated but kept in an interesting context.

• *Writing across the curriculum.* Journals and learning logs (students' observations of their own learning processes) are used in most content classes, and writing topics often grow out of these. Just as in Glassboro, the process writing workshop format underlies writing in all subject areas.

In commenting on teacher roles at MKA, Av Green says,

In these classrooms, the role of the teacher has changed from manager of commercial systems to creator of learning environments and experiences. Rather than dispenser of information, the teacher in this new setting becomes coach, collaborator, and cheerleader.

The program change has given a new definition to the role of the reading specialist. Formerly sequestered with a small group of youngsters in need of help, the specialist now helps all students by co-teaching with classroom teachers and by providing resources and expertise for the program.*

GUIDELINES FOR ADMINISTRATORS WHO WANT TO MOVE TOWARD A PROCESS APPROACH

Based on the real experiences of administrators who have initiated and implemented a process approach, the following guidelines are offered.

1. *Begin by visiting exemplary schools.*
Observe good programs in action. In-class observations are a must when getting started.

2. *Make contact with a recognized resource.*
One of the national writing projects or NDN centers such as Project WR.I.T.&E. can help you learn about current offerings and locate consultants to assist you in planning and delivering inservice workshops. (See resources at end of chapter.)

3. *Form a committee of teachers who are interested in process teaching.*
Usually there are some already working in your district. Invite them to join

---

*Av Green (1987, March 4), Personal communication.

you in your observation visits and in your contacts with resource centers. (Actually, teachers who have taken workshops and have read the current literature are often the best sources to help you locate the experts.) A reading leadership team comprised of reading specialists, librarians, and grade representatives can be formed to work with the administrator who is spearheading the move.

4. *Select a key person to coordinate the events and to implement the emerging program.*
In the systems surveyed, all the initiators (most of whom are still in charge) were either reading or language arts supervisors or coordinators. Strong administrative support seems to be a key to success. The administration should take the initiative and encourage continuation and expansion.

5. *Build a library of relevant professional materials on process teaching.*
Publications from NCTE, International Reading Association (IRA), Boynton/Cook Publishers, and Heinemann Educational Books will be particularly helpful. (Addresses may be found in the resources section at the end of the chapter; the reference list for this chapter is a good beginning.)

6. *With the help of your leadership committee, begin to plan for staff development in the areas of process teaching in reading and writing.*
This cannot be done in a one-shot deal but must evolve over time. Since writing is a popular issue, it might be good to start with workshops on teaching writing as process, then move to writing across the curriculum and connecting reading and writing in your reading/literature programs. (See Chapter 9, "Staff Development," for a full treatment of planning and implementing change through inservice training.)

7. *Once started, encourage teachers to form networks with teachers in their own school and with process-oriented teachers in other systems.*
Such networks provide support and a constant exchange of ideas. Administrators and supervisors should be a part of these networks so that they can help with present problems and anticipated needs.

CONCLUSION

In this chapter I have supplied administrators and supervisors with background information on the process approach (sometimes called whole-language or holistic approach) to the development of reading and writing, and I have shared with them some ideas gleaned from interviewing reading/language arts coordinators and supervisors in systems selected because of their commitment to this approach. Guidelines on how to get started, based on the real experiences of these supervisors, have been offered. Also included are resources for help in implementing change and sustaining interest.

Supervisors and administrators are encouraged to use these ideas and resources to lead their schools toward an integrated, process approach to developing literacy. This approach is recommended in *What Works: Research About Teaching and Learning* (U.S. Department of Education, 1986) and *Becoming a Nation of Readers* (1985), and its rewards are many. Instead of eschewing writing, as decades of schoolchildren before them did, students want to write more as they begin to view themselves as "published" authors. They read the writing of others in a more critical manner, searching first for meaning and then for style. They see writing as a tool for learning, as they write logs, response journals, and reports. According to Green and Parker (1985), the connections their students make between reading and writing and their independence in taking charge of their own learning have been some of the most notable strengths of their process-oriented program. They say,

> As our students progress through the grades, the connections between their own writing and the writing techniques of published authors are focused on in greater depth. Our readers and writers become increasingly familiar with the techniques and strategies of reading and writing as they begin to look at their reading from the perspective of writer and their writing from the perspective of reader.
>
> Throughout all grade levels the independence of our students is emphasized. Independence and responsibility are fostered through peer collaboration for problem solving, self-selection of books and responding activities, and self-selection of topics for writing. Student choices are set within a carefully structured, non-competitive framework in which rules and expectations are clearly established. [pp. 11–12]

RESOURCES

Boynton/Cook Publishers, Inc., 52 Upper Montclair Plaza, Upper Montclair, NJ   07043, (201) 783-3310

Heinemann Educational Books, Inc., 70 Court Street, Portsmouth, NH   03801, (603) 431-7894

International Reading Association, 800 Barksdale Road, P.O. Box 8139, Newark, DE   19714-8139, (302) 731-1600

National Council of Teachers of English, 1111 Kenyon Road, Urbana, IL   61801, (217) 328-3870

National Writing Project, School of Education, 5627 Tolman Hall, University of California, Berkeley, CA   94720, (415) 642-0963

Project WR.I.T.&E., Glassboro Public Schools, Annex A-N, Delsea Drive, Glassboro, NJ   08028, (609) 881-2290

REFERENCES

Applebee, A. N., Langer, J., & Mullis, I. (1987). *Learning to be literate in America: Reading, writing, and reasoning* (Report of the National Assessment of Educational Progress). Princeton, NJ: Educational Testing Service.

Banks, P., & Feeley, J. T. (1987). *Characteristics and administrative influences of exemplary reading/writing programs.* Unpublished manuscript, William Paterson College, Wayne, NJ.

Becoming a nation of readers: The report of the commission on reading. (1985). Washington, DC: National Institute of Education.

Botel, M., & Seaver, J. T. (1986). *Language arts phonics.* Jefferson City, MO: Scholastic.

Boutwell, M. (1983). Reading and writing process: A reciprocal agreement. *Language Arts, 60,* 723–730.

Britton, J. (1970). *Language and learning.* New York: Penguin Books.

Calkins, L. (1983). *Lessons from a child.* Portsmouth, NH: Heinemann.

Calkins, L. (1986). *The art of teaching writing.* Portsmouth, NH: Heinemann.

Camp, G. (Ed.). (1982). *Teaching writing: Essays from the Bay Area Writing Project.* Montclair, NJ: Boynton/Cook.

Emig, J. (1983). *The web of meaning: Essays on writing, teaching, learning and thinking.* Montclair, NJ: Boynton/Cook.

Fulwiler, T. (1987). *Teaching with writing.* Montclair, NJ: Boynton/Cook.

Giacobbe, M. E. (1981). Who says that children can't write the first week of school? In R. D. Walshe (Ed.), *Donald Graves in Australia* (pp. 99–102). Portsmouth, NH: Heinemann.

Graves, D. (1983). *Writing: Teachers and children at work.* Portsmouth, NH: Heinemann.

Green, A., & Parker, M. (1985). *The reading/language arts program of the Montclair Kimberley Academy.* Unpublished manuscript. Montclair Kimberley Academy, Montclair, NJ.

Holdaway, D. (1979). *The foundations of literacy.* Sydney, Australia: Ashton Scholastic (distributed in the United States by Heinemann).

Moffett, J. (1981a). *Active voice: A writing program across the curriculum.* Montclair, NJ: Boynton/Cook.

Moffett, J. (1981b). *Coming on center: Essays in English education.* Montclair, NJ: Boynton/Cook.

Murray, D. (1985). *A writer teaches writing* (2nd ed.). Boston: Houghton-Mifflin.

Shanahan, T. (1986). An analysis and comparison of theoretical models of the reading–writing relationship. *Journal of Educational Psychology, 78*(2), 116–123.

Tchudi, S. N., & Huerta, M. C. (1983). *Teaching writing in the content areas: Middle school/junior high*. Washington, DC: National Education Association.

Tchudi, S. N., & Tchudi, S. J. (1983). *Teaching writing in the content areas: Elementary school*. Washington, DC: National Education Association.

Tchudi, S. N., & Yates, J. (1983). *Teaching writing in the content areas: Senior high school*. Washington, DC: National Education Association.

Thaiss, C. J. (1986). *Language across the curriculum in the elementary grades*. Urbana, IL: National Council of Teachers of English.

Tierney, R., & Pearson, P. D. (1984). Toward a composing model of reading. In J. Jensen (Ed.), *Composing and comprehending* (pp. 33–45). Urbana, IL: National Council of Teachers of English.

U.S. Department of Education. (1986). *What works: Research about teaching and learning*. Washington, DC: U.S. Government Printing Office.

Young, A., & Fulwiler, T. (1986). *Writing across the disciplines*. Montclair, NJ: Boynton/Cook.

Zinsser, W. (1985). *On writing well* (3rd ed.). New York: Harper & Row.

13 Integrating Computers into Reading/Language Arts Instruction

SHELLEY B. WEPNER
William Paterson College of New Jersey

DAVID REINKING
University of Georgia

Dr. H. has been employed for the last twelve years as a supervisor of reading, for kindergarten through grade twelve, in a large school district. He has been instrumental in designing a districtwide reading curriculum that goes well beyond the scope-and-sequence chart of the district's basal reading series. For his efforts, Dr. H. enjoys the respect and camaraderie of his colleagues. His reading staff, which reflects his knowledge and enthusiasm, has helped him to implement an instructional program to meet the students' needs and interests. Known as hardworking, sincere, reliable, and knowledgeable, Dr. H. is confident in his own professional development. Until the advent of computers in reading/language arts instruction, he was secure in his knowledge about the teaching of reading. However, not only was he not knowledgeable about computers, but he had anxieties about using them in any context. These anxieties stemmed from his own failure at a programming course in college. He rationalized away others' attempts to interest him in computers by saying that computers were nothing more than expensive workbooks and elaborate typewriters. Yet he also knew that computers were quickly becoming an important new variable in the teaching of reading and that he would have to change his attitude.

He didn't have to wait long. The new assistant superintendent had a keen interest in computers, based on her experience in her former school district. She intended to emphasize computers in this district, and she asked the subject-area supervisors to develop a five-year plan for integrating computers into the teaching of their subjects. This was a difficult task for Dr. H., given his reluctance to embrace wholeheartedly the idea of using computers for reading instruction.

Dr. H. decided to hire a consultant to help him develop his plan. His consultant, Ms. C., had been working with computers for seven years. In her quest to discover some appropriate uses for computers in reading/language arts instruction, she had adopted a model for use in situations like the one Dr. H. was facing. Dr. H., having heard about her success in other districts, invited her to help him decide what equipment he would need and, more important, how to use it in the district's reading program.

Although the people are fictitious, this situation is real. Those in supervisory positions may find themselves coerced into becoming experts in educational computing. In our observations, we have found that many school districts choose one of two alternatives in using computers in schools. They either focus on adding a curriculum designed to help students learn about computers (often referred to as "computer literacy") or they focus on integrating computers into existing curricula. While we favor the latter choice, its implementation in subject areas such as reading is often haphazard or, if systematic, is carried out by personnel who lack the appropriate background. Dr. H. is a case in point. As a reading supervisor, he is knowledgeable about reading instruction, but he is uneasy about integrating computers into the curriculum. Yet, as an instructional leader, Dr. H. needs to know how to assist teachers in integrating computers into their teaching, and he has been given the task of developing a coherent plan for doing so. What should he and others like him do? That is the question addressed in this chapter.

GETTING STARTED

Obviously, those in positions similar to Dr. H.'s could hire consultants to solve their problems. But consultants usually provide short-term assistance for long-term concerns, as Ms. C. is doing for Dr. H. Clearly a major commitment is necessary and probably will require activity over a period of years. It is thus very important for supervisors to become informed about and work with computers long enough to understand the computer's advantages and limitations for reading/language arts instruction. We firmly believe that those in leadership positions should feel reasonably comfortable with computers if they wish to influence how computers can be used by the teachers they supervise. There are no shortcuts to learning about computers in reading and language arts; an investment of time and effort is required.

First, one must set out to become informed about computers. There are several options for doing this: (1) college reading courses that deal directly with the use of computers in the teaching of reading; (2) workshops and conferences at the local, state, regional, and national levels, given by reading and other professional organizations; (3) fact-finding visits to schools or districts to learn about successes to model and mistakes to avoid; and (4) books devoted to the topic of computers and reading/language arts (e.g., Balajthy, 1986; Blanchard, Mason, & Daniel, 1987; Geoffrion & Geoffrion, 1983; Rude, 1986; Strickland, Feeley, & Wepner, 1987) or reading methods texts with chapters on the use of computers in reading instruction (e.g., Robinson & Good, 1987; Vacca, Vacca, & Gove, 1987).

Second, one must explore options for the most suitable computer uses in one's situation, preferably with guidance from the literature on computers and reading. Third, this information must be coalesced into cohesive plans for integrating computers into reading/language arts. It is these last two efforts that need to be addressed in depth and to which this chapter is devoted.

EXPLORING OPTIONS FOR USING COMPUTERS

"The question is not whether computers should be allowed into classrooms but how they are to be used" (Smith, 1984, p. 32). Computers have become a significant factor in reading/language arts instruction. According to a survey conducted by *Electronic Learning*, 24 percent of *all* educational software released during a recent year was for reading/language arts instruction (Balajthy & Reinking, 1985). Despite the fact that there is much software available for such computer use, superficial reasons seem to be the motivation in many schools. For example, we know of schools where administrators have mandated that computers be used in the reading program for no other reason than the board of education insisted that they be used in every area of the curriculum. We also are aware of one state that would approve a basal reading series for a state textbook adoption list only if it had a computer component for instruction; there was little concern for what the computer's role would be. Although left with no choice but to contend with these forces, informed reading supervisors should be able to rise above some of them when planning for computer-based reading instruction. They need to become convinced that computers offer important new opportunities for enhancing reading/language arts instruction. They also need to remember that using computers should be based, first, on a sound understanding of reading/language arts (Miller & Burnett, 1986) and, second, on an understanding of what computers can contribute to this instructional area (e.g., Reinking, 1986).

Reading supervisors also need to be aware that some questions and concerns have been raised regarding the use of computers for reading. These include the ways that the computer's unique features may affect reading development (Henney, 1987), whether computer software matches our current understanding of reading (Cook, 1986; Miller & Burnett, 1986), and that the quality and usefulness of instructional software lags behind the development and potential uses of computer technology (Balajthy, 1986). Finally, supervisors need to know about recent developments in which researchers are exploring theory-based applications of computers to reading to help guide the development of new software applications (e.g., Reinking & Schreiner, 1985; Roth & Beck, 1987).

To help reading supervisors explore options for using computers for reading, we offer a few guidelines based on our experience in working with schools and teachers. Together, these provide a broad perspective for making decisions.

1. Rely on your reading knowledge.

As a reading supervisor, first and foremost, you need to rely on your knowledge and beliefs about reading when making decisions about computers. What do you believe is the nature of reading? How do you think reading is best taught? What is the importance of phonics? Vocabulary development? Critical reading skills? What reading diagnostic techniques are the most valid and reliable? The supervisor who can clearly articulate answers to these and similar questions will be in the best position to make informed decisions about using computers. Miller and Burnett (1987) have argued that having an understanding of reading theory is more important than technological knowledge, when implementing computers in reading/language arts instruction.

2. Consider intended uses.

Before making other decisions, you should consider how you will use the computer for instruction. Acquiring appropriate hardware is only one decision that will be affected by thinking first about intended uses. For example, the decision as to whether or not you will have a central computer lab with many computers or a single computer in each classroom will be made more easily and logically if it has been decided beforehand how the computer will be used for instruction.

In our experience, forethought about how computers will be used has not typically accompanied the acquisition of computer hardware and software in many schools. A few years ago one of us was asked to help an elementary school principal whose district had acquired ten new microcomputers and placed them in his school. This created several dilemmas for the principal: No money had been provided by the district to buy software, the school had little extra space for the computers, and no one in the school knew how to set up and turn on the computers.

Unfortunately, this situation is not uncommon. For several years, the acquisition of computers in many schools was an end in itself, instead of a means to achieve well-specified academic goals. Once the computers are in place (as is the case in many schools today), justifying their existence by acquiring and using software, sometimes any software, becomes paramount. We have seen some reading supervisors join in this activity because of their unbridled enthusiasm for computers or because they are competing for computer resources with teachers in other subjects. Or, as in the case of Dr. H., they have a mandate to use computers to teach reading. Focusing on acquiring or using computers without a specific concern for academic goals may address short-term needs but dilute efforts to establish a coherent, purposeful use of computers in a reading program.

3. Balance structure and flexibility.

When integrating computers into a reading program, strive for a balance between structure and flexibility. Because the existing array of computer applications in reading is impressive (Blanchard et al., 1987), it is important to encourage teachers to experiment with new applications. For instance, adopting only the software developed to accompany a particular basal reader and requiring all teachers to use this software three times a week in the computer lab reflects structure and organization, but it stifles creativity and overlooks the versatility of the computer. Part of this flexibility also involves considering the various ways a particular program might be used for instruction. Many software packages are not designed specifically to teach reading (e.g., word-processing programs, data bases, adventure games, social studies and science simulations, and even some programming languages), yet they may be used to address instructional goals in the reading/language arts curriculum. Thus, supervisors need to be aware of the general characteristics of commercial software and be familiar with the full range of options available.

In following these three guidelines, reading supervisors will be less likely to consider the use of computers as an end in itself. There may come a time when computers will affect the broad goals of reading instruction, but for the present the relevant issues revolve around how computers can contribute to achieving widely accepted goals for reading instruction. Although these guidelines define a broad perspective for considering the use of computers in reading/language arts instruction, they do not address specific concerns for implementation. In the remainder of this chapter we describe a framework that will enable a supervisor to address systematically the major concerns related to integrating computers into programs of reading instruction.

CREATING A FRAMEWORK FOR COMPUTER INTEGRATION

As referred to elsewhere in this volume, curricular decision making is a cyclical process (see also Campbell, Corbally, & Nystrand, 1983). Four curricular questions should be addressed in this process: Where Are We? Where Do We Want To Be? How Do We Get There? and How Do We Know We Are There? To help supervisors of elementary and secondary reading programs develop viable short-term and long-term goals for integrating computers into the reading curriculum, each of these questions will be addressed for the following five areas: curriculum, hardware, software, staff development, and facilities. As each question is addressed, a chart of points to consider in each area will be provided. Together, these four charts comprise a model for making decisions about using computers in reading instruction; we call it RECAP (REading/Computers Assessment Plan).

Phase 1: Where Are We?

Before you can plan, it is important to consider systematically the context in which you work. What are your students like, and what are the characteristics of the community or communities in which they live? Will using computers in reading instruction have parental support? Administrative support? Board support? Consider also the support you can expect from colleagues and the teachers with whom you work. You may need more than moral support. For example, you may also need technical assistance. By analyzing how much support you have, you will acquire a sense of how much you can accomplish and how long it will take. You also need to consider what investment already has been made by your district in educational computing. Figure 13.1 provides a listing of questions organized into the five major areas to be addressed in Phase 1 of the RECAP model. Responding to these twenty-four survey questions will help supervisors define the status of educational computing in their school districts and assist in determining what changes may be necessary and how much they will cost. If external funding will be necessary, several sources of funding are possible; for example, federal and state grants, parent–teacher associations, and private foundations. A number of reading books (e.g., Bean & Wilson, 1982) and computer resource books (e.g., Bullough & Beatty, 1987) can be used to help identify how additional private and public funds can be solicited.

Curriculum.   Making decisions about integrating computers into the reading/language arts curriculum undoubtedly will be influenced by existing curricula that involve computers. An important first step, therefore, is for the supervisor to examine how computers have been or are being used. Are computers integrated in any way? If so, for which subjects, grade levels, and students? The supervisor also should attempt to find out whether computers are used as an integral part of the reading/language arts curriculum.

Hardware.   Another critical component of the "Where are we?" question is compiling a complete inventory of the equipment available for instructional computing. By knowing what hardware exists and how it is being used, future expenditures can be planned. Answers to the following questions help focus this inquiry.

What hardware exists in the district? It is not unusual to find many computer brands in the same school or district. (One district visited has three different brands of computers at the elementary level alone.) Where is the hardware located (e.g., computer labs, classrooms, offices)? What peripherals (e.g., printers, voice synthesizers) are available? How are they used? Where are they located? Does the district budget include money to buy hardware on a regular basis, or is it purchased sporadically when funds are available? How are expenditures initiated (teacher request, administrative decision, parent pressure)? How often is the hardware used? Is the hardware stationary or mobile?

If accurate information is not readily available, we suggest that you visit each school and perhaps informally interview each teacher, to obtain the information you need.

Figure 13.1   Questions to Be Addressed in Phase 1

CURRICULUM

1. Are computers integrated in any way into existing curricula in our district?
   Yes _____   No _____
   (If yes, answer the remainder of curriculum questions.)
2. In which subjects?
3. For which grade levels?
4. For which students (e.g., basic skills, gifted and talented)?
5. Is a computer literacy curriculum in place? (Courses in computer literacy familiarize students with computers and their uses.)
   If so, what skills are emphasized?
6. Are computers used as an integral part of the reading/language arts curriculum?
   Yes _____   No _____   If so, how?

HARDWARE

7. What hardware exists in the district?
   Elementary
   _____ School: Number _____ Type _____ Memory _____
   Secondary
   _____ School: Number _____ Type _____ Memory _____
8. What peripherals (e.g., printers, joysticks) exist in the district?
   Elementary
   _____ School: Number _____   Kind/Type _____
   Secondary
   _____ School: Number _____   Kind/Type _____
9. Attach a list of hardware by school and by program use.
10. How often is the hardware used during the school day?
    0–25% of the time _____   25–50% _____   50–75% _____   75–100% _____
11. Is the hardware confined to one location, or mobile? If mobile, how often is it moved and to what locations?

SOFTWARE

12. What software exists in the district?
    Elementary
    Name/Publisher _____   Location _____
    Secondary
    Name/Publisher _____   Location _____
13. Who is/are the person(s) responsible for software purchases?
14. Does the district have any licensing agreements?
    Yes _____   No _____   Companies _____
15. Does a software inventory exist?
    If yes, what information does it include and to whom is it distributed?
16. Are computers used to manage instruction?
    Yes _____   No _____   If yes, how are they being used and by whom?
17. Attach a statement, identifying how software acquisition/use is coordinated with a curriculum guide?

Figure 13.1 *(continued)*

STAFF DEVELOPMENT

18. How many teachers/administrators have been trained to use computers, and what is their skill level?
19. Are the teachers making use of inservice offerings?
    Yes _____   No _____If so, how?
20. Is inservice training in educational computing available to teachers?
    Yes _____   No _____If so, what types?
21. Explain how administrators make use of inservice?
22. Do teachers want/need more training in educational computing?
    Yes _____   No _____If yes, specify what they need.

FACILITIES

23. What educational computing facilities exist in the district (e.g., central computer labs vs. computers distributed to individual classrooms)?
24. Are these facilities adequate for current needs? (Consider factors such as space, furniture, lighting, electrical outlets, maintenance, and security.)

Software. As with a hardware inventory, a software inventory can be painstaking, time-consuming, and frustrating. However, try to find out the following: What software exists in the district? What types of software packages have been ordered? For example, is the software designed primarily for drill and practice, word processing, and/or record keeping, or is it designed to create instructional materials? Are there certain packages that all schools have? Many districts, for instance, order the same word-processing package for all the schools, for the sake of uniformity.

Are there more software packages available at the elementary level than at the secondary level? This is often the case, since the majority of reading software programs focus on reading skills normally taught in the elementary grades. Who is responsible for ordering software? Does the district have licensing agreements for certain packages or with certain companies? (Licensing agreements are contracts between software vendors and, in this case, school districts, enabling districts to make and use multiple copies of specified software at reduced rates.) Does an inventory exist? If so, what kind of information was included on the inventory (e.g., subject area, description, rating) and by whom?

Again, this information can help shape future plans. In helping two districts gather this information, we found that, while it was a difficult and time-consuming task, it helped these districts immeasurably to clarify their thinking about using computers and to develop a plan for future use.

Staff Development.   An important component of implementing an instructional program that uses computers is staff development. Without teachers who are reasonably proficient at using hardware and software, it is impossible to integrate computers into the reading/language arts curriculum. Not only do teachers need to be familiar with computer technology, they also need to be aware of the possible role of computers in the reading/language arts curriculum. The following questions help identify what the district has done in the area of staff development or inservice training.

Has any of the staff had an opportunity to learn about computers in reading/language arts instruction? Who has been trained (teachers, staff, administrators, parents, paraprofessionals)? What kind of inservice training is available to teachers? Is there any follow-up to the training? Are teachers making use of the inservice? Administrators? If so, how?

Has the inservice training had a narrow or broad focus? For example, one district devoted two years to training teachers to use the programming language Logo. The superintendent of schools came from a mathematics background and knew that Logo was designed to help users learn mathematics. Another district devoted several inservice sessions during a school year to train teachers to use a word-processing package because the district believed that word processing would facilitate a process approach to writing. Consequently, the staff in these two situations knew a great deal about specific applications but very little about other alternatives.

Facilities.   Creating adequate work space for instructional activities in pleasant surroundings is an important administrative concern. Overcrowded rooms or work areas that are noisy, dark, or cluttered with outmoded or broken-down equipment have a negative impact on morale and learning. When educational computing is introduced into a school, unique challenges face an administrator who wishes to create suitable facilities (e.g., Bullough & Beatty, 1987). The first step in a school that already has computers is to find out where the computers are located. If more space is needed, can it be found without adversely affecting other programs? Can certain teachers or departments be relocated? Is there someone responsible for overseeing present facilities? Have questions about maintenance and security been addressed? Have students had suitable access to the computers?

Phase 2: Where Do We Want to Be?

Confronting this question will help a supervisor set realistic goals and guide decisions. Using the data gathered in phase 1, it is possible to develop short-term and long-term goals. A five-year period is recommended for considering long-term goals, although it is necessary to take into account that it is difficult to predict what technological developments will be influencing educational computing in five years. Figure 13.2 shows the second phase of the RECAP model, which is aimed at helping a supervisor develop long- and short-term goals.

Before planning in phase 2 can be addressed, a supervisor needs to consider her or his knowledge about the use of computers in reading. The

Figure 13.2   Chart for Developing Long-Term Goals in Phase 2

	Where do we want to be in year:				
	1	2	3	4	5
GENERAL READING/LANGUAGE ARTS/ COMPUTER GOALS					
INSTRUCTIONAL/CURRICULUM GOALS					
Elementary					
Classroom teachers					
Remedial reading					
Basic skills					
Gifted and talented					
Special education					
Other					
Secondary					
Developmental reading					
Remedial reading					
Language arts teachers					
HARDWARE/PERIPHERAL ACQUISITIONS AND LOCATION					
Type/memory					
Budget (district/government)					
SOFTWARE					
Type					
Licensing					
Budget (district/government)					
STAFF DEVELOPMENT					
Type					
Person(s) responsible					
Participants					
Time frame					

questions that guide planning in this phase presume a knowledge about computer applications in reading/language arts and information about how computers can best be used to accomplish specific objectives in the reading/language arts curriculum. For this phase, some supervisors may feel more comfortable seeking the help of a person knowledgeable about computers in reading/language arts.

The primary concern in phase 2 should be to determine how computer-based activities will be integrated into the curriculum. In ideal situations, where teachers are knowledgeable about computers and how to use them for a variety of instructional activities, general computing skills such as using data bases can parallel more traditional academic skills. For example, Strickland et al. (1987) provide a sample of this type of curriculum planning for fourth-grade students. The curriculum combines ideas from districts in Teaneck, New Jersey (Schweitzer, 1985) and Montgomery County, Maryland (Hunter, 1983) and uses three major computer approaches within the same academic disciplines. These three are tutor (instruction/drill and practice), tool (assistance), and tutee (programming). Based on Taylor's (1980) framework and similar to other instructional models proposed for using computers (Luehrmann, 1982; Sherwood, 1986), this type of curriculum delineates how the computer can be used in a variety of capacities.

It is important, however, to establish realistic goals. If your district has done little in the area of educational computing, you will want to start small. Examine your reading curriculum, focus on those objectives that may be problematic, and investigate what the computer may offer in these areas. For example, one district we worked with was concerned with students' ability to understand the main idea in a story. They were not satisfied with existing instructional activities in this area, and they decided to look at some computer software with the hopes of finding alternative instructional activities. For this district, a narrowly defined goal was a good way to begin learning about computers in the reading/language arts curriculum. Another district, intent on helping its students to pass the statewide literacy test, decided to examine how computers might assist them in addressing statewide reading objectives. They began to look for software that pertained to those objectives causing their students the most difficulty. After finding appropriate software, they used this goal as a rationale for a proposal to acquire additional hardware. Finally, a reading supervisor in East Brunswick, New Jersey, decided to use reading specialists as resources for classroom teachers who needed help with computer initiatives. The five-year plan for implementing this decision is shown in Figure 13.3. Although the yearly changes are not dramatic, the figure is evidence that computers are being used for a wider variety of applications.

Figure 13.3   Reading Supervisor's Computer Goals for Reading Specialists (K–5)

	Year 1 1987–1988	Year 2 1988–1989	Year 3 1989–1990	Year 4 1990–1991	Year 5 1991–1992
GROUP A					
4 pilot teachers to begin 1987–1988	within-room experimentation	pilot teachers act as resource to classroom teachers	continue with instructional/ resource role	explore telecommunication, within class	demonstrate telecommunications to classroom teachers
GROUP B					
4 pilot teachers to begin 1988–1989		within-room experimentation	pilot teachers act as resource to classroom teachers	continue with instructional/ resource role	explore telecommunication, within class

Source: Caccavale, P. (1987). Reading/Computer Goals for Reading Specialists in East Brunswick, N.J. Reprinted with permission.

Once curricular goals are set, goals for hardware/software acquisitions, staff development, and facilities need to be established and documented.

Phase 3: How Do We Get There?

After a general plan for five years has been outlined, a detailed plan for the first year should be developed. If thoroughly researched and thoughtfully developed, this first-year plan will make planning in subsequent years more efficient (Wepner & Kramer, 1987). Strickland et al. (1987) state that "a sensible procedure for planning is to form a committee of teachers and administrators representing the district's different schools and grade levels. A committee plan would embody all the goals and needs for the entire district" (p. 141). Also, several writers have emphasized the importance of involving teachers in decision making, to insure acceptance of districtwide plans (Barnard & Hetzel, 1986; English, 1975; Likert, 1969). If this is not feasible, enlist input from as wide a group as possible. The stronger their feelings of ownership for the district's computer integration plan, the more motivated the teachers will be to implement changes (see Veatch & Cooter, 1985–1986).

A time frame should also be established for implementing changes in the five areas addressed in phase 1 (refer to Figure 13.1). This should be similar to other models of curriculum planning, such as the Program Evaluation Review Technique (see Burg, Kaufman, Korngold, & Kovner, 1978), in that it should have both serial and parallel listings of events. For example, staff development sessions on word processing may have to wait until after enough hardware has been purchased but may be able to occur during curriculum committee revisions.

Although not presented chronologically, important considerations for this phase of the process are presented in Figure 13.4. An example of how this phase can be implemented is illustrated by our experience in helping one school district. Previously mentioned as the district intent on passing the statewide literacy test, it had invested substantial time and money in its computer program. Seven of the eight elementary schools had a computer lab for purposes of helping students acquire basic skills; however, they were underutilized because of scheduling conflicts that had not been resolved. Also, the computer curriculum, as specified in a handbook for teachers, focused primarily on computer literacy skills and did not include the use of computers in reading/language arts. Through the cooperative efforts of the reading supervisor and the computer coordinator, a plan to expand computers into the reading/language arts curriculum was developed and implemented. The goal was to integrate the district's microcomputers into the revised reading curriculum, which aligned the district's reading objectives with the state's high school proficiency test.

The assistant superintendent designated a school to test the plan. The principal of that school, in conjunction with the reading supervisor and the district computer coordinator, worked with the school's computer lab teacher to devise a plan to bring the school's basic skills teachers and remedial reading teacher into the lab on a regular basis.

In designing this one-year plan, the district computer coordinator and reading supervisor considered each of the five essential areas, as the following five descriptions of what was done in each area will verify. To these we have added our own suggestions.

1. The district's computer curriculum had to be reworked to include the revised reading curriculum.

   The key to curriculum planning is to address reading skills and general computing skills simultaneously.

2. A hard disk system was ordered to help with skill management. This made it possible to put the information from many floppy disks onto one hard disk. Also, a budget was created for the replacement of broken machines.

   Hardware replacement is as important as hardware expansion, if a program is to be fully operative (see Bullough & Beatty, 1987).

Figure 13.4   Chart for Developing the First-Year Plan in Phase 3

Year 1: 19____ to 19____

Instructions: Specify how you intend to accomplish each goal for the first year. For example, in the area of curriculum, your specific objective might be to integrate your first-grade computer objectives with your first-grade reading objectives. You identify the need for a committee, including two first-grade teachers, to accomplish this objective. You decide on specific tasks, a budget, and a time frame to accomplish each of the curricular objectives listed.

Curriculum
Specific objectives
Tasks required
Task assignments
Time frame
Budget

Hardware
Purchase plan (new or trade-in): type, quantity, features, cost, software compatibility
Peripherals (printers, Koala pads, speech synthesizers)
Local area network
Location
Budget for purchase (district and government monies)

Software
Type
Quantity
Hardware required
Reading/language arts objectives
Guides/resources used in evaluation
Budget

Staff development
Person(s) responsible
Purpose
Participants (teachers and participants)
Schedule
Location

Facilities
Student/teacher assignments (equity)
Physical conditions/changes
Security/maintenance

3. Objectives from each software application, both those available and those to be ordered, were matched to the objectives from the existing reading curriculum.

   Similar to textbook purchases, software purchases should reflect the district's instructional philosophy. More useful than a collection of the most popular software is a collection that matches the district's instructional objectives.

4. An extensive staff development schedule was planned, to acquaint teachers with the new curriculum. This included a series of sessions in the computer lab so that the teachers could experiment with the software.

   Because teachers want to do what is expected (Barnard & Hetzel, 1986), inservice training that simulates anticipated instructional situations with computers is most beneficial.

5. The test school's computer lab schedule had to be reorganized to accommodate the schedules of the remedial reading and basic skills teachers, so that all these students could use the computers for reading instruction.

   Providing equal access (across race, gender, and ability) to the largest number of students for the maximum amount of time is one concern for any computer facility (Bullough & Beatty, 1987).

Although the project in this district required several months of intense planning, its chances for success were increased because of the cooperative efforts of the reading supervisor and computer coordinator. This led to the involvement of the assistant superintendent, building principal, and computer lab teacher, so that, by the time the plan was ready to be explained to the teachers, it embodied the needs and goals of the entire district.

Phase 4: How Do We Know We Are There?

The last phase in the RECAP model focuses on evaluation and is included for two reasons: to determine if the program objectives are being achieved and to identify needed adjustments in the original plan. Phase 4 enables a supervisor to evaluate specifically what changes are occurring in the five areas outlined in phase 1. Figure 13.5 lists what factors should be considered. The project in the district just discussed, for instance, included in its assessment both formal data such as standardized tests and informal data such as pupil attendance, student journals, student interviews, monthly progress reports, and observations. These were used to evaluate the effects of the changes that had been implemented. Again, the reading supervisor and computer coordinator worked together to gather these da-

Figure 13.5   Factors to Consider in Phase 4

Evaluation techniques
  Teacher observations and
    conferences
  Review/analysis of standardized and
    informal test data
  Informal student assessments
  Interviews
  Communication with board and
    community
  Survey questionnaires

Evaluation sources
  Administrators
  Teachers
  Students
  Community
  Outside consultants

Contents of evaluation
  Curriculum
  Hardware
  Software
  Staff development
  Facilities

Follow-up
  Program maintenance
  Transition plan
  Recommendations from evaluation
  Monitoring plan
  Continued communication

ta. They also reported findings in the school and district newsletter, to highlight different facets of the program.

Although data gathered during this phase may not indicate dramatic improvements in academic achievement, using a variety of informal measures will allow the supervisor to document subtle changes that may otherwise have gone unnoticed.

Another important consideration is follow-up. Pilot projects such as the one discussed earlier require planning for subsequent stages, since only one segment of the population will be affected (in that case, it was basic skills students). Full-fledged programs, on the other hand, need time to evolve as program adjustments contribute toward their development. Another important aspect of follow-up should be a way to shift ownership of the program from districtwide coordinators to those directly involved with it on a daily basis. In this way, it can be constantly monitored and maintained. While district administrators may have good intentions to oversee programs, it is more difficult for them to insure the appropriate day-to-day use of reading software. This type of monitoring must occur in each school.

SUMMARY

The foregoing discussion provides administrative guidelines for using computers in reading/language arts instruction, followed by an organizational framework for integrating computers into such a curriculum. The organizational framework, RECAP (REading Computers Assessment Plan), attempts to address systematically major administrative concerns needed for effective change.

As professionals, we must continue to develop as computer technology evolves. As reading supervisors, we must prepare ourselves for these changes so that we can lead our districts forward. This chapter provides information that should assist in achieving such professional growth.

REFERENCES

Balajthy, E. (1986). *Microcomputers in reading and language arts*. Englewood Cliffs, NJ: Prentice-Hall.

Balajthy, E., & Reinking, D. (1985). Micros and the first R. *Electronic Learning, 5*(1), 45–50.

Barnard, D. P., & Hetzel, R. W. (1986). *Principal's handbook to improve reading instruction* (2nd ed.). Lexington, MA: Ginn.

Bean, R. M., & Wilson, R. M. (1981). *Effecting change in school reading programs: The resource role*. Newark, DE: International Reading Association.

Blanchard, J., Mason, G., & Daniel, D. (1987). *Computer applications in reading* (3rd ed.). Newark, DE: International Reading Association.

Bullough, R. V., & Beatty, L. F. (1987). *Classroom applications of microcomputers*. Columbus, OH: Charles E. Merrill.

Burg, L. A., Kaufman, M., Korngold, B., & Kovner, A. (1978). *The complete reading supervisor: Tasks and roles*. Columbus, OH: Charles E. Merrill.

Campbell, R. E., Corbally, J. E., & Nystrand, R. O. (1983). *Introduction to educational administration* (6th ed.). Boston: Allyn and Bacon.

Cook, D. M. (1986). *A guide to curriculum planning in reading*. Madison, WI: Wisconsin Department of Public Instruction.

English, F. W. (1975). *School organization and management*. Worthington, OH: Charles A. Johnes.

Geoffrion, L. D., & Geoffrion, O. P. (1983). *Computers and reading instruction*. Reading, MA: Addison-Wesley.

Henney, M. B. (1987). Computer text vs. printed material text and the effect on reading. *The Reading Instruction Journal, 31*(1), 14–18.

Hunter, B. (1983). *My students use computers: Learning activities for computer literacy*. Reston, VA: Reston.

Likert, R. (1969). The nature of highly effective groups. In F. D. Carver & T. J. Sergiovanni (Ed.), *Organization and human behavior: Focus on schools* (pp. 360–361). New York: McGraw-Hill.

Luehrmann, A. (1982, September). Don't feel bad about teaching BASIC. *Electronic Learning*, pp. 23–24.

Miller, L., & Burnett, J. D. (1986). Theoretical considerations in selecting language arts software. *Computers and Education, 10*, 159–165.

Miller, L., & Burnett, J. D. (1987). Using computers as an integral aspect of elementary language arts instruction: Paradoxes, problems, and promise. In D. Reinking (Ed.), *Reading and computers: Issues for theory and practice* (pp. 178–191). New York: Teachers College Press.

Reinking, D. (1986). Six advantages of computer-mediated text for reading and writing instruction. *The Reading Instruction Journal, 29*(3), 8–16.

Reinking, D., & Schreiner, R. (1985). The effects of computer-mediated text on measures of reading comprehension and reading behavior. *Reading Research Quarterly, 20,* 536–552.

Robinson, R., & Good, T. L. (1987). *Becoming an effective reading teacher.* Cambridge, MA: Harper & Row.

Roth, S. F., & Beck, I. L. (1987). Theoretical and instructional implications of the assessment of two microcomputer word recognition programs. *Reading Research Quarterly, 22,* 197–218.

Rude, R. T. (1986). *Teaching reading using microcomputers.* Englewood Cliffs, NJ: Prentice-Hall.

Schweitzer, P. (1985, August). *Computer curriculum course guides, grades 3–5.* Unpublished report. Teaneck Public Schools, Teaneck, NJ.

Sherwood, R. D. (1986). Models of computer use in school settings. In C. K. Kinzer, R. D. Sherwood, & J. D. Bransford (Eds.), *Computer strategies for education: Foundations and content-area applications* (pp. 105–129). Columbus, OH: Charles E. Merrill.

Smith, F. (1984). *The promise and threat of microcomputers in language education.* Victoria, British Columbia: Abel Press.

Strickland, D. S., Feeley, J. T., & Wepner, S. B. (1987). *Using computers in the teaching of reading.* New York: Teachers College Press.

Taylor, R. (Ed.). (1980). *The computer in the school: Tutor, tool, tutee.* New York: Teachers College Press.

Vacca, J. L., Vacca, R. T., & Gove, M. K. (1987). *Reading and learning to read.* Boston, MA: Little, Brown.

Veatch, J., & Cooter, R. B. (1985–1986). Suggestions to school administrators for involving teachers in the selection of reading programs: The California study. *National Forum of Educational Administration and Supervision Journal, 3*(1), 1–6.

Wepner, S., & Kramer, S. (1987). Organizing computers for reading instruction. In J. Blanchard & G. Mason (Eds.), *The computers in reading and language arts* (pp. 53–66). New York: The Haworth Press.

14 Students with Special Needs

MICHAEL LABUDA
Jersey City State College

JOAN T. FEELEY
William Paterson College of New Jersey

WARREN E. HEISS
Montclair State College

Cathy A. Labate © 1988

Diversity in the American classroom is the norm rather than the exception. According to May (1986), a typical class contains children who are gifted and those who are learning disabled. Because of the waves of new immigrants from Spanish-speaking countries, Southeast Asia, and the Middle East, children whose first language is not English may be found in classrooms everywhere.

Reading/language arts supervisors and administrators must be prepared to deal with the reality of this diversity and be able to help schools to provide for the special needs of these learners. The purpose of this chapter is to provide background information about these special-needs students, describe ways of working with them, and suggest guidelines for supervisors and administrators to follow in planning and implementing literacy programs. We will discuss these issues with regard to three special populations of learners: gifted and creative children, children with learning disabilities, and children with limited English proficiency.

GIFTED AND CREATIVE CHILDREN

Who are the children we call gifted and creative? They are students who are above average in intellectual ability and creativity, who can make a commitment to a task or problem over an extended period, who function appropriately for different kinds of reading as they adjust and adapt to all kinds of text, and who repeatedly perform remarkably in most tasks (Gardner, 1983; Labuda, 1985; Renzulli, Reis, & Smith, 1981; Witty, 1958). Since classes for gifted and creative students are formed in relationship to school tasks, it behooves educators to think about a definition of this group that relates to the school's program goals.

Identification Procedures

Identification procedures for gifted and creative students depend on the types of programs that districts want to offer. Program goals may be established to provide for those with high IQ, extraordinary achievement, marked creativity, demonstrated leadership, and/or outstanding performance in the visual or performing arts (Bloom, 1982; Khatena, 1982; Labuda, 1985; Marland, 1972; Richert, Alvino, & McDonald, 1982; Saunders, 1982; Witty, 1985). Assessment procedures are employed to identify the following:

- *Intellectual ability.* Intelligence tests provide one practical way to predict general academic performance, by assessing the degree of rapid learning, alertness, common sense, and originality.
- *Academic achievement.* Special-ability or achievement tests are used to identify present academic achievement and to predict future talent in verbal, communication, and abstract ability skills.
- *Creativity.* Tests of creativity are used to identify creative or divergent productive thinking ability, such as coming up with new ideas, using materials in new and different ways, displaying curiosity, and engaging in experimental and inventive activities.

• *Leadership ability.* Actual performance measures and rating scales are utilized to indicate students' ability to influence others, be liked and respected by peers, and be regarded as a leader.

• *Visual and performing arts.* Tests, rating scales, and performance measures are used to reveal how well the student draws, paints, dances, and develops stories that are interesting and creative. Students gifted in an art form almost always show exceptional sensitivity to the emotional nuances of their specialty.

Regardless of the program, assessment procedures should include aptitude, achievement, and creativity measures. A search must be made for students of all abilities, not just students with high verbal aptitude. In addition, identification needs to be based on talents pertinent to the main instructional purpose of the school. Individual rather than group testing techniques must be used. Administrators must use tests that are appropriate for the specific purpose intended, employ culturally fair assessment practices, and make certain that qualified examiners administer the tests (Howley, Howley, & Pendarvis, 1986; Marland, 1972).

Many tests are available for identifying gifted and creative students; in general, federal regulations governing protection in assessment have provided some type of framework (PL 94-142, 1975). However, many of the tests used are either invalid or misused. As Stein (1986) says that it is quite common to use tests/instruments in a way that does not match what is described and intended in the test manuals. Emerging identification practices seem to indicate a harmful trend. Using tests for populations for which they have not been normed nor validated will most likely exclude underachievers and disadvantaged and multicultural/multilingual students. And, unfortunately, children in these groups account for a very small percentage of the students in programs for the gifted and creative.

One of the fairest ways of overcoming scores that do not reflect the true abilities and potential of minority students is to make use of the Baldwin Matrix (Baldwin & Wooster, 1977). This method of assessment enables one to pull together all of the scores of the various measurements used, into a workable, practical, and nondiscriminatory format. As this matrix formula weighs all test scores, one is able to assess all abstract and functional abilities, thus enabling culturally different students to compete for recognition. In addition, strengths and weaknesses are easily identified for all students.

Learning Environments

Research reveals that there is no single program concept that can effectively meet the needs of all gifted students (Labuda, 1985; Witty,

1971). A variety of program options must be designed and implemented. Prior to designing a program, one must determine the philosophical and psychological precepts that will guide the content, pace, methodology, and materials for the program. Administrative responsibilities must be spelled out. Federal efforts have encouraged differentiated services for the gifted but have not mandated specific types of programs. As a result, and as it should be, a variety of program options have been designed and implemented. States and local districts have initiated programs ranging from changes within regular school settings to special classes and schools. This wide diversity of programs reflects the schools' attempts to meet the needs of the gifted. Although there are differing views on program needs, there is general agreement on educational objectives. They include (1) mastery of important conceptual systems in various content fields; (2) development of skills and strategies that enable the gifted to become independent, creative, and self-sufficient; and (3) development of pleasure and excitement in reading and lifelong learning as a regular routine process (Gallagher, Weiss, Oglesby, & Thomas, 1983).

Although the regular classroom teacher can meet some of the goals for gifted children, special programs are essential to achieve all of them. Every subject should be taught to these students in a quantitatively and qualitatively different way. By changing the learning environment, it becomes possible to bring gifted children together for a period of time. This is advantageous for several reasons. It provides an opportunity for students with similar abilities and interests to interact and learn from each other. It reduces the instructional variance and enables the school to provide instructionally relevant materials. Finally, it provides instruction by teachers who have special expertise in meeting the needs of the gifted for a variety of content areas. Six common learning environments are described as follows.

Resource Rooms. In resource room pull-out programs, the student is removed from the regular classroom for several hours a week to work on special enrichment lessons with a trained teacher. Of all learning environment changes on the elementary school level, resource room pull-out programs are by far the most popular (Gallagher et al., 1983). Both parents and teachers prefer this method, since it provides special curricula and does not remove the child from total contact with peers, an important social consideration. Resource rooms provide accelerated classes for students with high IQs and/or special abilities in a variety of subject areas. Activities generally range from literature projects to classes in science, problem solving, and the arts. Usually this individualized instruction cannot be offered in the regular classroom. The chief advantage of resource classes is flexibility in scheduling.

Special Classes.   In this environment, gifted students are grouped together most of the time, for instruction with a specially trained teacher. Special classes may be self-contained, pull-out for all or part of a day, or homogeneous cluster groupings for special interests. This learning environment change is the most popular modification at the secondary school level and the second choice for the elementary grades (Gallagher et al., 1983). Special advanced-level classes permit students to earn college credit for special courses while still in high school. Termaine (1979) reported that participants in high school programs for gifted students earned high grades while taking more demanding classes, scored higher on the SATs, received more scholarships and awards, and were more involved in school activities, when compared to other gifted students.

Independent Study.   Independent study allows students to select topics of special interest while working under the supervision of a qualified teacher. This is a suitable method of study for any subject; however, student characteristics will determine the scope, procedure, and structure of the study. This is the second most popular method on the secondary school level (Gallagher et al., 1983). Renzulli and Smith (1979) and Reis and Cellerino (1983) provide detailed ways of planning and evaluating independent study.

Special Schools.   In this environment, gifted students receive differentiated instruction in a special school by specially trained teachers. Special schools are most popular where major population centers exist. For instance, New York City's high schools for the gifted (e.g., Bronx Science and Stuyvesant) have achieved high rates of success because of specialized instructors, ongoing acceleration, coordinated enrichment, and continuous articulation (Morgan, Tennant, & Gold, 1980). The "magnet school" concept may be employed to offer specialized study in one area; for instance, a language arts school may provide advanced classes in creative writing and journalism.

Community Consultants/Teachers.   Community consultants/teachers are mentors from local private sectors who are willing to participate in the school program. When mentors are available, this type of learning environment is quite popular. For instance, in the New York City public schools, an engineer/architect became involved with culturally disadvantaged gifted junior high school students. She visited the school once a week to help the students develop a project on environmental planning. Initially, she took the students to visit a local construction site, to help them visualize the land on which they would create their architectural designs and participate in environmental planning. Subsequently, she used a manual on architecture and engineering and a variety of inexpensive materials to help the students plan and construct buildings for this piece of land in the inner city. Throughout the semester, these "at-risk" gifted students were actively involved in using scientific principles to help discover how their visions for this land could be implemented.

In-Class and Pull-Out Enrichment Programs.   Enrichment programs usually include instruction in academics at an accelerated rate, as well as training in independent study techniques, creativity, and problem solving. Usually these programs focus on divergent rather than convergent thinking patterns. Often, the classroom teacher conducts a differentiated program of study without outside assistance; however, planning appropriate enrichment activities may tax the energy and resources of regular classroom teachers and require special training for them. Potential pitfalls include teachers defining the program as "more of the same," using students only as tutors, prescribing special study projects, or providing unique experiences that are not integrated into a comprehensive plan.

Within enrichment programs, there are three types of instructional objectives: process, content, and product. Process-oriented objectives attempt to develop high mental processes, informational techniques, and/or creative production. Bloom (1956), in his ranking of the process of cognition, and Guilford (1959), in postulating 120 potentially measurable cognitive processes, have influenced this type of instruction. Process or problem-solving instructional approaches include an abundance of commercial materials that enhance productive thinking, such as game-type strategies used in chess, self-paced "think lab" materials, and mind benders or logic exercises such as those developed by Harnadek (1982). Karnes and Collins (1980) have provided a comprehensive guide for selecting and adapting such materials.

Content-oriented objectives help students to develop factual knowledge and problem-solving strategies (Bloom, 1956; Bruner, 1960; Parnes, 1963). Research and critical thinking skills are utilized to identify a problem, analyze the results, evaluate the merits, and synthesize the findings.

Product-oriented objectives emphasize the end results. Regardless of the type of end result, whether it be in the form of a painting or piece of writing, the product justifies the program. Renzulli's (1977) "enrichment triad" offers suggestions for enrichment in exploratory activities, group training, and individual and small-group investigations of a real problem. Renzulli states that "the chief characteristic is that [students] are producers who use investigative techniques to solve real problems" (p. 29).

We offer the following two examples of the pull-out enrichment learning environment, to illustrate its use more fully. The first, a suburban-rural school in Warren County, New Jersey set up an effective pull-out enrichment program for its twenty gifted students, grades four through eight. They identified participants mainly through IQ test scores and teacher judgment. Students met for enrichment classes with a special teacher, outside their classrooms, for two days a week.

We observed the class as they were completing a literature unit. It was exciting to see a program in which children were taking responsibility for their own reading development. They selected literature suited for their needs and interests, worked at their own rates, and practiced communication skills in context. A framework of well-understood ground rules conducive to natural learning had been established earlier. They moved through a cycle consisting of sustained silent reading of self-selected books; an array of elective postreading activities such as producing filmstrips or illustrations and writing editorials or character analyses; compulsory activities such as summarizing or evaluating, assigned by the teacher according to skill needs; and "going public" activities, involving sharing and critiquing their products with each other.

For instance, after reading Paula Fox's *One-Eyed Cat* (1984), three eighth-grade students brainstormed on the content, process, and product objectives suggested in the Guilford-Bloom modality taxonomy (Labuda, 1987) (see Figure 14.1). In the content category, as suggested by the figure, they first identified the "kinds of themes" that ran throughout the book: guilt, forgiveness, illness and death, and living up to other people's standards. For process, they zeroed in on the higher thinking skills of analysis and synthesis. For the analysis process, they agreed to "explore" the illness-and-death theme by developing a diary of how the main character, Ned, felt about his mother's illness at different periods of time. For the synthesis process, they used the theme of "living up to other people's standards" to develop a list of figures of speech that revealed a code of behavior that was important to them as individuals. During sharing time, these eighth graders utilized a "going public" activity to share their products with their peers and invite their critique. This product sharing also allowed the teacher to check the students' comprehension of the book.

The second illustrative example of an enrichment program involves a fifth-grade student in another Warren County school where a similar model had been adopted. He read Katherine Paterson's *Bridge to Terabithia* (1972). Using the content theme of "Kids' Secret Kingdom" and the synthesis process, this student chose to predict how love, fairness, the arts, privacy, and education would fare in his kingdom. For his product, he portrayed his predictions through illustrations done in colored markers. During his "going public" activity, he had to explain his product and defend the integrity of his predictions.

Figure 14.1 Guilford-Bloom Modality Taxonomy

CONTENT	PROCESS						PRODUCT
	KNOWLEDGE	COMPREHENSION	APPLICATION	ANALYSIS	SYNTHESIS	EVALUATION	
History of . . .	show	explain	organize	analyze	revise	determine	Oral a. Panel b. Debate c. Teach a lesson d. Cassette e. Film/slide-tape f. _____
Kinds of . . .	explain	group	apply	classify	predict	rank	Written g. Journal/diary h. Letter i. Report j. Editorial k. _____
Purpose of . . .	list	describe	order	compare	estimate	measure	
Influences of . . .	discover	translate	relate	explore	develop	defend	Visual l. Display m. Collage n. Timeline o. _____
Characteristics of . . .	demonstrate	summarize	classify	categorize	adapt	justify	Kinesthetic p. Model q. Puzzle r. Sculpture s. Worksheet t. _____

Source: Labuda, M. (1987). *Using Literature to Develop Higher Thinking Comprehension Skills.* Unpublished manuscript.

Guidelines

In closing this section, we offer the following guidelines to administrators and supervisors:

1. Establish a committee, including specialists, administrators, classroom teachers, and parents, to determine what would constitute gifted and creative students in your school district.
2. Use this representative committee to select culturally appropriate assessment tools and develop quantitatively and qualitatively different curricular goals for this special population.
3. Based on predetermined curricular goals, set up appropriate learning environments so that these students can continue to develop their literacy skills and use their special talents to become lifelong learners and contributors to society.

CHILDREN WITH LEARNING DISABILITIES

Current practice in special education requires that instruction be provided for a variety of children who meet eligibility requirements for certain classifications. In addition, instruction for classified children must be made available along a continuum that includes settings that are "least restrictive" (regular classrooms) to "most restrictive" (homebound instruction). Federal guidelines in the form of the Education for All Handicapped Children Act (*Federal Register*, 1977) and the rules and regulations of each state govern these instructional delivery models.

Federal and state guidelines also require the development of an individualized education plan (IEP) for children who are eligible for special education services. Included in this plan are specific objectives for the child and for the placement of the child within the range of special education service delivery options.

Within the broad context of those who are eligible for special education, children with learning disabilities represent the largest group (Lerner, 1985). It is also likely that children from this group will be the ones placed in the "least restrictive" settings for instruction. Many of these children will be in regular classrooms and will receive support from resource-room teachers or supplemental instructors. A small proportion of them will be in self-contained special classes. Both the characteristics of and the instructional settings for children with learning disabilities create challenges for supervisors and administrators of reading programs.

Learning Characteristics

Lists of characteristics of children with learning disabilities abound in the literature. Bryan and Bryan (1986) summarize those characteristics and show how the influences of definition and research create shifts in emphasis. From an instructional perspective, however, two pervasive characteristics emerge. Both of these—poor incidental learning and dissociation—must be taken into account when designing instructional activities (Heiss, 1979).

Poor incidental learning skills result in an uneven accumulation of basic information. Academic tasks such as reading comprehension assume that a fundamental store of facts and concepts is present. The unevenness of these stores often accounts for the "peak and valley" assessment profiles of youngsters with learning disabilities. Dissociation refers to the difficulty that these children have in making connections between and among what appear to be logically related matters. This manifests itself in difficulty in reaching generalizations.

Because poor incidental learning and dissociation exist side by side, they exert an enormous negative influence on academic progress in all areas of the curriculum. An understanding of the effects of incidental learning difficulties on the availability of information and of dissociation on thought processes leads to making instructional decisions about what and how to teach children with these problems. Both content and process must be taken into account when designing instruction.

Beyond these general characteristics, there is a growing body of research showing the intimate connection between language disorders and learning disabilities (Vellutino, 1977; Wigg & Semel, 1984). It is clear that reading instruction cannot be separated from instruction in other aspects of language function.

Instructional Setting

Most children with learning disabilities are receiving instruction in more than one setting. Frequently this includes regular classroom placement with support provided by resource-room teachers and/or supplemental instructors. A complete description of various instructional delivery options and their combinations is offered by Lerner, Dawson, and Horvath (1980).

While it would appear that a combination of settings would be conducive to growth in reading and other skill areas, evidence shows that this is not always the case. Kimbrough and Hill (1981) found that pull-out programs are often self-defeating. Among their findings were that such programs

- Are viewed as replacements for instruction that goes on in the classroom
- Take time away from exposure to the core curriculum
- Confront the child with conflicting methodologies

Children with learning disabilities may in the course of a week see three or four different professionals for instruction. This array could include a regular classroom teacher, a resource-room teacher for reading instruction, a speech/language clinician, and a supplemental instructor for arithmetic tutoring. If there is no provision for integrating these various instructional efforts, their impact is likely to be minimal, since, as noted already, one of the major characteristics of children with learning disabilities is dissociation.

Resolving the Challenges

Addressing the challenges just delineated requires an examination of the assessment and instructional models that appear to be most responsive to the needs of these youngsters.

Assessment.   Yssledyke (1983) has studied the use of assessment data in making decisions regarding the development of programs for students with learning disabilities. His findings show that most of the assessment effort does not result in guidelines for instruction. Assessment models and the decision making that goes on within them are directed instead at defining the appropriate placement for the child. Yssledyke argues for a shift in that process so that the dynamics of the instructional intervention are addressed directly.

Principles and techniques for assessing children who require special interventions have been outlined by Salvia and Yssledyke (1985). What makes assessment for special children different is its emphasis on addressing the questions of *what* to teach as well as *how* to teach. Responding to these questions appropriately requires that the nature of the curriculum and its demands be understood fully. An extensive discussion of curriculum-based assessment has been developed for this purpose by Howell and Morehead (1987).

For children with learning disabilities, appropriate assessment of reading skills is critical for instructional planning, for several reasons. First, reading must be viewed as a means to an end. Nearly all areas of the curriculum have unique reading demands. To be successful in mathematics, social studies, and the sciences, students must be able to read proficiently. Because they have uneven information stores *and* because they have difficulty in generalizing, it is important to assess these students' skills in a context. Assumptions cannot be made that a skill that appears intact in one context will be usable in another. This is illustrated by examining the contextual shifting demanded by the curriculum for a simple word such as *table*. Table 14.1 lists the subject-matter contexts and word meanings for *table*.

The second reason that appropriate assessment in reading is important is in the larger framework of the life-adjustment goals of education. Functional literacy is an objective within life adjustment, and daily survival calls for functional literacy. For youngsters with learning disabilities, a major focus must be social and vocational adjustment. Within these contexts there is a critical need to assess reading skills that have functional applications.

Instruction.   Approaches to teaching children with learning disabilities must be well integrated. The more connections that are made among the parts of the curriculum for these students, the more likely it is that skills and concepts will be learned and retained. For this reason instruction in reading is best accomplished in the framework of the broader demands of the curriculum and with an emphasis on functional outcomes.

Lerner (1985) argues that a false dichotomy has evolved which pits the "specific-skill" approach against the "holistic" approach. She states that

> The two approaches to teaching reading comprehension are complementary and must be combined for effective reading. Specific skills give direction to remedial instruction. The holistic approach stresses the reader's experience, motivation, and participation in reading. . . . While good readers readily

Table 14.1   Contextual Shifts in Meaning for Word *Table*

SUBJECT-MATTER CONTEXT	WORD MEANING
Mathematics	"Turn to the square root *table*."
Geoscience	"Let's discuss the water *table*."
Social Studies	"The legislature *tabled* the bill."
Language Arts	"We will read stories about the Knights of the Round *Table*."
Woodshop	"Here are some of the uses of a *table* saw."

learn the subskills and then intuitively combine and integrate them, less accomplished readers may be still struggling to acquire specific reading skills and therefore using them in an unintegrated, splintered manner. [pp. 366–367]

It is important to recognize that, within Lerner's context, specific teaching methodologies are valuable to the extent to which they work in individual cases. This model accommodates the need to balance content decisions (what to teach) and process decisions (how to teach).

While Lerner's (1985) perspective is an eclectic one and allows for an array of methodologies, recent studies have shown that a "learning strategies intervention model" is beneficial for teaching reading to secondary-level students with learning disabilities (Deshler, Schumaker, & Lenz, 1984). Developed at the University of Kansas, this model has taken the position that specific learning strategies must be taught to these students if they are to cope effectively with the secondary school curriculum. Continuing to teach basic skills to these students fails to equip them to handle the curriculum. In essence, the learning strategies model employs tightly structured organizational devices and systems which can be applied across the curriculum (Alley & Deshler, 1979).

Summary

It is clear that children with learning disabilities require instructional approaches that are integrative. Instructional activities that promote skill development in reading must lead to direct application in the larger context of the demands of the curriculum. In addition, because these students are taught more often than not by several people, every attempt must be made to assist them in tying together the results of all instructional efforts.

This section has examined current practices in special education for students with learning disabilities. To be successful, assessment and instruction in reading must take into account not only the learning characteristics of the students but also the variations in settings for which the instructional objectives are applicable. Within these settings, the instructional objectives should be applied across the curriculum, so that students understand the functional value of reading for life.

CHILDREN WITH LIMITED ENGLISH PROFICIENCY

Today, children whose first language is not English can be found in almost all schools. Added to large numbers of Spanish speakers from Cuba, Puerto Rico, Mexico, and Central and South America are the new immigrants from Asia and the Middle East. It is not unusual for large urban districts like Paterson, New Jersey, to have to deal with speakers of fifty or more different languages. Suburban districts, too, are experiencing an influx of "limited-English-proficient" (LEP) children, as businesspeople from around the world move their families in and out of American towns that had previously known few nonnative English speakers.

Traditional Approaches

Traditionally, there have been two main approaches to handling LEP populations: transitional bilingual programs in which children learn in their native language until they know enough English to move into regular classes and English-as-a-second-language (ESL) programs that are aimed at teaching English and all content areas in English only. More and more, the differences between these two approaches are becoming blurred, as some federal Title VII (Bilingual Education Act, 1984 Amendments) grants, originally intended to promote bilingual education, may now go to English-only programs (Crawford, 1987a). On the other hand, contrary to popular belief, transitional bilingual education employs English as the medium of instruction from 72 to 92 percent of the time (Ovando & Collier, 1985).

The advantages of using the child's native language as a bridge in transitional situations are self-evident. We are building on what children know (their own language, learned naturally, and their own cognitive framework), promoting self-esteem by accepting what is an integral part of them, and making them feel comfortable during the difficult transition to speaking and learning in English. (An illustration to make English-only advocates stop and think is to ask them to imagine themselves as eight-year-olds whose parent has been transferred to rural Brazil where there are no schools with instruction in English. They would have to enter a world in which only Portuguese was spoken all day long. They soon acknowledge that it would be a very difficult situation and that they would appreciate having someone around who spoke English.)

Certainly, when it comes to learning to read and write, there is universal agreement that it is best to learn first in one's native tongue, building on what has been learned naturally about the syntax, semantics, and grapho-phonemics of the first language (Feeley, 1970; Feitelson, 1979; Hakuta, 1986; Hudelson, 1987; Krashen, 1985a). While it is still possible and most advantageous to offer this option to LEP children from the larger language minorities like Spanish and Chinese, it is becoming increasingly difficult to find teachers for the myriad of languages found in today's schools.

Whole-Language Approach

One answer to this problem of educating a multilingual population is a whole-language approach, such as those described in chapters 3 and 12 for the general population. This is in contrast to traditional ESL programs, where students are drilled on selected grammatical structures with an audio-lingual method (ALM). Termed *communication-based ESL* by Ovando and Collier (1985), the whole-language approach sees a second language developing in much the same way as the first language. This happens in language-rich, comprehension-based environments in which children are free to experiment with speaking, reading, and writing, with feedback given by understanding peers and adults (Krashen, 1985a; Tough, 1985).

Krashen (1985b) has coined the term *comprehensible input* and has stressed the importance of context in second-language learning. Moustafa (1987) has described a method built on these principles, called Comprehensible Input *plus* the Language Experience Approach (CI+LEA) and has used it successfully to teach newly arrived speakers of Spanish, Cambodian, Korean, Vietnamese, Farsi, and Urdu to speak, read, and write English in record time. Her technique is to show a picture of a familiar situation (e.g., children playing in a schoolyard) to the students. They discuss the picture through questions, answers, and gestures, until the children have acquired the language orally. Then she introduces the major content words in written form on cards (*boy, ball, throwing*) and has the children match the words to the picture. Next, using these key words, the children dictate sentences about the picture, which Moustafa writes on chart paper or an overhead transparency. Finally, she has them read the text in unison and individually and work with it in the same way as would any primary teacher using LEA.

These dictated stories become the basis from which the children learn grammar, spelling, and print conventions. Before long, after the "comprehensible input" stage, many begin writing their own compositions and eventually demonstrate their ability to transfer what they have learned by reading stories from other groups and printed materials that have not been directly taught in their lessons. While most of the fifty-plus children in Moustafa's (1987) class were at the zero-year level in aural English (Peabody Picture Vocabulary Test) at the start of the year, all made gains, with many scoring at the four-, five-, and six-year levels by May. Their writing samples were impressive, appearing quite natural, with invented spellings but clear messages.

Another "comprehensible input," whole-language practice has been described by Aida Montero.* When she was a teacher trainer in Brooklyn's District 15, she successfully used Holdaway's (1979) "shared reading" of big books (see chapters 3 and 12) with LEP children of various language backgrounds. After she explained the pictures and introduced the vocabulary to the children, they would read the story in unison several times until the children could read it by themselves. Since the children were writing in a writing workshop (see chapter 12), they gradually began to add text to their picture stories. Through shared book experiences they learned to speak, read, and write English within a holistic, literature-based, meaningful context.

Hudelson (1987) describes a bilingual program in Arizona which has incorporated many of the writing-as-process techniques described in chapter 12. For example, the children, who learn to read in Spanish first, are encouraged to write for different purposes and audiences. In their Spanish writing they behave much as English-speaking beginners do, using invented spelling and unconventional punctuation. By the end of the year, children write their pieces in Spanish and English. Hudelson says, "Writing fluency in their native language gave these children confidence that they could write in English. . . . Rather than avoiding or refusing to use English, these children moved themselves from monoliteracy in Spanish to biliteracy in Spanish and English" (pp. 835–836).

Other whole-language activities are suggested by Feeley (1979; 1983) and Rigg and Enright (1986). Most of the teaching strategies described in chapters 3, 4, 12, and 15 can be adapted for LEP populations. The important thing is to keep the focus on comprehensible input and language learning in holistic, fully contextualized situations.

Guidelines

Based on the problems and teaching approaches just discussed, we offer the following guidelines (adapted from Reisner, 1983) for administrators and reading/language arts supervisors to use as they try to provide appropriate learning experiences for various LEP populations.

1. *Determine the district's legal responsibilities regarding LEP students and communicate them clearly to the board and the public.*
If your state mandates native-language instruction, make every effort to be in compliance or make adjustments where possible. For instance, although Paramus, New Jersey could not find a qualified teacher of Japanese when

---

*Aida Montero (1988, January 6), personal communication.

their Japanese-speaking student population reached the state quota, they did hire a competent aide. A middle-class suburb of New York City, Paramus has some thirty languages represented in its LEP population. Accordingly, it has developed an exemplary, communication-based ESL program to meet the needs of its multilingual students.*

2. *Establish an administrative steering committee that includes representatives from mainstream and other special programs, to help set up and implement your program.*

Successful bilingual/ESL programs cannot operate in a vacuum. Since LEP students are mainstreamed for part of the day, classroom teachers must be involved. Because reading teachers usually deal with these students eventually, their assistance is invaluable. Special education personnel and child study team members should round out the committee.

3. *Develop the approach that is best for the LEP students in your district.*

In response to a federal investigation that found them failing to meet their obligations to LEP students (Lau Decision), the Alhambra School District in suburban Los Angeles set up a transitional bilingual education plan in which LEP students began instruction in their native language (Spanish, Cantonese, Mandarin, or Vietnamese). Because of the success of their students in eventually learning to read and write English, Alhambra, whose LEP students had been failing miserably, has become a model district. Bilingual education, which worked well for them, was their "Lau remedy" (Crawford, 1987b).

On the other hand, Fairfax County, Virginia, with students from fifty different language groups, won a battle with the Office of Civil Rights for its Lau plan that featured ESL instruction only. They argued that finding bilingual teachers for their language-diverse population was impossible; instead they opted to spend additional money ($750 per LEP child) and keep their student-teacher ratio at about twelve to one (Crawford, 1987a).

The Dual Language Program at P.S. 84 in New York City offers instruction in both English and Spanish to Hispanic students and monolingual English-speaking students. Their goal is to produce children who will graduate from P.S. 84 with full command of communication skills in both English and Spanish.†

There is no one program that is best for all LEP situations. It is up to your steering committee to decide which approach is best for your district.

---

*Dr. Harry Galinsky, Superintendent of Schools, Paramus, NJ (1988, January 8), personal communication.
†Ruth A. Swinney, Program Coordinator (1988, January), personal communication.

4. *Highlight similarities between the LEP and general school populations.*

Encourage the sharing of cultural heritage through assemblies, writing assignments, and festivals with broad, general themes such as holidays or foods. One local school district recently presented Winter Holidays Around the World, complete with piñatas, menorahs, and manger scenes.

5. *Group students according to their instructional needs.*

With the help of your steering committee, develop screening procedures to identify and group LEP students according to first language or English proficiency. Usually screening is done by parental interview, an oral/aural language test, and teacher observation. It is important to seek parental approval of your recommendations; placement should be flexible and subject to change. Also, exit criteria should be established so that children can be completely mainstreamed as soon as they are able.

Although children need to be grouped for language study, they should be with regular classes for noncognitively based subjects. For instance, in the Case-Studies Curriculum Model (Crawford, 1987c), an experimental transitional bilingual program in California, LEP students study language arts, math, science, and social studies in Spanish, learn ESL in a "sheltered" English class (meaning is stressed in a communications context), and are mainstreamed for art, music, and physical education. Gradually, math and science are moved into the "sheltered" mode, soon to be joined by English language arts and social studies; after this, children are mainstreamed for math and science. When proficient in English (usually by grades four to six), they are fully mainstreamed.

Even if your program is ESL only, it is good to alternate children between ESL small-group pull-out classes, "sheltered" English for some cognitive areas, and mainstream classrooms in which they are paired with an English-speaking buddy. LEP children learn from English-proficient classmates, through what is called "the missionary child syndrome." Isolation prevents this natural acquisition phenomenon.

6. *Offer staff development for mainstream teachers, bilingual/ESL teachers, and other specialists.*

Classroom teachers need to be informed about sociolinguistic and psycholinguistic principles of language acquisition and language functions. Characteristics of the special language populations in your district should be highlighted. Informed strategies are better than an "I give up," sink-or-swim approach.

Both classroom teachers and bilingual/ESL teachers need to be informed about the latest research and concomitant strategies for teaching reading and writing. For example, schema theory (see chapter 15) and writing-as-process findings (see chapter 12) need to be communicated on a practical level to all teachers involved. In one exemplary bilingual district, the bilingual/ESL teachers specifically asked for inservice training on the teaching of reading (Reisner, 1983).

7. *Involve parents whenever possible.*
The key to successful programs for LEP students is strong support from the home. P.S. 84 has a drop-in room for parents to use when they bring children to school. There parents find coffee, literature, and people to help in filling out forms. This gesture gives parents a sense of belonging to the school community.

Newsletters and special invitations to PTA meetings and school functions, written in the parents' language, and opportunities for parents to evaluate and participate in your program will garner much-needed parental support.

SUMMARY

In this chapter we have described the problems and most current approaches to providing appropriate literacy experiences for gifted and creative children, children with learning disabilities, and children with limited English proficiency. All these types of students with special needs are found in today's schools. Since most school populations are more diverse than they are homogeneous, we have offered suggestions and guidelines for administrators and reading/language arts supervisors to use as they attempt to develop reading/writing programs to meet the needs of all learners.

REFERENCES

Alley, G. R., & Deshler, D. D. (1979). *Teaching the learning disabled adolescent: Strategies and methods.* Denver, CO: Love.

Baldwin, A. Y., & Wooster, J. (1977). *Baldwin identification matrix.* Buffalo, NY: Dissemination of Information Publishers.

Bloom, B. (1956). *Taxonomy of educational objectives, handbook I: Cognitive domain.* New York: David McKay.

Bloom, B. (1982). The role of gifts and markers in the development of talent. *Exceptional Children, 48,* 510–522.

Bruner, J. S. (1960). *The process of education.* New York: Vintage Books.

Bryan, T. H., & Bryan, J. H. (1986). *Understanding learning disabilities* (3rd ed.). Palo Alto, CA: Mayfield.

Crawford, J. (1987a, April 1). Bilingual policy has taken shape along two district federal tracks. *Education Week*, pp. 21, 23–25.

Crawford, J. (1987b, April 1). California program grapples with problems, scores successes. *Education Week*, pp. 47–50.

Crawford, J. (1987c, April 1). Project aims to bridge gap between research, classroom. *Education Week*, pp. 40–43.

Deshler, D. D., Schumaker, J., & Lenz, B. (1984). Academic and cognitive intervention for learning disabled adolescents, Parts I, II. *Journal of Learning Disabilities, 17,* 108–119, 170–187.

Federal Register (Part IV). (1977, August). 42 (163).

Feeley, J. T. (1970). Teaching non-English-speaking first-graders to read. *Elementary English, 47,* 199–208.

Feeley, J. T. (1979). A workshop tried and true: Language experience for bilinguals. *The Reading Teacher, 33,* 25–27.

Feeley, J. T. (1983). Help for the reading teacher: Dealing with the limited English proficient (LEP) child in the elementary classroom. *The Reading Teacher, 37,* 650–655.

Feitelson, D. (1979). *Mother tongue or second language?* Newark, DE: International Reading Association.

Fox, P. (1984). *One-eyed cat.* New York: Bradbury Press.

Gallagher, J., Weiss, P., Oglesby, K., & Thomas, T. (1983). *The status of gifted and talented education: United States surveys of needs, practices and policies.* National/State Leadership Training Institute on the Gifted and Talented. Ventura, CA: Office of the Ventura County Superintendent of Schools.

Gardner, H. (1983). *Frames of mind: The theory of multiple intelligences.* New York: Basic Books.

Guilford, J. P. (1959). Three faces of the intellect. *American Psychologist, 14,* 469–479.

Hakuta, K. (1986). *Mirror of language: The debate on bilingualism.* New York: Basic Books.

Harnadek, A. (1982). *Thinking skills.* Pacific Grove, CA: Midwest Publishers.

Heiss, W. E. (1979). Relating educational assessment to instructional planning. In E. L. Meyen, G. A. Vergason, & R. J. Whelan (Eds.), *Instructional planning for exceptional children* (pp. 390–405). Denver, CO: Love.

Holdaway, D. (1979). *The foundations of literacy.* Sydney, Australia: Ashton Scholastic (distributed in the United States by Heinemann).

Howell, K. W., & Morehead, M. K. (1987). *Curriculum-based evaluation for special and remedial education.* Columbus, OH: Charles E. Merrill.

Howley, A., Howley, C., & Pendarvis, E. (1986). *Teaching gifted children: Principles and strategies.* Boston: Little, Brown.

Hudelson, S. (1987). Language minority children. *Language Arts, 64,* 827–841.

Karnes, F., & Collins, E. (1980). *Handbook of instructional resources and references for teaching the gifted.* Boston: Allyn and Bacon.

Khatena, J. (1982). *Educational psychology of the gifted.* New York: John Wiley.

Kimbrough, J., & Hill, P. T. (1981). *The aggregate effects of federal education programs.* Santa Monica, CA: Rand.

Krashen, S. D. (1985a). *Inquiries and insights: Second language learning, immersion and bilingual education, literacy.* Hayward, CA: Alemany Press.

Krashen, S. D. (1985b). *The input hypothesis: Issues and implications.* London: Longman.

Labuda, M. (1985). *Creative reading for gifted learners: A design for excellence* (2nd ed.). Newark, DE: International Reading Association.

Labuda, M. (1987). *Using literature to develop higher thinking comprehension skills.* Unpublished research paper.

Lerner, J. (1985). *Learning disabilities: Theories, diagnosis, and teaching strategies.* Boston: Houghton Mifflin.

Lerner, J., Dawson, D., & Horvath, L. (1980). *Cases in learning and behavior problems: A guide to individualized education programs.* Boston: Houghton Mifflin.

Marland, S. (1972). *Education of the gifted and talented: Report to Congress by the U.S. Commissioner of Education.* Washington, DC: U.S. Government Printing Office.

May, F. B. (1986). *Reading as communication: An interactive approach* (2nd ed.). Columbus, OH: Charles E. Merrill.

Morgan, H. J., Tennant, C. B., & Gold, M. J. (1980). *Elementary and secondary level programs for the gifted and talented.* New York: Teachers College Press.

Moustafa, M. (1987). Comprehensible input PLUS the language experience approach. *The Reading Teacher, 41,* 276–287.

Ovando, C. J., & Collier, V. P. (1985). *Bilingual and ESL classrooms: Teaching in multicolor contexts.* New York: McGraw-Hill.

Parnes, J. (1963). *Creative behavior guidebook.* New York: Scribners.

Paterson, K. (1972). *Bridge to Terabithia.* New York: Thomas Crowell Company.

Reis, S. M., & Cellerino, M. (1983). Guiding gifted students through independent study. *Teaching exceptional children, 15*(3), 136–139.

Reisner, E. R. (1983). *Building capacity and commitment in bilingual education: A practical guide for educators* (Report by the Education Policy Department Center). Washington, DC: U.S. Department of Education.

Renzulli, J. (1977). *The enrichment triad model: A guide for developing defensible programs for the gifted and talented.* Wethersfield, CT: Creative Learning Press.

Renzulli, J., Reis, M., & Smith, L. (1981). *The revolving door identification model.* Mansfield Center, CT: Creative Learning Press.

Renzulli, J., & Smith, L. (1979). Issues and procedures in evaluating programs. In A. H. Passow, (Ed.), *The gifted and the talented: Their education and development* (pp. 289–307). Chicago: University of Chicago Press.

Richert, E., Alvino, J., & McDonald, R. (1982). *National report on identification and recommendations for comprehensive identification of gifted and talented youth.* Sewell, NJ: Educational Improvement Center, South.

Rigg, P., & Enright, D. S. (1986). *Children and ESL: Integrating perspectives.* Washington, DC: Teachers of English to Speakers of Other Languages.

Salvia, J., & Yssledyke, J. (1985). *Assessment in special and remedial education* (3rd ed.). Boston, MA: Houghton Mifflin.

Saunders, R. (1982). Screening and identifying the talented in art. *Roeper Review*, 4(3), 7–10.

Stein, M. J. (1986). *Gifted, talented, and creative young people: A guide to teaching and research*. New York: Garland.

Termaine, C. (1979). Do gifted programs make a difference?: *The Gifted Child Quarterly, 23*, 500–517.

Tough, J. (1985). *Talk two: Children using English as a second language in primary schools*. London: Onyx Press.

Vellutino, F. (1977). Alternative conceptualizations of dyslexia: Evidence in support of a verbal-deficit hypothesis. *Harvard Education Review, 47*, 334–354.

Wigg, E. H., & Semel, E. (1984). *Language assessment and intervention for the learning disabled* (2nd ed.). Columbus, OH: Charles E. Merrill.

Witty, P. (1958). Who are the gifted? In N. B. Henry (Ed.), *Education of the gifted, part II* (pp. 41–63). Chicago: University of Chicago Press.

Witty, P. (Ed.). (1971). *Reading for gifted and creative students*. Newark, DE: International Reading Association.

Witty, P. (1985). Rationale for fostering creative reading in the gifted and creative. In M. Labuda (Ed.), *Creative reading for gifted learners: A design for excellence* (pp. 8–25). Newark, DE: International Reading Association.

Yssledyke, J. (1983). Current practices in making psychoeducational decisions about learning disabled students. In G. Senf, & J. Torgesen (Eds.), *Annual review of learning disabilities* (Vol. 1). Chicago, IL: Professional Press.

15 Cultivation of Lifetime Readers

DIXIE LEE SPIEGEL
University of North Carolina at Chapel Hill

What is a "lifetime reader"? Surely once a person learns to read reasonably well, he or she doesn't forget how to read (barring neurological problems). True. People usually don't forget how to read, but sometimes they forget *to* read. Lifetime readers never forget to read. They choose reading as a leisure-time activity. They automatically use reading to gain information and solve problems (What is the best way to train a dog to heel?). They escape from their everyday lives into worlds of adventure, romance, and exotic lands. "Real" lifetime readers take a book with them to the doctor's office, knowing that they will probably have to wait. They plan their weekends carefully to be sure that they have enough books to see them through while the library is closed. They experiment with reading while mowing the lawn (the vibrations will defeat you), ironing (you need a good book rack), and vacuuming (this works well, especially if you have low standards for cleanliness).

As a nation we are coming closer to the goal of creating a nation of individuals who can read (National Assessment of Educational Progress, 1981). But we have yet to reach the goal of developing students who *will* read, who will become lifetime readers who choose reading voluntarily as a source of pleasure or information.

In this chapter, two solutions to the problem of cultivating lifetime readers will be described. Each of these solutions goes beyond the bounds of the usual "reading program," and both are appropriate at all levels of schooling, K–12. One solution is to promote leisure reading by providing time within the school day to do recreational reading of self-selected materials. The other solution is to integrate literature into the regular content-area curricula. Both of these programs have the advantage of providing the learner with "real reading" experiences like the ones lifetime readers have. Furthermore, both recreational reading and integrated literature programs promote the habit of reading as a voluntary activity, but without sacrificing the rest of the curriculum.

THE RECREATIONAL READING PROGRAM

What Is It?

In a recreational reading program, students read. They read what they want, at their own pace, and without the burden of having to prove that they have "really read." This, of course, is what lifetime readers do. The teacher's job is to "provide time for [the students] to read, materials for them to read, and places for them to read. And then let them do it, with a minimum of interference" (Spiegel, in press).

In a recreational reading program, time for self-selected pleasure reading is provided during the regular school day, as a valued part of the curriculum. In some instances an entire school will shut down for thirty minutes once or twice a week while everyone, including the custodial staff and the principal, reads. (This is called sustained silent reading.) In other cases, specific time for recreational reading is set aside on a daily basis, within individual classrooms. Students might read the first thing every morning for ten minutes, or they might be required to read for a minimum of twenty minutes during independent seatwork time in the elementary grades. At the middle and high school levels, ten minutes of reading might be taken from homeroom period or drawn from first period one week, second period the next week, and so on. The frequency and duration of the "chunk" of time allowed for free reading will vary, but what is important is that on a regular basis students are given sustained periods of time to immerse themselves in a reading activity of their own choice. They may choose to read anything they wish (pornography excluded), including *Sports Illustrated*, comic books, and their favorite Dr. Seuss book for the fifth time that month. There is really only one rule: Read.

Why Would This Program Create Lifetime Readers?

A recreational reading program is likely to develop lifetime readers for three important reasons. First, the students actually act like lifetime readers. For much of a student's schooling, she or he is told what to read, when to read it, how fast to read it, and what to learn or enjoy from it! None of that mimics what a lifetime reader does. If we want students to develop the independence of purpose and application that a lifetime reader has, we must allow them to practice these activities in school. In some ways we as educators may create "learned helplessness" in pleasure reading by tightly controlling so many of the reading experiences in school. Students learn to wait to be told what to do. But in a recreational reading program, the students practice taking these responsibilities upon themselves.

A second reason for the likely success of a recreational reading program in creating lifetime readers is that learners develop positive attitudes toward reading during a recreational reading program. They experience the "down time" of reading that comes when one reads in an unthreatening, psychologically safe environment that is free from competition and accountability. They are free to explore whatever nooks and crannies of the world they wish, without explaining what they are doing or why. And they will find that, the more reading they do, the easier it becomes and therefore the more they enjoy it. McCracken (1971) likens recreational reading to the reinforcement step or drill of silent reading. It is the time that the student "puts it all together" as a whole, rather than continuing to practice on isolated pieces.

The third way that recreational reading promotes lifetime reading is that students begin to perceive recreational, self-selected reading as something that is valued, because it is a real part of the curriculum, just like science and social studies. Time is built into the school day for this activity; it is not relegated to the status of a frill, something "we'll get to if we have time." Furthermore, in the most successful recreational reading programs, free reading is something the teacher also does. That is, while the students read, the teacher also reads something solely for pleasure. Thus the students are viewing a real-life model of a lifetime reader. Free reading therefore is not perceived as "good for you young folks, like milk," but something that a relatively normal adult actually looks forward to and enjoys.

Will Recreational Reading Detract from Other Curriculum Areas?

No, the rest of the curriculum will actually be enhanced, because recreational reading advances that most basic and transferable of all curricula, learning and using reading. Anderson, Wilson, and Fielding (1986) found that even ten minutes of free reading a day had an enormous impact on reading comprehension scores on a standardized measure. There are many plausible reasons for this relationship. Practice with easy, enjoyable reading develops fluency or automaticity (LaBerge & Samuels, 1976), which is the ability to read the words without conscious attention to the words. The greater the degree of automaticity, the less the reader's attention is drawn away to deal with words and the more attention is available to deal with ideas. Comprehension also improves.

Another link between free reading and increased comprehension is based on the fact that reading is a valuable source of vicarious experience. As such, reading develops one's schemata. A schema is a cognitive network of information, containing what one knows about a topic and the way in which the various pieces of this information are interrelated. As an individual reads, new information is added to old, thus elaborating already existing schemata, and new information is distinguished from old, thus setting up new schemata. The facilitative relationship between prior knowledge and comprehension is well documented (Johnston, 1984; Langer & Nicolich, 1981; Steffensen, Joag-Deu, & Anderson, 1979). In this way, reading might be said to have a cumulative effect on comprehension: The more you read, the more you know, and the more you know, the better you comprehend new information.

A third hypothesized connection between free reading and growth in reading comprehension is the development of meaning vocabulary. A person's meaning vocabulary is the set of words for which that individual has at least one meaning. Meaning vocabulary is very important to reading comprehension, and one of the most effective ways of expanding it is through reading. As students meet new words in the context of free reading, they gradually learn the meanings of these words and continue to refine and elaborate on these meanings as the words are encountered in new contexts.

It is important to note that all of these suggested relationships between free reading and comprehension apply to curricular areas beyond reading. It is not just that reading comprehension improves. A student reads content—social studies, literature, science. Comprehension in all curricular areas should improve.

INTEGRATING LITERATURE AND THE CONTENT AREAS

What Is It?

In a recreational reading program, time is taken from other curricular areas and given over to free reading. When literature is integrated into the content areas, reading is placed into other curricular areas in a way that enhances those areas. There is a synergistic relationship in which the total growth is more than the sum of the individual parts.

Literature can be integrated into the content areas in many ways. A piece of fiction, such as *Johnny Tremain* (Forbes, 1943) or *War Horse* (Morpurgo, 1983)—a tale of World War I as seen through the eyes of a cavalry horse—might be used to set the ambiance for the study of a particular period of history. The teacher could read selected portions of the novel to the class for five to ten minutes at the beginning of each period. Another procedure is to have students read excerpts from a variety of pieces of literature about one topic and compare the information gleaned across these pieces with the information from their "official" assigned textbooks. The class might make a bulletin displaying information they have learned about a topic solely from their reading of literature. Students might use a piece of literature such as Dillard's *Pilgrim at Tinker Creek* (1974) as a model for writing their own descriptions of the wonders of biology, or *Ben and Me* (Lawson, 1939) to create a diary of the Revolutionary War period. These are only a few of the many ways literature can be integrated into the content areas.

Why Would This Program Create Lifetime Readers?

One of the joys of reading is the broadening of one's world. Avid readers learn when they read, whether they are reading Agatha Christie and learning about life in sleepy English villages, or Bill Cosby and learning to use humor in dealing with the perils of parenting, or *The Joy of Cooking* (Rombauer & Becker, 1975) and learning the best way to make a meringue. When literature is integrated into the content areas, students become sensitive to how much reading, especially literature, expands their knowledge about the world. They will learn that information about the world can come from many sources, not just texts, if only one is open to receiving this information. Conversely, they will learn that reading is not either for pleasure or for gaining information, but often for both. This is what lifetime readers know.

Will an Integrated Literature Program Detract from Other Curriculum Areas?

Adding literature to the content areas does not mean that less content will be learned, but more. Adding literature to social studies, science, and math units will not detract from the enjoyment of and interest in these content areas, but will enhance them. Artley (1967) expresses this reciprocal relationship well: "The content being studied is clarified, enriched, and dramatized through literature. In turn, good reading is motivated and becomes functional as it relates to content being studied" (p. 214).

Integration of literature into the content area makes the content more memorable and relevant. Literature captures the mood of a time or event, not just the facts; it transplants the reader. Literature adds depth and detail to the study of content, often with images that are more vivid than those of traditional textbooks. Who could not gain a more humble perspective of our own place in the scheme of things after reading the following?

> Consider the ordinary barnacle, the rock barnacle. Inside every one of those millions of hard white cones on the rocks — the kind that bruises your heel as you bruise its head — is of course a creature as alive as you or I. Its business in life is this: when a wave washes over it, it sticks out twelve feathery feeding appendages and filters the plankton for food. As it grows, it sheds its skin like a lobster, enlarges its shell, and reproduces itself without end. The larvae "hatch into the sea in milky clouds." The barnacles encrusting a single half mile of shore can leak into the water a million million larvae. [Dillard, 1974, p. 169]

Literature stimulates transfer, generalization, and application of concepts. It provides a broader base of information for concepts, by providing more examples. Hennings (1982) suggests that literature enhances transfer of concepts because readers have to process concepts more deeply, since "the messages in story form are generally implied rather than stated explicitly" (p. 288).

Last of all, students who have had a tendency to view chemistry or history or civics as dry, dull, and dead may find their interest piqued and their view of these content areas dramatically changed. As literature provides additional detail and perspective, the students become more active learners; they may become involved interpreters and synthesizers rather than mere passive receivers of "facts."

THE ADMINISTRATOR'S ROLE

The administrator's role in supporting the development of lifetime readers through recreational and integrated literature programs is crucial. Such programs can limp along with administrative neglect, but they can thrive with just a bit of careful nurturing. This comes in four ways: through administrative support at the curricular level, through financial support, through support within the school and across the school system, and through liaison activities with forces outside the school.

Support at the Curricular Level

Administrators at both the school and system level need to support efforts to create lifetime readers as legitimate and valued parts of the regular, whole-school (or system) curriculum. The most crucial aspect of treating a recreational reading program or an integrated literature program as a real part of the curriculum is to provide substantial and sustained periods of time for these activities on a regular and protected basis. For the recreational reading program, in which a specific time period may be designated solely for this activity, "protected" means that the recreational reading time is not the automatic sacrificial lamb when more time is needed for special activities such as assemblies or parent conferences. It also means that this time is not viewed as an opportunity to talk with the teacher, make announcements, or schedule fire drills. In other words, this time period should be viewed as dedicated exclusively to recreational reading.

Teachers' efforts to find time for recreational reading and an integrated literature program in their already overcrowded curricula will undoubtedly require creative reshuffling of schedules. Administrators need to assist teachers in examining the ways they organize their days, looking for additional ways to combine, coordinate, and integrate. Both groups need to keep in mind that there is nothing sacred about having spelling every day at the elementary level or about using an entire fifty-minute period at the high school exclusively for biology. Furthermore, pressure to get through the entire curriculum may need to be replaced by acceptance of teaching most of the curriculum very well rather than speeding through all of the curriculum just to be able to say, "We covered that."

Although these efforts to promote lifetime reading need to be viewed as full-fledged components of the curriculum, there is one area in which a difference ought to occur: accountability. If administrators insist on requiring a mass of record-keeping or a set of specific measures to prove that the children are learning to enjoy reading in these programs, the very nature of the programs will be violated. Lifetime readers do not write book reports or take quizzes after they read!

Financial Support

Both the recreational reading program and the integrated literature program are relatively inexpensive to operate. They require books — lots of books, to be sure — but mostly just books. These books need to be in both classroom and school libraries. The students must have reading materials of a wide variety of genres and reading levels easily accessible. Powell (1966) found that this availability of materials was a crucial factor in the amount of recreational reading done, and Bissett (1969) found that students in classrooms without classroom libraries read 50 percent fewer books than children with access to them.

For an integrated literature program, both variety and amount of reading materials within a topic are important factors. Teachers will need to indicate to the school librarian what topics will be included in the integrated literature program in the forthcoming year, so that the librarian can take this information into consideration when ordering new materials. If funds are limited, teachers may need to work with the librarian in order to list topics by priority, so that at least a few topics can be examined fully rather than all topics superficially.

Support Within School and Across School System

Administrative support for recreational reading and integrated literature programs can be provided in at least two ways within the school and across the school system. First, the administrator can sponsor and encourage a wide range of whole-school and systemwide reading activities. Second, the administrator can serve in a very personal way as a resource for the programs.

Whole-school and systemwide activities that celebrate reading and encourage the development of the habit of lifetime reading are numerous, and most are appropriate for all levels, K–12. One of the more serious factors that limit the development of the reading habit is lack of access to books outside of school. The school itself can ease this problem in many ways. Worn or outdated books that are culled from school libraries (and even discarded textbooks) can be given to interested students. Contests can be sponsored, with competition by classroom, grade, or school, to see which unit can have the largest percentage of members obtaining public library cards. Maps can be sent home illustrating the location of the public libraries and bookmobile stops, along with a schedule and list of public library services.

Books can be ordered cheaply by individuals, through a wide variety of children's book clubs. Book swaps can be organized, with students taking books they no longer want to a central location and receiving markers for that number of books. Then each student can browse throughout the room and leave with the same number of books as she or he came in with. Administrative support can be given to these efforts by supplying clerical help (often parent volunteers) to relieve teachers of the burden of organizing these activities.

The school or system might wish to participate in a Reading Is Fundamental (RIF) program.* This nonprofit program used to be funded by the federal government but is now privately funded. Its purpose is to promote voluntary reading and the development of lifetime readers by getting self-selected books into the hands of students. Local funds are matched by RIF funds at a specified ratio. All funds are used to purchase books for free distribution to children several times a year, and the children must be allowed total freedom of choice for their free books. No local or matching funds can be used in the administration of the program; therefore, the use of volunteers is almost a necessity. This, of course, meets another goal of the program: the involvement of the community.

Other administrative efforts can focus on the celebration of reading as an interesting and worthwhile activity for all students at all levels. Book clubs based on areas of interest can be formed across grade levels, with children who wish to read about computers or horses or fairy tales meeting with each other on a regular basis to share what they have learned and to learn about new sources of information. Bulletin boards in the halls might be set up for different topics on a monthly basis, with teachers, librarians, parents, and students contributing the names and short descriptions of relevant books. The librarian can set up consumable displays of books, by topic, in the library. Several books of a variety of genres and levels, dealing with a particular topic, can be displayed together for two weeks in the library. Sign-up lists can be available for each part of the display. At the end of the two weeks, the display can be dismantled and the materials begin circulating.

Contests at all levels (classroom, grade, or school) can be sponsored to encourage free reading. However, the criterion of what equals one "point" in the contest must be varied according to grade level and ability level within grades, based on equal amounts of effort, not numbers of pages. That is, one point may be earned by a kindergarten child when a parent has read two picture books to the child. One point for an average fourth-

---

*Additional information on RIF programs can be obtained from Reading Is Fundamental, 600 Maryland Avenue, S.W., Suite 600, Washington, DC 20560.

grade reader might mean that the child has read one fifty-page book independently. For a less capable eighth grader, a point might be given for fifteen pages of a book usually read by third graders. If the contests are run on the basis of one point for one book, the very students who need the most practice and the most encouragement in reading will do the least amount. These students will immediately feel like failures because they can never match the productivity of the high-achieving students who have already developed the reading habit.

Cross-age reading is another way to support a reading ambiance within in a school and especially to promote reading among less able students. In cross-age reading, older (and perhaps low-achieving) students prepare selections to read aloud to younger groups. Thus the older students get practice reading successfully, at an appropriate level for their expertise, but without the onus of reading "baby books." Rather than being perceived as poor readers, the older readers serve as models of good reading for a much younger (and often very supportive) audience. Conversely, the older students can also serve as audience for younger readers who also have prepared selections to read aloud. Cross-age reading can sometimes be one of the few really positive interactions with reading that poor readers have and can serve as a confidence builder that encourages these students to become more involved with reading.

All of the activities just described can thrive with the active support of the administration, even though administrators may not become personally involved to a great degree. But at the personal level, administrators can also do a lot to promote both recreational reading programs and integrated literature programs. They can serve as classroom models in many ways. During sustained silent reading, an administrator can simply come into a classroom, sit down, and read like everyone else. At other times, he or she can listen to a child read, discuss a book with a student, or read to the class. If provided by the teacher with a rough schedule of topics to be covered in an integrated literature program, the administrator might be prepared to share a literature experience with the entire class. "Book Look Lunches" (Hunter, 1980) can be instituted, where a student signs up to have lunch with an administrator, for the purpose of discussing a particular book. During lunch, the student has the sole attention of the administrator, who strengthens the association between reading and adult attention and approval.

Liaisons Outside of the School

One of the most important functions that an administrator serves is as liaison between the schools and the community. Reading as a lifetime habit can be furthered by the support of parents, businesspeople, and members of the community at large. It is the administrator who is in the best position to solicit this support.

The involvement of parents in promoting lifetime readers is, of course, crucial. Their support is needed in several ways. First of all, parents need to understand and reinforce the within-school efforts to promote reading, but they may have a variety of concerns about recreational reading or integrated literature programs. These questions are best answered at the administrative level. In this way the administrator can not only address the specific concerns but can also give an overall endorsement of the programs. Morrow (1986) found that parents ranked voluntary reading as the lowest priority in reading, believing that comprehension, word identification skills, and study skills were more important. Furthermore, even though teachers and principals also ranked voluntary reading as lowest, parental ratings of recreational reading were significantly lower than those of the other two groups. Thus, many parents are going to need to be convinced that creating lifetime readers is an important part of the curriculum.

Administrators can work to involve parents at home with the cultivation of lifetime readers. Monthly newsletters can be used to inform parents of the within-school efforts to promote voluntary reading and to detail activities that the parents can do at home to provide a "reading culture" (Cain, 1978). One of the most important ways that parents can help their children develop the habit of reading is to serve as reading models themselves, both by reading to their children and by reading for their own pleasure. Morrow's (1983) research provides persuasive evidence of this. She found that 76.8 percent of kindergarten children identified as having a high interest in reading were read to daily at home, whereas only 1.8 percent of the low-interest children had this daily interaction. An even larger percentage (78.6 percent) of the high-interest kindergartners had mothers who spent some of their own leisure time in reading, compared to 28.1 percent for the low-interest children.

Administrators can encourage parent involvement in the school's programs by making them feel welcome in the schools and by suggesting a wide variety of ways in which they might become involved. Some parents may particularly enjoy working with the children themselves, and these individuals can be asked to read to children in the classroom and to listen to children read on a one-to-one basis. They can take orders from the children for paperback book clubs. They can share their own literature experiences with the class. Other parents may wish to contribute in ways that involve less direct contacts with children. These parents can serve as models during silent reading time; they can tape books for children to listen to; they can keep the classroom library organized and stocked; they can collect literature resources for units in various content areas. Even parents who cannot come to the school can be actively involved in the school's efforts. They can work with community groups, such as fraternal organizations, businesses, and church groups, to sponsor classroom libraries or to provide incentives for reading contests.

Administrators can work directly with business leaders and service clubs in sponsoring support for reading programs. Many businesspeople like to deal with "the top" and may respond more positively to overtures by administrators than by either parents or teachers. Many of the activities described here — serving as models, listening to children, providing incentives — can be participated in by community members who are not parents but who are simply interested in promoting reading. If community members do not have time to give, administrators can encourage them to give financial support.

One of the most spectacularly successful examples of business involvement in promoting reading is the National Reading Incentive Program, BOOK IT!* This program is sponsored by Pizza Hut, Inc. In its very first year of existence, this program involved 7 million children. For its second year, more than 11 million children in 375,000 classrooms were expected to participate (*Reading Today*, 1987). The BOOK IT! program provides Personal Pan Pizzas, buttons, diplomas, and classroom pizza parties as incentives that children earn by reaching individually negotiated reading goals.

One last way that administrators can promote the development of reading is through frequent interactions with the media. Often the attention of the media is drawn to schools only when there is something negative to report. A regular system of press releases about what is going on in the schools to promote reading and what the community can do to support these efforts can be of great benefit.

CONCLUSION

Our schools can develop lifetime readers who choose to read for both pleasure and information. Most of the activities described in this chapter are relatively simple to put into effect and are not prohibitively expensive. Their most important quality, however, is that they give students opportunities to act like lifetime readers in ways that most reading programs do not. One result of these programs should be that students learn what it is to be "real readers."

---

*Further information can be obtained from BOOK IT!, P.O. Box 2999, Wichita, KS 67201, (316) 687-8401 or (800) 4-BOOK-IT.

REFERENCES

Anderson, R. C., Wilson, P. T., & Fielding, L. G. (1986). *Growth in reading and how children spend their time outside of school* (Technical Report No. 389). Urbana: University of Illinois.

Artley, A. S. (1967). Literature in the language arts program. In I. M. Tiedt & S. W. Tiedt (Eds.), *Readings on contemporary English in the elementary school* (pp. 214–219). Englewood Cliffs, NJ: Prentice-Hall.

Bissett, D. J. (1969). The amount and effect of recreational reading in selected fifth grade classes. *Dissertation Abstracts International, 30,* 5157-A. (University Microfilms No. 70-10, 316)

Cain, M. A. (1978). Born to read: Making a reading culture. *Teacher, 95,* 64–66.

Dillard, A. (1974). *Pilgrim at Tinker Creek.* Toronto: Bantam Books.

Forbes, E. (1943). *Johnny Tremain.* Boston: Houghton Mifflin.

Hennings, D. C. (1982). Reading picture storybooks in the social studies. *The Reading Teacher, 36,* 284–288.

Hunter, J. (1980). Hooks to catch "on level" readers. *The Reading Teacher, 33,* 467–468.

Johnston, P. (1984). Prior knowledge and reading comprehension test bias. *Reading Research Quarterly, 19,* 219–238.

LaBerge, D., & Samuels, S. J. (1976). Toward a theory of automatic information processing in reading. In H. Singer & R. Ruddell (Eds.), *Theoretical models and processes of reading* (2nd ed.) (pp. 548–579). Newark, DE: International Reading Association.

Langer, J. A., & Nicholich, M. (1981). Prior knowledge and its relationship to comprehension. *Journal of Reading Behavior, 13,* 373–379.

Lawson, R. (1939). *Ben and me.* Boston: Little, Brown.

McCracken, R. A. (1971). Initiating sustained silent reading. *Journal of Reading, 14,* 521–524, 582–583.

Morpurgo, M. (1983). *War horse.* New York: Greenwillow.

Morrow, L. M. (1983). Home and school correlates of early interest in literature. *Journal of Educational Research, 76,* 221–230.

Morrow, L. M. (1986). Attitudes of teachers, principals, and parents toward promoting voluntary reading in the elementary schools. *Reading Research and Instruction, 25,* 116–130.

National Assessment of Educational Progress. (1981). *Reading, thinking, and writing.* Denver, CO: Education Commission of the States.

Powell, W. R. (1966). Classroom libraries: Their frequency of use. *Elementary English, 43,* 395–397.

Reading Today. (1987). BOOK IT! program enters second year. *4,* 7.

Rombauer, I. S., & Becker, M. R. (1975). *The joy of cooking.* Indianapolis: Bobbs-Merrill.

Spiegel, D. L. (in press). Initiating the classroom recreational reading program. In B. Hayes (Ed.), *Reading instruction and the effective teacher.* New York: Allyn and Bacon.

Steffensen, M. S., Joag-Deu, C., & Anderson, R. C. (1979). A cross-cultural perspective on reading comprehension. *Reading Research Quarterly, 15,* 18–29.

Epilogue:
Connections and Directions

SHELLEY B. WEPNER
William Paterson College of New Jersey

JOAN T. FEELEY
William Paterson College of New Jersey

DOROTHY S. STRICKLAND
Teachers College, Columbia University

As we began to explore the connections among the many messages in this book, we realized that making connections is what *The Administration and Supervision of Reading Programs* is all about. As we see it, the essence of supervision is the ability to make connections among administrators, teachers, parents, and students; between recent research and current practices; and between professional relationships and theoretical conceptions.

Although each contributor spoke to a particular topic, a common philosophy was revealed regarding their beliefs, practices, and ideals. What they communicated is an *esprit de corps* for finding ways to connect the reading research of the last few decades with the realities of today's supervisory responsibilities. For example, even as they grappled with unresolved issues, they never let go of their holistic perspective on reading. It is clear that reading, as described throughout this text, is one facet of the language arts. It is a functional, constructive process that must be used — not simply taught — in order to be developed for lifelong literacy. Instant formulaic answers to the many complex queries surrounding reading supervision are neither sought nor offered. Instead, numerous research-based guidelines for productive supervisory practices are presented.

What follows here is a summary of the themes that recur throughout the text. Restated as connections and directions, they represent the key ideas presented in this book.

CONNECTIONS

1. *Initiating program change is a systematic, ongoing, collaborative process.* A supervisor's role is to initiate, implement, and evaluate reading programs. In order for this to occur, it is essential to have planning and involvement with key participants — reading specialists, reading coordinators, teachers from appropriate subject areas and grade levels, building and district-level administrators, school board members, and parents.

   Committees must be responsible for devising a systematic procedure for assessing the district's status, planning accordingly, implementing a plan, and evaluating for future program decisions. Committees also need to invest organized time and constructive energy to get first-hand information about how the proposed change could impact upon their school and district, by participating in fact-finding visits to schools and workshops, completing course work, and conducting interviews and independent reading research. Well-researched information will give committee members the knowledge needed to make informed decisions and sound judgments about the proposed program changes.

   Teachers and others directly or indirectly involved with the committee's work will develop a sense of ownership in program change and serve as collective agents for change in the school or district.

2. *Sound instructional reading programs are created at the school and district levels, not purchased.* In order to build an atmosphere for success, respect, and individuality, we must build instruction on what children know. We must recognize that each child is unique and that all children have different, special abilities and needs. We must become sensitized to the needs of all types of students, so that the texts and tasks assigned will match them. To facilitate functional instructional decisions, we need to understand the nature and use of tests for screening and achievement and, when appropriate, supplement existing tests with developmentally and culturally appropriate evaluation procedures.

   In a similar vein, we must insure that teachers understand how to match the learner with texts and tasks. Clearly, it is the teachers, not the programs or guides, that are the key to successful reading programs. Thus, teachers must understand what learners know and need to learn. As supervisors, we can work cooperatively with teachers, either individually or collectively, to plan and analyze how they can best provide instruction for their students. Teachers also need to understand how to select and use suitable texts, including high-quality fiction and well-written expository texts. Teachers also need to understand how to use reading and writing so that these communicative processes span the curriculum in a way that makes students actively involved in literacy tasks and, consequently, in the learning process.

As initiators and leaders, we need to assist other administrators with scheduling patterns and documented support, to help them see the value in providing time for independent, recreational reading and narrative and expository writing. Since the best reading programs often are invisible, especially at the secondary level, it is important that administrators and teachers see reading as a communicative process, rather than a separate subject area. Students then have a chance of becoming "real readers."

3. *Communication among colleagues and with the community is indispensable.* Reading supervisors should communicate with parents, teachers, and principals so that the reading program is understood by all. In communicating with colleagues, reading supervisors must build a sense of mutual trust and respect, facilitating a free exchange of ideas and concerns. In addition, reading supervisors need to help school-based reading personnel communicate effectively with classroom teachers, so that students' assignments are better coordinated between pull-out programs and regular classroom programs.

Also important is an appreciation for the impact that parents and others have on children's literacy development. We should strive to make parents aware of the reading program. We also need to understand various community types, in order to open the appropriate communication channels for stimulating, promoting, and maintaining parent involvement.

4. *Realistic expectations inspire productive supervision.* As reading supervisors, we cannot expect to be expert in all developmental levels, disciplines, and areas of responsibility. What we can expect of ourselves is that we take the responsibility to be informed decision makers. We must commit our time and resources to learning about current research, newly developed theories, and applied practices. We also must keep abreast of national trends, statewide initiatives, and local changes. Finally, we need to realize that there is no best program for all children at every level, nor at any one level; nor is there any best way to supervise under all circumstances.

If we realize our strengths and limitations and know how to connect with the appropriate people and resources in order to become better informed, we can begin to create a balance between our role responsibilities, our characteristics, our ideals, and the realities of our individual situations.

DIRECTIONS

As more and more connections are made between what we know and what we seek to learn, our understandings are fused into a fluid network for change. Upon thinking about the forward-looking comments of the authors of this book, we recognized common goals for some of the unresolved issues and unfinished searches in reading. As we move toward the twenty-first century, we anticipate that many of the following ten directions will be pursued.

1. The nature of the reading process will be better understood by those in the position to initiate change — politicians, state boards of education, building- and district-level administrators, and school board members.
2. The nature of evaluation will be more broad-based, so that students' cognitive and affective gains are assessed and program components are reviewed from many different perspectives. In other words, the success of the total reading program and the individual students within that program will be measured by more than a standardized test score.
3. The resource roles and responsibilities of school-based and distict-level reading personnel will be more highly valued by teachers, administrators, and parents.
4. National and local reading organizations will do more to help connect researchers with administrators, through conferences, consultancies, journals, books, workshops, and other media.
5. New instructional modes, such as computer technology and the writing-as-process approach, will be more clearly understood theoretically and more effectively applied administratively.
6. Reading labs will be converted to reading/writing centers, so that students have a place to go to get assistance with any assignments involving literacy.
7. Students with special needs will be better understood in the context of the reading process, so that programs can be better adjusted to meet their specific requirements.
8. District-level administrators will establish interdistrict networks to facilitate idea exchanges about reading and writing.
9. As more public figures appreciate the value of parent involvement in cultivating children's reading habits, they will use the media as a forum for advocating and modeling parental involvement. More of the media also will be devoted to celebrating reading and writing activities for all students at all levels.

10. As increased information is available about the importance of providing time to read and write in the school day, building-level administrators will become more involved in working with students on reading and writing projects.

Even as we look toward the future, we realize how critical our current initiatives are. Informed by the best thinking available, we can begin to sharpen our vision in carving out future directions in literacy development.

About the Contributors

Kathryn H. Au is an educational psychologist and head of the Elementary Curriculum Department at the Kamehameha Schools in Honolulu, where she was formerly a classroom teacher. She received her Ph.D. from the University of Illinois, Urbana-Champaign. She has published more than thirty articles and book chapters and, with Jana Mason, is author of an introductory textbook *Reading Instruction for Today.* She has served on the editorial advisory boards of *The Reading Teacher, Reading Research Quarterly,* and *Journal of Reading Behavior* and was the first recipient of the National Scholar Award of the National Association for Asian and Pacific American Education.

Rita M. Bean is Associate Professor of Education at the University of Pittsburgh and Associate Director of the Institute for Practice and Research in Education. Before coming to the university, she taught in an elementary school and served as reading specialist and reading supervisor. Her publications include research and applied articles specifically focused on the role of the reading specialist, instructional procedures for teaching individuals with reading problems, and comprehension instruction. She is co-author of a monograph, *Effecting Change in School Reading Programs: The Role of the Reading Specialist,* and is a co-author for a basal program. Currently she is studying critical features of remedial reading programs and is also developing procedures for using curriculum-based measures in adult literacy programs.

Mark W. Conley is Assistant Professor of Reading at Michigan State University. He received his Ph.D. in reading education at the Syracuse University Reading and Language Arts Center. Professor Conley was an English teacher, reading specialist, and department chair at the middle and high school levels in upstate New York. His publications include research and applied articles concerning staff development and instruction related to content reading. Currently he is working on a methods textbook in content reading. He is co-editor of *Research Within Reach: Secondary School Reading,* with Donna Alvermann and David Moore.

Janice A. Dole is Assistant Professor of Education at the University of Utah. Before receiving her Ph.D. at the University of Colorado, she was a classroom teacher in California and Massachusetts. She later taught at the University of Denver and was a visiting assistant professor at the Center for the Study of Reading. There she was involved in a project designed to improve the evaluation and selection of reading textbooks. She has written many articles on reading and is co-author of the book, *Language Arts.* Her current research interests focus on instructional studies on prior knowledge, comprehension, and learning.

Roger Farr is Professor of Education and Director of the Center for Reading and Language Studies at Indiana University. He received his Ed.D. from the State University of New York at Buffalo. He has held various public school positions and has served as Associate Dean for Research and Graduate Development at Indiana University. Professor Farr has published on the teaching of reading as well as on the measurement and evaluation of reading and reading programs. He has just published the second edition of *Reading: What Can Be Measured?* which was co-authored with Robert Carey. Farr is the author or co-author of several nationally standardized reading achievement tests. His present research interests include the study of reading strategies and longitudinal studies of reading ability.

Joan T. Feeley is Professor of Reading/Language Arts in the Department of Curriculum and Instruction at William Paterson College, Wayne, New Jersey. She received her Ph.D. from New York University, where she served as a teaching fellow. Besides having taught in elementary and secondary schools in New York and New Jersey, she also taught at Seton Hall University. She has written many articles and chapters and has developed a series of filmstrips on beginning reading instruction. With Dorothy Strickland and Shelley Wepner, she wrote *Using Computers in the Teaching of Reading.* Her current research interests include computers and reading, prior knowledge test bias, and research-into-practice studies. She teaches courses in psycholinguistics and research.

Anthony D. Fredericks is Assistant Professor of Education at York College, York, Pennsylvania. He earned his Ed.D. in reading from Lehigh University. A former classroom teacher and reading specialist, he is a recipient of the Innovative Teaching Award from the Pennsylvania State Education Association. He has served as a contributing author for *Reading Today* and currently writes a column for *Teaching* magazine. In addition, he is the author of over 100 books and articles in the field of reading, including *The Reading Comprehension Idea Book* and *The Gifted Reader Handbook.* A frequent presenter at inservice meetings and reading conferences throughout the country, his interests include parent involvement, interactive comprehension strategies, and motivating reluctant readers.

Warren E. Heiss is Professor in the Department of Communication Sciences and Disorders at Montclair State College in Upper Montclair, New Jersey. He is Coordinator of Graduate Programs in Special Education. Professor Heiss received his Ed.D. from Yeshiva University in New

York City. Of particular note is Professor Heiss's work in curriculum development. He was instrumental in the design and field testing of major national curriculum projects for handicapped children in the areas of social learning and life sciences. Currently Professor Heiss is conducting a number of program evaluation studies in special education, to examine the effectiveness of a variety of service delivery models.

Maurice Kaufman is Professor of Education at Northeastern University. He holds a Ph.D. from New York University. He is a co-author of *The Complete Reading Supervisor* and author of *Perceptual and Language Readiness Programs* and of *Reading in Content Areas*. He has served as evaluator of numerous educational projects and has worked with school-based and college programs, adult literacy projects, ESL projects, and programs for the deaf. He has worked as a classroom teacher, reading specialist, and supervisor.

Michael Labuda is Professor in the Reading/Language Arts Department at Jersey City State College and a consultant in District 10, New York City. He received an Ed.D. from the University of Idaho. Professor Labuda taught in the elementary grades and was an elementary principal. He also taught at the University of West Chester, Pennsylvania; Long Island University; University of Idaho; and Curry College, Milton, Massachusetts. He has chaired the International Reading Association's gifted and creative committee and its special-interest group on the gifted and creative student. His publications include articles and the book, *Reading for the Gifted and Creative: A Design for Excellence* (2nd edition), an IRA publication. His current interest is in providing differentiated programs for gifted and creative children.

Jana M. Mason is Professor in the Department of Educational Psychology and the Department of Elementary and Early Childhood Education at the University of Illinois. She is also a member of the Center for the Study of Reading. She received her Ph.D. from Stanford University. She set up preschool programs in Pittsburgh and Champaign, Illinois, and taught in elementary schools in upstate New York and Chicago. She has written many articles and has written and edited several books on reading, including *Reading Instruction for Today* with Kathryn Au and *Comprehension Instruction* with Gerald Duffy and Laura Roehler. Her current work is on early reading and writing development, its instruction in classrooms, and intervention techniques for children who are at academic risk.

Jean Osborn is the Associate Director of the Center for the Study of Reading at the University of Illinois. She received her M.A. in Education at the University of Illinois. She taught in preschool and kindergarten programs at the university, developed curricula, and trained teachers. For fifteen years she worked with students and teachers in schools throughout the country as part of the United States Department of Education Follow Through Study. She has written many articles, edited several books, and is a co-author of numerous language and reading programs. Her current interests include the analysis of workbooks, the preparation of information for use by textbook adoption committees, and a comparative analysis of beginning reading approaches.

Robert H. Pritchard is Assistant Professor in the Teacher Education Department at California State University, Fresno. He holds a Ph.D. in reading education and second-language learning from Indiana University. Dr. Pritchard was a classroom teacher and reading specialist in public schools in New Jersey and California, as well as a teacher trainer and curriculum specialist in the Republic of Palau. His primary research interests are the investigation of reader strategies and the cultural and linguistic factors that affect the reading process.

David Reinking received his Ph.D. from the University of Minnesota. After serving on the faculty of Rutgers University, he moved to the University of Georgia, where he is currently Assistant Professor of Reading and Associate Director of the Reading/Language Arts Computer Resource Center. His experiences with computers and reading include conducting research on computer-mediated text, developing instructional software, and helping teachers implement computer-based activities for language arts instruction.

Dixie Lee Spiegel is Associate Professor of Education at the University of North Carolina at Chapel Hill. She holds a Ph.D. degree in curriculum and instruction, with emphasis in reading, from the University of Wisconsin at Madison. She is a former third-grade classroom teacher and a former elementary-grades reading teacher. Dr. Spiegel is particularly interested in applying research in reading and writing to classroom practice. She is the author of a monograph on recreational reading as well as several research and applied articles and a reading methods textbook.

Dorothy S. Strickland is Professor of Education in the Department of Curriculum and Teaching at Teachers College, Columbia University. She has been a classroom teacher, reading consultant, and learning disabilities specialist. She co-authored *Family Storybook Reading* with Denny Taylor and *Using Computers in the Teaching of Reading* with Joan Feeley and Shelley Wepner. Dr. Strickland has held offices in the National Council of Teachers of English and the International Reading Association, of which she is past president.

JoAnne L. Vacca is an Associate Professor and Department Chairperson of Teacher Development and Curriculum Studies at Kent State University, Kent, Ohio. She received her Ed.D. from Boston University. Professor Vacca taught at the middle school level and was a consultant with the

Illinois Office of Education. She is the author of articles, reviews, and chapters, and co-author of *Content Area Reading* (2nd ed.) and *Reading and Learning to Read*. She is interested in staff development and leadership and applications of qualitative research design.

Richard T. Vacca is Professor of Education and Director of the Reading and Writing Center at Kent State University. He completed his doctoral studies at Syracuse University and has been an instructor at Northern Illinois University and the University of Connecticut. Dr. Vacca has taught reading and writing at the junior high and high school levels. He is the co-author of *Content Area Reading* (2nd ed.) and *Reading and Learning to Read*.

Shelley B. Wepner is Assistant Professor of Reading/Language Arts in the Department of Curriculum and Instruction at William Paterson College, Wayne, New Jersey. She received her Ed.D. from the University of Pennsylvania. She held various public school positions in New Jersey, including Supervisor of Curriculum and Instruction. She also was an instructor at Trenton State College, Trenton, New Jersey. Editor of *The Reading Instruction Journal* and author of *Read-a-Logo*, a software program for beginning reading, Shelley Wepner has written many articles on beginning reading, computers and reading, administration, and prior knowledge test bias. She also co-authored *Using Computers in the Teaching of Reading* with Dorothy Strickland and Joan Feeley. She currently is working on a reading-writing software package for at-risk secondary school students.

Index